AVOIDING THE BLAME GAME:

Your (Legal and Holistic) Guide to No- Fault Divorce

Copyright

<u>Disclaimer</u>

a) Although the author and publisher have made every effort to ensure that the information in this book is correct at the time of press, the author and publisher do not assume and hereby disclaim any liability to any party for any loss, damage, or disruption caused by errors or omissions, whether such errors or omissions result from negligence, accident, or any other cause.

b) This book is not intended as a substitute for legal advice from solicitors or medical advice of doctors. The reader should regularly consult with their professionals.

c) This guide is intended only to be an overview of the practice and procedures introduced on no- fault divorce, and other family proceedings in England and Wales – it is not to be relied on as legal advice or as a substitute for obtaining professional guidance for your divorce, and other child related and financial issues. An overview is provided for cohabitees. It is not intended to be exhaustive. It covers some of the main matters and issues that are likely to be relevant, and that clients have commonly experienced in the past.

d) Case law and legislation changes frequently so you must receive up-to-date legal advice on your particular case. There are a collection of issues that are likely to be of concern or interest to you, which have been coupled with holistic methods to help you cope through the whole process. This book is not intended to replace therapy for mental health issues, but the support mechanisms should help you to cope better. Due to the recent introduction of no-fault divorce, procedures are likely to develop over time. Court fees change from time to time so always check with the court what the current court fees are before you make any application.

e) The outlined case scenarios referred to are fictitious and a loose amalgamation of circumstances from countless clients' divorce situations the author has come across, which may help you in your journey. Names do not refer to the original names of those clients who have been represented.

Table Of Contents

About the Author

Neeta Mardia helps individuals as a divorce consultant. Neeta also continues her part-time career as a qualified senior consultant solicitor specialising in family law for nearly 30 years and a member of Resolution (professionals committed to the constructive resolution of family disputes). Neeta has always been passionate about helping people and family law became her vocation. As a divorce consultant, she provides legal information combined with practical guidance and in parallel provides emotional support to individuals who sadly have to face this tough challenge. She has come across numerous people throughout her career going through similar situations. As a result, she wanted to bring together all the information they found helpful combining it with holistic support to benefit those now going through divorce. This led Neeta to write this book to share her best practice and tips gained throughout her career. For those embarking upon divorce this equips them with information to navigate the legal process and ultimately empower them to personally transform their lives.

Neeta has practised family law in different localities spanning the North and South of England including the Home Counties, and London to Leeds. She has been a consultant solicitor and worked for multi-disciplinary law firms and niche specialist family practices.

You can connect with Neeta at:
Website www.neetamardia.com
Email hello@neetamardia.com
LinkedIn linkedin.com/in/neetamardia

Introduction

Divorce is not easy. Most people say that going through divorce was probably one of the toughest challenges they had to face. Many of those who are breaking up and going through the divorce process just don't know where to turn and may not understand the legal and practical complexities involved. Knowledge of the divorce process and an understanding of available support gives individuals the power and the strength they need in order to deal with this challenge more easily.

Divorce is not the end of the road. It is a crossroads showing you a new path. If you are breaking up and just don't know where to turn, I will help point you in the right direction. My book provides a clear and in depth guide to no- fault divorce in England and Wales, and introduces a unique holistic approach to the legal process and practical steps surrounding divorce. Navigating you through the myriad of legal and personal issues this guide also gives you the benefit of case studies with specific situations you will be able to identify with. This book is a must for readers who want to be shown the best route through their divorce, and to go on to transform their lives.

I would suggest it is an important book to read before you start or respond to a divorce particularly if you are concerned about financial implications or arrangements for the children as a result of the marriage breakdown. Also covering immediate legal steps you should consider taking – such as injunctions, dealing with your property and updating your will, and separation deeds. Avoiding the Blame Game ultimately helps you cope positively throughout these turbulent times and grow steadily in both your outer and inner journey.

In reading this book I hope you receive guidance through your divorce and other legal procedures you are likely to come across, and at the same time achieve both personal and spiritual growth to transform your life and start again with positivity, strength and serenity.

What this book covers

Main Legal Issues

Over time I have come across common experiences, and encountered similar questions about the divorce process, and other legal matters. I will share with you the procedures and most likely issues that will be important to you, as you maybe start your divorce with deep trepidation and little knowledge of what to expect.

This book gives you a plain and simple overview of the divorce process, as no-fault divorce is now available to you from 6th April 2022 since the Divorce, Dissolution and Separation Act 2020 came into effect. I have covered finances and children issues in detail, including proceedings, as these are likely to be the main areas of concern for you. I have also covered several important side legal issues, such as injunctions, and updating your will.

In case you are thinking of cohabiting, or may do so in the future, I also cover cohabitee matters in outline, as the rise continues in couples choosing to cohabit, rather than marry.

Top Tips

I have added a few "Top Tips" along the way to help guide you, and make sure you do not become overwhelmed.

Case Scenario

Each chapter concludes with a case scenario which you will easily relate to. These scenarios show you the type of issues my clients have experienced, and many may be similar to yours. They ought to give you some insight into how to deal with your situation. You are likely to identify what you are going through, and your own personal journey, with these scenarios.

Supportive Holistic Tools

I have approached the topic of divorce in a holistic way, as it is one of the major crises of life. It will really help you if you also use this time to delve inwards and reflect. Spirituality helps maintain some equilibrium in this time of inevitable change. As a constant companion throughout the divorce process, I have outlined key practices to support you from the inside out. These methods encourage personal growth and transformation which I have seen many times over, is possible, as a conclusion to the divorce experience.

Meditation and Affirmation

I conclude each chapter with a simple morning, or evening, meditation; to start your day off well, or to end it peacefully. Meditation, and its benefits are widely accepted. I therefore introduce a meditation practice in every chapter and go into detail about the practice in Chapter 3. Meditation can help you in three major ways:
1. Addressing and solving personal conflicts.
2. Helping your body and mind to heal.
3. Encouraging your personal and spiritual growth.
Let the meditations comfort and help you, and your mind, at this time. Whilst I have included an appropriate meditation at the end of each chapter, if there is one you really feel you benefit from, you can make that one your daily practice. Repetition is the key to lasting results. If you can, also take the positive thought I finish with into the day or evening, almost like a mantra to keep your mind positive.

For Men and Women

I have written this book to help men and women. Regardless of gender, the same principles apply. From my experience, sometimes men become more isolated whereas women may have a support network of friends to lean upon. But, whichever of these applies to you, external support may only help at times and the only way to really work things out is to go inwards. It is nice to have a shoulder to cry on for a few hours, but afterwards, you are left facing the vacuum alone. It is an essential time for deep reflection if you wish to see the sky clearly again.

An Aid to Instructing Solicitors

I suggest you read this book before you start your divorce, and before you decide to engage a solicitor, so you have a basic understanding, and dip in and out of it when you wish to refer to some terminology or matters that crop up, or may be mentioned by your solicitor along the way.

I provide an overview of basic divorces, and cover financial and children issues, in addition to some common side issues, but for any complicated or involved matters you should always seek advice. The majority of family solicitors have entered this area of work as a vocation, and my opinion is that they are dedicated, hardworking and like helping people. They have a great deal of empathy and are equipped to deal with emotionally charged clients.

Embrace your Future

When I first see my clients and they are finding the whole idea of divorce a huge challenge, I always say that it may feel bad now, but I promise you it will get better, and you will get through it. Some, practically, get through quicker and easier than others: allow approximately six months to one year, or more than two years for the divorce if financial and children matters are more complex. The emotional side of getting through this may be longer. But be strong and positive, and you will not only survive the divorce, but your life will eventually flourish after it.

No- Fault

It may feel that no time is a good time to divorce! However, one advantage you have is that you are getting divorced after a monumental change to the law. After nearly 50 years of having to prove fault in the majority of cases to get divorced, you no longer have to show fault. I, like most family practitioners, have welcomed this change.

The divorce process has, for many years, been an administrative one, but now it will also be kinder and easier. The benefit of no allocation of blame is that you can proceed through divorce in a much less emotionally charged way. You can spend time on your personal growth after the breakup, rather than on paperwork outlining allegations. You no longer set out all the wrongdoings from the past, seeking to justify reasons for the marriage breakdown. The courts have also introduced an online system for divorce, so the procedures throughout England and Wales have become much easier to complete.

If you divorce outside of England and Wales, whilst the procedures differ in each jurisdiction, the holistic methods outlined in this book can still support you through the turbulent times. If you are still trying to cope from a previous divorce, much of the information I have outlined may help finally put the past behind you.

Summary of Each Chapter

What will you expect from each chapter of this book? I will talk about the legal and formal matters that will surround your divorce. I will couple this with the personal impact upon you and share tools that will help you use this as an opportunity for growth.

Each chapter starts with a short summary introduction to the law topic and why it is relevant to you. Following detailed information on the legal matters, I outline for you the legal process, and if you are likely to go to court, the proceedings. I give you my "Top Tips". We then turn to you, personally, and your emotions and needs during this tumultuous period of life. I share with you personal and spiritual tools for growth and guidance. These can be taken together at the same time with your legal matter, or just pick up a particular practice whenever you need a boost. There are many alternatives for personal support that may help you at this time. These range from internal to external sources of support. For instance, I cover mindfulness to seeking counselling. After the end of each topic, we turn our attention to a case scenario, and I hope this may help you put your situation in perspective. These cases serve as an example of what you may go through and what others before you have experienced and have come through the other side! We conclude each chapter together with a short reflective meditation to begin, or end, your day.

Final Question to You

As we start, I leave you with one question. Have you ever considered a divorce as an opportunity for positive personal and spiritual growth? Come back to this question and you may have your answer at the end of this book, and your divorce journey ....

Chapter 1

NO-FAULT DIVORCE

Introduction

In this chapter we discuss the ground for divorce and personal reasons you or your spouse may have come to a decision that the marriage is over– and how to move forwards to your next life chapter, without blame and recrimination. I invite you to reflect on whether you are blaming yourself, or your spouse, or others for the marriage breakdown. You may wish to act with both yourself and others in a more compassionate way. This leads onto considering your motivation for certain actions and reframing your thinking. We meet William and find out what he went through in his divorce, and his approach towards it. Finally, as your days may start with a sense of trepidation at this time, we conclude with our morning meditation on compassion, and a positive thought, "all is well".

What is No-Fault Divorce

In England and Wales, from 6th April 2022 you can now apply for no-fault divorce. What does this mean for you? It means that the legal divorce process no longer asks you to detail allegations about each other's conduct, state the cause for the marital breakdown, or allocate blame.

Until recently, in order to divorce, you had to give a reason for the marriage breakdown. In the majority of situations, you had to show that one spouse was at fault. No-fault divorce means that neither of you need to give a reason why your relationship is over, or prove "fault", which is any type of marital misconduct on the part of the other. With this change, in order to obtain a divorce, you can now just make a statement that the marriage has *irretrievably broken down*. This simplifies the divorce procedure and reduces conflict between couples.

The ability to contest a divorce has been abolished, so now you can move forwards with it freely. Previously, where a spouse did not want the divorce, they would regularly threaten to defend, dig their heels in, cause delay, and increase costs. Cooperation was difficult to obtain from an uncooperative spouse.

Ground for Divorce

The ground remains the same as for divorces before the new law came into being, which is "irretrievable breakdown of marriage". But you no longer need to prove a fact (i.e. a reason) to illustrate this. The person bringing the divorce makes a simple statement that the marriage has irretrievably broken down, and this statement is considered by the court to be conclusive evidence.

The Divorce, Dissolution and Separation Act 2020 is the legal statute governing no-fault divorce. The Act of Parliament which came into force on 25th June 2020 but not into practice until 6th April 2022 still keeps irretrievable breakdown of marriage as the sole reason for divorce but takes away the five facts upon which this was previously proved and replaces them with a single notification process. The court does not require any supporting reason or fact why you feel the marriage is over. Previously you were required to provide details of conduct or separation. Either of you, or for the first time, both of you, can simply state that the marriage is over.

Many of the legal profession and the public have been campaigning for this change in family law for a long time and the legislation is a historic change to UK law, after more than 50 years of divorce with blame. The legislation certainly makes the process kinder to both parties involved, and easier for practitioners.

As a result, divorce is easier, both practically and emotionally. With no-fault divorce, couples no longer play out the blame game at court, and whilst some may still wish to battle outside court with each other, the law is taking the lead to say it is unnecessary to do so. We have moved away from the dark ages and become more aware and enlightened. So now, more than it has ever been in the past, there is an opportunity to grow spiritually from the experience and avoid the blame game.

Under the old procedure, to avoid proving "fault" you had to be separated for two years to proceed with a consent divorce, or five years if a spouse failed to consent. For those who could not wait that long for financial or other reasons, pursuing "fault" divorce was the only option. Divorce is a very stressful experience and proving fault-based facts often exacerbates tensions between parties. For separating parents, it becomes even more difficult to focus on the needs of the children and the demands of co-parenting. It is not helpful for anyone for this to happen.

Timescale

There is now a minimum six-month timeframe which enables couples to reflect on their decision. This starts from the date of the initial application to the final order. For those who have already separated if they proceed under the new procedure, there will be no reduction in time even though they have already been apart for some time.

Provided that England and Wales hold jurisdiction for your divorce which relies upon requisite "residence", or "domicile", and you have a valid marriage, you will be able to proceed with your application. You must also have been married for at least one year before you can start divorce proceedings.

On 9th April 2019, when the Justice Secretary announced the forthcoming change in law, he said that hostility and conflict between parents leaves their mark on children and can damage their life chances. It was a forceful remark. It makes sense that hostility must at least influence anyone exposed to it and particularly, impressionable children. He stated that whilst the institution of marriage should be upheld, it was unacceptable that our out dated law increased conflict between divorcing couples. He announced the time for reform and an end to the blame game. Hopefully, this will make a genuine difference and will support divorcing couples, and you too, to move forwards constructively.

At the conclusion of this book, I will also briefly outline many other countries worldwide which have also introduced no-fault divorce, as these jurisdictions may also apply to you.

Also note, in the UK, Scotland and Northern Ireland have separate differing legal procedures from England and Wales.

No-Fault Divorce (Summary)

This relates to the divorce procedure and timescales in England and Wales. I provide a detailed step-by-step account of the process in Chapter 4.

In summary, The Divorce, Dissolution and Separation Act 2020 introduces the following:

- It replaces the previous requirement to provide evidence of conduct or separation, with a requirement to provide a statement of irretrievable breakdown followed by an overall period of notice of 26 weeks.
- It removes the possibility of contesting the divorce as the statement of irretrievable breakdown will be taken as sufficient conclusion of breakdown.
- It introduces the option for a joint application.
- The language has been updated to ensure it is fit for the modern age; previously used divorce terms have changed.
- The person bringing the application for a divorce order is the "Applicant". This replaces the previous term of the *Petitioner*.

- The form used to start off your divorce, is an "application", no longer a *divorce petition*, which was the previous form.
- There are two stages to the process. In the first stage you obtain a "conditional order", replacing the previous stage of *decree nisi*. In the second, and last, stage you obtain a "final order", replacing the previous termed *decree absolute*. Once the "final order" is obtained your marriage is over.
- There is a minimum 20-week period before a conditional order is granted, and then not until six weeks after a final order is made.

IMPORTANT POINT
This change in law applies to dissolution of civil partnerships (both for same sex, and since December 2019 heterosexual couples who have entered into formal civil partnerships). The conditional order and final order, are terms already used in the dissolution of civil partnerships.

Top Tips

DO

1. Discuss with your spouse if the relationship has in fact irretrievably broken down and the reasons both or one of you may feel this way to gain a better understanding of the situation. Keep the discussion calm and if either of you become upset agree to have another chat in a few days time.
2. Decide practically whether it would be better if one of you should move out, as the divorce process can be long and uncomfortable if you are in the same house. It also gives you both breathing space in case there is the opportunity for your relationship to be re-assessed, and possibly reconciled. If you take this step, work out between you how to deal with

the household bills in the interim, i.e. who should pay what, until your financial situation can be formally addressed later in the course of proceedings.

3. Keep discussions with your spouse general in nature, and as measured as possible, until you have sought legal advice.

DO NOT

1. Jump straight in with issuing a divorce application even if you have made your decision. Get legal advice early but do not ask your solicitor to send your spouse a letter or issue proceedings before you have had several discussions with your spouse.

Marriage Breakdown

There is a difference between marriage breakdown and divorce. Let's face it – unfortunately the marriage has already broken down. Even if divorce was abolished, relationships would still break up. Divorce is accepting what has already happened. None of us, including you and your spouse, entered into marriage thinking this would happen. So, it is a harsh reality to come to terms with when your marriage is no longer working. You may have tried over and over but the relationship has just gone beyond the point of no return.

It should not be a family expectation, or any other person's, for a party to stay in a marriage when they are suffering, just because they are married. I am pro divorce for this reason. The marriage contract is not absolute. Whilst, like any partnership, it takes commitment and effort from each of you, the marriage contract should not have significance over safety and long-term happiness.

My experience is that my clients, both men and women, do not take divorce lightly or eagerly. A person tries to keep the marriage together until impossible to do so, after many arguments and upsets. The marriage contract for life is the joining of equal partners but where a partner may fail to keep up their side of the bargain in the other's eyes and there is a breakdown of trust, this results in a breach of the marital contract. If there is a breach of any fundamental term of a partnership contract, it is hard and often untenable, to continue.

Personal Reasons often given for Divorce

If you make the decision to divorce, you know why. If you did not make the decision, you may not really know why your spouse has. Very often it is a culmination of many issues that have arisen over time between you. Sometimes one major issue between you can be pinpointed. There is very often a turning point, and "final straw" moment. It is sometimes hard to imagine when you are going through the breakup, that your personal set of circumstances have often been experienced by many others before you. Whilst you may feel alone, others have had similar experiences to you. Harsh times have been endured by many through a marriage, and often over a long period of time. Please be reassured that they have got through them and so you will too.

I have set out a few themes that may resonate on a subtle level, or really hit home with you, as being the main causes of your breakup. These may also serve as an indication, and understanding, of the reasons your spouse may want to leave your relationship.

Infidelity

Invariably infidelity comes up the most, whether it is a one-night stand, or an affair that has been carrying on in parallel to your marriage. It may also happen that an affair started before marriage or an earlier love may be rekindled. Affairs during marriage may have been for a few months, sometimes a few years, more than five years, or even for the whole marriage duration, and with one person, or a string of different affairs throughout.

It is often a startling wake-up call to the reality of the state of your marriage of which you may have been blissfully unaware. Or you may have suspected but chosen to turn a blind eye; perhaps now, somehow, the situation is different from before. Of course, once trust is broken it is very difficult to recover, and it takes a great deal of openness and willingness on both sides to put the past aside. It is unlikely that the relationship will ever be the same. Occasionally, one party will react to the other's infidelity by having an affair of their own. Otherwise, it ends up being a memory constantly thrown in the face of their partner in an argument.

An affair can often also be the catalyst for the person that has found love and companionship elsewhere, to end an unhappy marriage. As a society finally accepting of sexual orientation, perhaps your partner now wishes to be openly gay, and that can dramatically break the stability of a previously traditional heterosexual marriage.

Growing Apart

Over the last decade, it has become increasingly common for divorces to take place after the empty nest. Parties have grown apart by the time the children are due to leave home. This happens more and more. As we live longer, we will invariably go through different stages of life, and often the children having grown up and been the focus for a substantial period of time, are no longer a reason to stay together. As many of my clients have observed, they may have spent 25 or 30 years with their spouse, but what about the next 25 or 30 years – how do they really want to spend that? Several clients mentioned to me that, as their contemporaries started to develop health issues in their 50s and 60s, they looked towards the ageing process and decided the time they remained healthy was meaningful and precious, and they did not want to stay in an unhappy marriage for the sake of appearances. They sometimes unexpectedly have to navigate their grown-up children's feelings as well as their own. Even grown-up children often find their parents' breakup difficult. It is part of their identity so they can find it hard. Grown-up children can, on the other hand, also be a source of strength, as they may have the wisdom to support a parent's choice to live a happier and fulfilled life.

Couples also often seek a divorce where they have married young. For a similar reason, as they grow and mature, time shows that ultimately they have little in common unless they have been lucky to grow together.

Communication and Intimacy

Poor communication becomes a downwards spiral, and once communication breaks down it is hard to salvage. Patterns of negative talk, ignoring, or constantly rebuking or belittling the other, once established, are hard to break. Many of my clients say they feel their spouse looks to point out their faults, and the rest of the time the spouse hardly, if at all, acknowledges or compliments them. One, or both, lapse into long periods of silence, in between raised voices, or full blazing rows. Poor communication often leads to lack of intimacy. Nothing happening inside, or outside, the bedroom. Soon the hand holding and cuddling of those early days of marriage falls away. Frustration and antagonism sets in, and when respect and goodwill between you is lost, there is nothing left.

Domestic Squabbles

Frequently, domestic difficulties come up as reasons for divorce. Unmet expectations, and lack of attention or appreciation, often arise in any long-term relationship. Day-to-day mounting irritations, and the unequal division of labour are cited. Particularly the division of domestic chores. I have often heard that one person hardly lifts a finger in the house, expecting the other to take responsibility for the house, children and even looking after their spouse. This can often be tied to economic reasons and the breadwinner taking the view that they are doing their bit by going out to work. But this also follows many years of traditional stereotyped role models. After years of bearing the burden of cooking and cleaning, and feeling unappreciated and unsupported, one party – still usually the wife – gets fed up and wants something more than a life of drudgery. I have seen many highly skilled professional women with flourishing careers say they still have to do all the organising at home, the cooking and weekend chores. Over years, with no compromise in the home, one person often feels their life is better outside of the home, and away from the relationship.

Also, it is clear that over time, the other person's habits have continued to grate on them. This can be from leaving their clothes lying around and general untidiness, to dishes left in the sink and debris all over the kitchen surfaces. Generally, these habits result in one person having to clear up after the other and illustrate a general self-centredness and lack of consideration for their spouse.

Introvert/Extrovert Personalities

Socialising comes up quite a lot. The parties may have different interests or one person may just not want to go out. One person wants to go out more and the other refuses to socialise with them or their friends, and sooner or later they start to lead separate lives. This often applies to extended family. If one person does not get on with their in-laws, this increases tensions between the couple, and their spouse is caught in the middle. This puts a lot of strain on the marriage.

Finances

Financial reasons also tie into the relationship issues. There can be control issues. A situation can arise where one party controls the money that is brought into the house by them, and in many cases, even controlling the money earned by their spouse. I have seen instances where one party will even question their spouse spending £10 whilst clearly spending hundreds of pounds on themselves. A party may also keep their finances secret from the other, leading to mistrust.

Sometimes one party may be a spendthrift and often gets into debt, exacerbating the couple's financial worries and placing a great deal of pressure on the relationship. This may also go hand in hand with responsibility and views on work. One person may work hard, and the other may not be interested in working, leaving the full financial burden on one person.

Children

Although children can be the glue between a couple, they may not always be, depending on both party's outlook. Sometimes one party may not have really thought about the responsibilities that come with looking after children. Deep down, they may not have really wanted to have children, or the extra duties, and limit on their personal freedom, that having children entails. Also, if a child has any disabilities, it is sad when one party cannot cope and leaves for a new life, often leaving one parent with the care. If there are children from a previous relationship, this often does not work – neither spouse, nor child, really accept each other.

Addictions

Alcohol, drug taking, gambling and all addictions can wear down the other party over many years, who may try to help the addict to no avail, and often the only option is to separate or divorce.

Domestic Violence

Domestic violence is still a very real issue in many relationships. These situations are much harder to get out of and need a lot of support. The relationships thrive on control and fear. If you are suffering any type of abuse, emotional, psychological, physical or financial, it will have worn you down over a period of time. Please know that all types of violence and abuse go across all social classes regardless of education. It may feel hard to talk about as it is deeply personal but is nothing to be ashamed about. Get support, and get out as soon as you can, is my advice.

Avoiding the Blame Game

With a significant change in the legal process, this should influence the overall tone of the divorce procedure and how each party interacts with the other. Ideally, blame can be put firmly to bed, and whilst there will inevitably still be painful human emotions, the divorce can go through with collaboration and understanding. Blame can be avoided if you and your spouse choose to avoid it in all your interactions with each other. The relationship has come to an end, and with hindsight you both may have done various things differently. But no one person should feel the brunt of responsibility, and definitely there is no place for blame. Responsibility for one's own actions is as far as you should go. As there is no legal process provoking you to divulge intimate details of the other's behaviour and mud- sling in front of the courts, this is an opportunity to discard anything negative, and leave the past in the past. The procedure no longer has to start by blaming the other, and it should make the whole thing much kinder and hopefully a little easier.

Both legally and personally, the advantages of having the mental fortitude to avoid the blame game are numerous. You have the potential to stay friends and have support for the future. Finances and children issues are resolved much easier. Future social occasions for the children and eventually grandchildren can be attended in unison. Ultimately you come out the other side much less tarnished.

Understanding Blame

1. Firstly, do not blame yourself; this is really important. It can feel as though you have failed – a very significant part of

your identity is often parcelled up in the status of being married – my husband, my wife. What do others think now? You always thought your marriage was for life; you were secure. As other friends and family went through divorce, you never thought it would be you. There may be cultural issues. Do people think you must have done something wrong? You are hugely disappointed; it is easy to question what you did wrong, what you should have done better. It is best to use the reality of the current situation to ground you. Don't look back. It is as it is, and you are at this point.

2. Secondly, do not blame your partner. In my experience over the years, this will be the most difficult to overcome. We all know of married couples constantly complaining about their spouse. Well, it gets much worse on divorce, particularly if either has found a new partner. Where trust breaks down, it is easy to blame. Also, a party often thinks they were constantly putting up with the other's behaviour. They often justify any part they may have had to play in the breakdown by looking at the other's faults. Well, ideally try to stop right there. No need to blame or complain; you will now have your own life. Even in the worst of marriage situations, you will have learnt something – and this is your journey. They have not ruined you; they have not ruined anything. You now control how you live the rest of your life. They are not the movie star in your movie, you are, so don't spend your time for the rest of your movie on anger and resentment when you could choose joy, compassion, love and so many other ways to be.

3. Thirdly, do not blame others. Do not think, if only your parents had been happy in their marriage, been better role models, been around more for you, things could have been different. It is not the case; they did the best with what they knew. Do not blame your in-laws, or your spouse's friends, for interfering. I would even go so far as stating that any other person involved in an affair is not to blame. They were only able to influence if the relationship was not solid. The breakdown is no one else's fault or responsibility.

It is a good time to check your own emotions. I have found some unusual and unexpected responses. On many occasions now I have seen the spouse who may have had an affair, blaming and being resentful of the other spouse, which I did not expect. The stance is almost that they were driven to that position rather than there being any sense of regret. Or after separation, when one party has moved on to a new relationship, the other party wants to make them suffer. They do not want them to find happiness, even though they themselves did not want to stay with them, and often the marriage partnership was simply a front for many years.

It is hard to hear, but if you feel anger and blame, unfortunately this is now of your own making. No one else can make you feel this way. That is the very deep truth of any situation. It is easy to point the finger of blame at your spouse, and no doubt you can justify this by recounting numerous episodes of their behaviour. It takes deep knowledge of how things really are, and wisdom to finally understand that ultimately it comes down to what causes you yourself have created. Who knows, in addition to our past conditioning, maybe there are karmic reasons behind each relationship. Blame and resentment simply avoid responsibility for your actions, and part, in the relationship and the breakdown. If you are in this cycle, try to break it urgently otherwise it will affect your emotional, mental and physical health in the long run. Let resentment go, as you let the situation go. Accept the position for what it is now, regardless of how you got to this point.

A helpful way to look at the situation now is that whatever is happening, is for your highest and greatest good. However it appears, if you believe it is for your very best, you will find it easier to go through the changes and it will finally conclude this way. Concentrate on growth and optimism as much as possible.

The best way to proceed with your divorce, if you can, is to make the joint decision that the marriage has irretrievably broken down. This is going to be effective on many levels. Neither of you can then say it was the other person's choice, so you both take equal responsibility. Then, with that, comes equal commitment to the decision, together with its implications;

financial and children considerations which will still remain to be resolved.

Being Gentle on Yourself and Others

Another way of putting this is to be kind and compassionate to yourself and others. Do not be harsh – do not judge yourself, the situation or the other. This is a really important time to take stock and nurture yourself and others. Really take it easy – don't give yourself a hard time. There may be some days you really do not feel like doing much. On those days, maybe pick one thing to do that makes you feel good, to uplift you. If you do this daily, over time your outlook will seem brighter as you start to feel better.

Divorce is one of the most self-isolating life events. We hear and see many stories in the media of celebrity divorces as if they are just the everyday situation. In fact, it is particularly harsh for those exposed to the media. It is not a glossy occurrence. It comes with a lot of heartache and self-introspection. I remember one of my clients saying she felt that she became insular and inward looking. Sometimes it is just enough to get through the day.

Going in is the only way to come out of this, and there is nothing wrong with doing so. It is a period of growth, and that comes from within. Let the external world spin while you resolve your inner turmoil and only listen to your inner voice. Everyone will have a view – they are entitled to it – but don't get sidetracked. If you can retain your awareness, however, you can get the best of both worlds. You can grow from within and be open to external opportunities for support.

So how to be gentle on yourself? Let go of all expectations of how things should be, or how you should cope, and allow yourself a long period to adjust. No should or should not. Be patient with yourself, and your emotions, which can vacillate considerably over this time. Let go of time in particular. A breakup situation always lasts longer than anyone would anticipate. Make each decision moment by moment. Appreciate your life fully and realise that what you are experiencing is just one aspect of that. Above all, nurture yourself – you are a precious human being. Go to bed each night counting your blessings; be grateful for what you have and who you are and ask for a peaceful night's sleep.

How to be gentle with others? Be kind to your spouse, soon to be ex-spouse. Treat him or her with compassion and kindness. Treat him or her as you would do a friend. Bring space into your emotions and act objectively. It may not initially come easily, if you are feeling hurt, but with time how you act will affect how you both interact, and the responses you get should eventually reflect this. You can still be clear and firm but act with dignity and integrity.

Albert Camus, French philosopher, author and winner of the Nobel Prize in Literature in 1957, refers to having found, in the depths of winter, an invincible summer. That is how it can be experienced through your divorce.

"In the midst of winter, I found there was, within me, an invincible summer. And that makes me happy. For it says that no matter how hard the world pushes against me, within me, there's something stronger – something better, pushing right back."

When we have been in the depths of despair and encountered suffering, we are forced to go inwards to transform our misery and find the true, never-ending lightness of our being. We can make small outer changes but they do little to help us long term. It is some relief that suffering not only forces our hand to look at ourselves for who we really are but can also get us to a better place.

Using seasons and weather is a good analogy – you can use it daily in your reflection of your feelings and your situation. It is helpful to sit at the breakfast table, or in the office, and just spend a few moments looking out of the window at the weather. If it is pelting down with rain, let your sadness float away with it; if it is windy, remind yourself you will weather this storm; and if it is sunny, appreciate the sun rays and bathe in the warmth and comfort for a few moments. It is all impermanent: the weather, the seasons, your situation. You may be in the darkest winter, but the summer sunshine will inevitably make its appearance.

Tool for Reframing

Reframing, in a therapeutic sense, is about looking at a situation, thought, or feeling from another angle. A technique that leads to reframing your thoughts, is the process of inquiry, advocated by Byron Katie. She developed a process of self-inquiry which she now calls "The Work", which is a form of self-directed cognitive therapy. It has helped many thousands of people to get out of their mental ruts. It involves asking four simple questions about each belief that causes us pain and suffering:

- Is it true?
- Can you absolutely know that it's true?
- How do you react when you believe that thought?
- Who would you be without the thought?

After answering these questions, you are asked to come up with a turnaround thought, which is in the form of a sentence expressing the opposite of what one believes. So, for instance, "my spouse doesn't understand me" could become "I don't understand them or, I don't understand myself." This process of inquiry is particularly helpful in break-up situations. You may feel unless they apologise you won't be happy. The turnaround could be that you actually don't need anything from them to be happy, and maybe you need to apologise to yourself, or even to them. The inquiry process helps you to come out of destructive thought patterns and expands your awareness.

It is worth looking at these questions and how to apply them to your situation – Byron Katie's website is as follows and provides a free step-by-step guide to the process of inquiry:

https://thework.com

Checking your Motivation

If you can check your motivation often, this will help you make the right choices. We need to take control of our mind rather than being controlled by it. As you delve deeper inwards, you start to check your motivation for each action and consider the consequences. This is important as you will be making constant decisions throughout the process.

By coming out of the reactive patterns, even how you interacted in the past can slowly change. When you would perhaps have attacked or defended, you can now pause and think about how you are going to respond. Also, to really listen to what the other is saying. This is particularly key to better communication as you will have to engage over many months with your spouse to bring the relationship, and the divorce process, to a close.

There are a few key questions to check your motivation to assist rather than hinder the situation between you and your spouse:

Will it create happiness or suffering for myself and others? Am I motivated by selfish concerns at the expense of others? Is there a more skilful way to handle this situation? Can I bring in forgiveness?

Do I want to be right or happy? How can I have compassion for myself in this moment? How can I have compassion for my spouse right now?

Case Scenario

Situation. William did not want a divorce. He had been married to his wife Constance for over 10 years and thought they were happy. They had not been arguing and he thought their relationship was fine. He treated her children from a previous relationship as his own, as they were unable to have children together. Suddenly, out of the blue, his wife wanted a divorce. They were both in their late 30s. He was very upset and approached the possibility of trying again with her as he wanted to stay in the marriage, but she was adamant she wanted a divorce. He felt she wanted to be free and single again, as they had both been working hard over the last few years and her children were now more independent.

How we helped him. We advised him to let his wife apply for divorce and offer her 50% of the equity in the house, as she wanted to move quickly. We prepared a financial remedy order transferring the property to him and providing for his wife to receive a lump sum and be released from the mortgage. The divorce went through easily as a result of letting his wife start off the proceedings. All he had to do was acknowledge he had received the application. This really suited him as he did not like paperwork! The court approved their financial provision and ordered there should be a clean break of all further claims between them. The divorce and finances were amicable and everything was concluded in six months.

How he coped. He had to quickly come to the point of acceptance that the marriage was over and come to terms with the early start of divorce proceedings.

As he needed to work some extra hours to support the higher mortgage he now had, he undertook some decorating work. He knew that by doing some more work for a period, it would take his mind off the situation but also lessen the financial stress.

Where he is now. He worked hard for many months, and then out of the blue one of his clients called him and asked him for coffee. It was the start of a new romance. They went out and got on so well that a year later they married, now have two lovely children and are very happy. He did not expect to be able to have children, nor meet his future wife in this way. If you had asked him a few years earlier, or even when he was getting divorced, if he thought this would happen, he would not have guessed it! By listening to what his wife needed, and letting his first marriage go easily and amicably, maybe he brought good fortune into the next one? It was nice to see him open up to a new and exciting chapter in his life.

Morning Meditation

When you wake, you may have that sinking feeling of what the day ahead will be like. You may have a sense of apprehension at what your spouse will say or the next step forwards today. Take a seat for five minutes somewhere comfortable where you won't be disturbed. Close your eyes and take a few deep breaths. As you breathe in, let compassion for yourself flow into your lungs and say to yourself, all is well. Breathe out any stress. Breathe in that compassion. Breathe in compassion and breathe out stress. Keep doing this until you feel more settled. If it helps to concentrate and soothe you can cross your hands over each other at your heart centre. After a few minutes, breathe in compassion and breathe out kindness to your spouse. They may also be feeling stressed, regardless of how they appear. Anything today is possible with kindness. Keep breathing in this way until you feel kindness and compassion, and then open your eyes. If you feel a bit wobbly through the day, remember to look after yourself with compassion and repeat to yourself "all is well". You will remember this as any challenges arise today. You will keep that thought as you move into your day.

Opening Thought of the Day
Anything today is possible with kindness and compassion. All is well.

Chapter 2

DECISION TO DIVORCE
(AND MINDFULNESS)

Introduction

The decision to divorce is going to impact many areas of your life. Whoever makes the decision to proceed with divorce, when your marriage breaks down it is inevitably a sad day. You promised each other when you married that you would live together happily ever after. The fairy tale is over. No wonder, therefore, painful emotions akin to grieving a loss on death, are keenly felt. We will go through the emotions in this chapter and discuss tools to help you process them effectively. We start with recognising your emotions, using tools to lift those emotions, and mindfulness methods. By allowing ourselves to be present, we let go of our habitual thought patterns. I will also cover professional and personal support groups you should take full advantage of at this time. We meet Debra, who was married for over 25 years, what she went through in her divorce, and how her life unfolded afterwards. Evenings and weekends may be difficult, particularly if you are in the same house. I therefore suggest you take a walk to get a break and try a short meditation in nature to engage all your senses. We end this chapter with letting go of judgment.

Making the Decision

Your Decision

Have you made your mind up? Maybe you have reached that "final straw". It is more than likely you have taken a long time to reach the painful fact that your marriage cannot be salvaged. If you are the one who made the decision to divorce, it tends to be a little easier to process but painful, nevertheless. Emotionally, you may still swing wildly between differing emotions. However, you are probably starting to get mentally prepared and may have already partly, or fully, detached yourself from your spouse. As soon as you have withdrawn energy from someone, or towards some situation that no longer serves you, you have detached from it. You are more likely to have disengaged over time than encountered a more stark epiphany. Or perhaps you may have had growing concerns and then reached a "final straw" situation.

However, this does not mean it is going to be an easy ride. Your husband or wife are still catching up; generally, they feel out of control if it has not been a mutual decision that you bring the marriage to an end. If your spouse does not accept it, there will be resistance so you need to be mentally prepared for this. Their emotions may bring unpredictability in how they now relate to you, the news, and the situation generally, as you proceed through divorce.

If you are getting a lot of negativity from your spouse, the only way to deal with this is through understanding with constant patience, forgiveness and compassion. If you react or retaliate you will end up in a battle and the situation will become more complicated and even turn out nasty at times.

In certain situations, it may be important to be clear with your own boundaries. If your spouse wants to confront you, you may need to walk away, or disengage, where you have to. Make it clear that you are available when your spouse wants to discuss matters sensibly, and hopefully this time will come.

If you can just sit, really listen and try to acknowledge and understand how the other is feeling, this is the best way for communication to slowly turn around between you, to become more positive. We are all familiar with getting things off our chests. If you can allow the other to do so without reacting, they will start to feel better as they process what is happening.

Not your Decision

This is numbingly hard for you. We've all been in that place where the decision is made for us. If it is not your decision, your emotions will be painfully raw. You need as much support as possible and many of the practices I outline in this book will be of great help to you as you work your way through your divorce. You may sometimes feel confused. You will at times have a resigned acceptance. Or you may swing between resistance, confusion, and acceptance. There will be a whole heap of emotions that you may experience, that I will outline for you, to help you to come to terms with what is in effect a grieving process.

You will begin the process of letting go. Letting go does take awareness, and a certain faith that everything will be all right. It is hard to let go of all the hopes, dreams and memories you had. It is a major loss, yet you may have no control over the situation. So how you manage the transition is important.

If you want your spouse to continue to be part of your life in the future, for instance, if you have children, or value their friendship, then you have the opportunity to resolve your relations and build a different relationship with this person moving forwards. But this comes down to good communication, and often resolving your own emotions, in favour of the greater good. I have known of some situations where the ex-husband or wife still spend Christmas together for the sake of the children, and even when one or both has met a new partner, they are also invited. This shows how, with a fresh outlook and kindness and consideration towards each other, new positive situations are still possible. There is a phrase sometimes referred to as "conscious uncoupling" and brought into popularity through

couples separating in the public eye. This is actually what it is –
bringing a level of consciousness into the decision.

Is the Decision to Divorce too Easy?

There are some that say that it is far too easy to divorce in
England and Wales, and most other countries, and that it is
made even easier with the commencement of no-fault divorce.
However, this does not take into consideration what has already
driven couples to this point. A divorce may be a relatively
straightforward process but I have not met one client who has
not come to the decision after painstaking consideration and
often after enduring misery for years. More often than not it is
long marriages that are being brought to an end, and the couple
have waited for the children to grow up before they start
proceedings. Even with shorter marriages, it is still often after
much agonising before the final decision is made that it is over.
That being said, currently you cannot issue for divorce in
England and Wales until after one year has elapsed since you
married. I have rarely seen couples who have entered into the
marriage with the thought that they can get divorced if it does
not work out – it is a disappointment when things go wrong and
generally one person, or both, have tried hard to make it work.

It is unhealthy for a person to carry on in a relationship,
marriage or otherwise, where they are unhappy. It is, of course,
a much tougher decision if there are children involved but
squabbling couples are not good role models. It is not good for
the spirit; it saps the good and vibrant energy of everyone
involved. As human beings we are not meant to be unhappy; we
almost condition ourselves to be this way and trap ourselves in
situations that unconsciously follow our belief systems.

I have not previously had a situation where the marriage was
salvageable once proceedings were issued. Sometimes a divorce
gets put on hold where there is doubt but I have often seen it
resurrected at a later date. It remains to be seen with no-fault
divorce whether one party, or both, do in some cases, have
second thoughts once the process has started. I have come

across couples remarrying again in the future, but these are few and far between.

What is the Impact of the Decision?

There will be inevitable changes to all aspects of life.

Social Impact

There is a social impact. To an extent, divorce is still stigmatised by society and everyone else will have an opinion regarding what went "wrong". The spiritual way of looking at this is that you have learnt what you were meant to learn from that relationship and it is no longer relevant to your growth. At the end of the day, it is your movie, and people will come and go from it.

I was once told by a good friend that a relationship is there to show you what you want from the rich buffet of life, not necessarily to give you it. It is helpful to treat divorce as a valuable life lesson which has brought a catalyst for change to open your life up to more freedom and possibilities.

Your relationship with friends may change. It is particularly hard when you have been together for a long time and your social network is the same. Suddenly, your social world will never be the same as you are now two separate units. The couples you used to see together may start to favour your ex over you, or you over your ex, or simply find it awkward. As a result, you will see them less and no longer be invited to "couple" get-togethers. You can also initially be invited by friends to get the up-to-date gossip on your situation and this too wanes as it becomes old news. This is the time to make new friends and try new interests. Your true friends will always stand by you, but even with them after a while you will not want to regurgitate the same old stuff about your relationship. It is boring, and you, and they, will be bored and exhausted. So, let your feelings out initially as much as you can, and start to process them and the situation in a positive way.

Be prepared that your relationship with your in-laws is likely to change. The saying that blood is thicker than water is never truer than on divorce. Even after long marriages where a spouse has thought they were close to their mother and father in-law, it can dramatically change on divorce where camps are quickly made and the family stick with their son or daughter regardless of the situation. It is sad but it invariably happens. Often, extended family and particularly parents, or grandparents, can bring wisdom to the situation to achieve a compromise for the couple on issues but sometimes they do just the opposite.

Financial Impact

The financial impact should not be underestimated as you separate out combined marriage resources. The security of your home will be turned upside down and your finances stretched. At least one of you will be moving out of the family home. You may both end up moving out to a new house as your home may need to be sold as you downsize to afford your individual new properties. There will soon be the outgoings of two separate households to cover from available income.

Divorce is one of the most stressful life events, generally cited after bereavement, in terms of stress. As it is often coupled with moving home, two major stressful life events are often experienced at the same time. Nothing can really prepare you for the upheaval of no longer being in a marriage and being displaced from your home. Even where your relationship may have been less than satisfying, two important anchors in your life – marriage and home – are pulled from under you and you will move from comfort to discomfort.

Impact on Health

A breakup of any kind, whether or not you made the decision, can be a shock to the system and you may suffer mentally and physically. This can have a direct impact on your mental and physical health. It is not unusual to suffer from depression and lose or gain weight at this time.

Impact Longer Term

The personal ramifications do not disappear overnight. I always say to my clients that the first six months are the worst, and generally, the first year anniversaries and other special occasions such as birthdays and Christmas may, as with bereavement, bring the feeling of loss and loneliness. It may feel like you have been a failure and it may be difficult to grasp the reality that either you, or your spouse, is letting go. The marriage has failed. The picture you once had in your head of marital bliss has been ripped to shreds. It can feel extremely brutal for some time.

You will need to get comfortable with some, or even a high level of, uncertainty with your situation. We can feel particularly traumatised by the uncertainty of what is going to happen next. Just be content with the knowledge that everything is happening for a reason and serves a purpose. Keep as a mantra, your wish that everything is happening for your highest and greatest good.

Support

This is a difficult period, and you need as much support as possible. The support you seek will vary depending upon the issues that crop up over this time. There are various sources of support through divorce. Professional: from your solicitor, financial advisor, and accountant. Personal: support from family and friends. Both professional and personal support can be found from your GP and a counsellor. If you have a religious affiliation, your community will also help to support you.

Counselling

Support from family and friends is really important at this time and if you do not have this, do seek some counselling. It really helps to get your mind straight but it is not necessary to remember and revisit every detail of the past. You just need to take control of the here and now and your emotions, and counsellors can often facilitate this. You can then put things in perspective and make clearer decisions.

Counselling can also be a helpful step to ensure you are moving forwards with no regrets if you have the made the decision. Before you make your final decision, you may also make a last attempt to go through counselling together. If we apply our work life to our home life, we would first explore solutions and discuss options and only if all else fails, do we feel the need to resign. So, it is worth a final push with the help of expert counselling if you think the relationship is still worth salvaging.

If you do not have a recommendation for a counsellor, search on the internet, www.nationalcounsellingsociety.org or www.bacp.co.uk (British Association for Counselling and Psychotherapy).

Religion

In times of crisis, many people turn to faith for comfort. Support from any spiritual organisation – a church, temple, mosque, synagogue or otherwise – is also a great help. Choose one that you already have a belief in, or attend, or used to attend. You will be sensitive at this time so be aware not to become involved in any cult or anything that doesn't feel right. You may wish to deepen your religious practices and faith at this time.

GP/Doctor

Your GP will have a supportive network in place to help you and they often have a sympathetic ear. Your GP will have a list of counsellors they can recommend and your workplace may have insurance in place to fund the sessions. Your GP can make suggestions to help you cope with the mental and sometimes physical stress, particularly if you are not sleeping which is often the case when you go through a divorce.

Family

Support from family can often be the best support at this time. I have had many clients who bring their parents to the first meeting, and very often this is helpful for them. Also, their parents as observers are likely to absorb more of what is being said and can confirm the advice given when they go home and translate it to the rest of the family (so you don't have to repeat it). Family provide important emotional support throughout the process. Family also often provide invaluable financial support at this time, from helping to pay legal fees to helping to raise a settlement. You will often find different family members will bring varying perspectives. Parents, with their life experience, often have a broader viewpoint. They also know you well. If your family lives abroad, still confide in them as they will sense there is some issue and would prefer to be involved. Do not be concerned they will worry. Whatever age you are, parents will always worry but still be there for you. They just want your happiness. Keep in regular touch with any member of your family who supports your decision and can provide emotional or practical help. If, on the other hand, they do not support your decision then keep true to yourself and just tell them the outline of what is happening. You only need to give the detail you feel comfortable with.

Friends

Good friends are there for solid support – they are willing to listen time and time again and may give you some helpful tips and advice in addition to spending time with you or going out for the evening and distracting you from the situation. Don't underestimate how nourishing friends can be for you at this time. Being able to verbalise what we are going through starts off the healing process. They can pick you up emotionally and give you strength. They can have abundant patience – you need to be looked after and cossetted at this time. Even simply going to them and having a weekly cry over coffee with a few laughs interspersed, helps with the release.

I remember one of my friends who had a young family and still just dropped everything and drove miles to visit me when I had my breakup, and it was greatly appreciated. I have heard from my clients, many tales of friend's kindnesses at this time, from inviting them to stay to going on holiday with them. Just taking you out of your usual environment and feeling cared for can give you a temporary lift and reprieve from your agony. Also, their kindnesses will not be forgotten and will build a strong lasting friendship. They may also accompany you to the solicitor or your GP. Even if they just stay in the waiting room whilst you have your meeting, you can then discuss anything that is said to you whilst it is fresh in your mind. Your solicitor may also be agreeable for them to sit in your first meeting but check when you make your appointment.

Workplace

You will know if the culture in your workplace is likely to be sensitive and supportive whilst you go through divorce, and if so, you may choose to put them in the picture. Most modern employers are, and Human Resources departments do not share your personal details with your colleagues. Although sometimes, with their own personal experience, colleagues can often be a helpful support. If you work in a team, they can help you on "off" days. You may wish, therefore, to share with your workplace the fact you are going through a divorce so they understand if you need flexible time off, or some days you are just not 100%. Most companies are supportive during these periods, and hard times can bring you closer to your boss/team. Most people will have gone through a relationship breakup so they ought to be able to understand and empathise.

Financial Advisors/Accountants

Engage early on with practical advisory support on your finances, particularly if you have not dealt with finances through the marriage, which you will now be confronted by. Speak to your bank and ask if your friends can recommend a financial advisor. You can discuss matters with them and seek their clarity and guidance on your and your spouse's assets, and the practical financial options available to you. Check that they are members of the Institute of Financial Advisors https://www.ifa.org.uk. If you have complex finances, for instance, more than one property, you should also instruct accountants to advise you on tax implications.

Top Tips

DO

1. Spend time writing down the reasons for your decision to divorce to gain clarity that you are taking the right step and consider whether counselling could help salvage the marriage.

2. Engage the professional support of a financial adviser (IFA) to help you navigate your finances and understand your spouse's financial situation.

3. Instruct a chartered accountant if your joint finances are more complicated, particularly if you and your spouse have more than one property, or a business.

4. Discuss with your spouse whether the next step should be to divorce and which one of you, or whether both of you, should bring the divorce application. I still always prefer you to issue the application, rather than your spouse, as you can then ensure the divorce goes through in a timely manner.

DO NOT

1. Shy away from asking your spouse questions to enable you to process your situation and receive the correct support. Be clear and brave. It may be easier to get your spouse to provide information and open up in the earlier stages of a marriage breakdown.

2. Do not take to processing your situation and emotions all over social media. This will not be helpful. It may also be advisable to disconnect from your partner's Facebook, Twitter, Instagram and all other social media accounts. This will assist

you to disengage and concentrate on your own new life rather than your spouse's.

Mindfulness and Emotions

You may find that the most natural way to get through this period is to look inwards. After all, your external world is spinning. Calm down your inner world to keep as centred and grounded as possible, and regain some overall balance.

Check your emotions. There are a whole range of emotions you are likely to experience, ranging from deep anxiety and despair, to sadness, disappointment, and a feeling of failure. These may be intertwined with a heavy dose of anger, hostility and resentment thrown in. These emotions come in waves and it is often possible to feel a whole range of emotions in the same day, or to become overwhelmed by a negative emotion over time, or even suddenly in a moment when you least expect it.

It is better to feel and heal the emotions than avoid them. It is easy to suppress them by drinking, taking drugs and partying hard or even working to extreme. It is ideal to process your emotions as early as possible and to let them go. You do not want to be left with deep-seated emotions such as resentment. These emotions will only eat you up in the future and cause you more pain. In contrast, your pain will have no effect on your spouse or ex-spouse.

Even the most confident person is likely to hit low self-esteem at the point of divorce. Just remember that none of us are born with low self-esteem and it is ok to "fail" in the eyes of the world as it really does not matter what anyone else thinks. You have not failed; your outer situation has failed (only if it is labelled this way). Another way to look at it is that your outer situation has just changed. Build on your inner self-esteem and growth as being your true success to come through your divorce.

The Grief of Divorce

There is often a comparison between bereavement and divorce. There are key similarities as on divorce you have no choice but to let the other person go, and often the same feelings have to be processed. Death of a beloved, as they say, is not a conscious choice on the person left and divorce can often feel the same. Whether your spouse takes the first step to bring the marriage to an end or you make that decision, you may both still take time to adjust to the new reality.

Be aware that you are likely to encounter many negative emotions through divorce – grieving emotions akin to those felt when suffering loss on bereavement. The Kubler-Ross model in 1969 initially outlined the five stages of grief. These were stated as denial, anger, bargaining, depression and acceptance. Over the years, these were adapted and additional emotions included. The grief model or curve, as it was initially outlined, has been updated as the emotions do not necessarily follow sequentially. It is quite frequent for these emotions to overlap, for several to be experienced at the same time, and also experienced again and again, over time.

Denial (and shock). The first emotion of denial is often preambled by the initial shock. In my experience, if your spouse has made the decision to divorce and you are on the receiving end of being told that the marriage has broken down – and that is the end – you are first likely to go into a state of shock. I have had clients who have seen me at the very early stages after they have been told who are in shock. This appears to be part of the fight or flight syndrome and the brain's supporting mechanism to protect us.

If that is you, you may find it hard to deal with any task where you may need to concentrate. Even mundane tasks may become more challenging for you. You may find it difficult to work. One way to focus is to concentrate on getting through each day at a time and decide you will perform your daily tasks to the best of your ability for that day.

It is a good idea to take more periods of rest than usual. You may also need to see your GP to provide some medical guidance to help you through. It is sometimes helpful to see a solicitor if you need some reassurance regarding implications for finances and children, but you are unlikely to take much in. An idea may be for a helpful friend or family member to accompany you to any meeting to take notes for you.

With the initial feeling of shock often comes the mental processing and seeking more information from your spouse, together with an overwhelming fear of the unknown. At this point you may feel completely immobilised to take any action and need to digest the situation. You may be desperate for answers. You may fixate on things said during your relationship, or even recently, that may possibly contradict the reality that a breakup is actually happening. You may debate about it with friends and family to justify why the relationship shouldn't be over and may still not be convinced it actually is.

Following shock, denial is the next step. Many of my clients whose husbands or wives have told them the marriage is over, still show signs of disbelief and often think that their partners will change their mind. It is likely at this point that they may have been burying their heads in the sand. Perhaps their spouse has previously said that they would be issuing divorce proceedings but have not done anything about it and they feel that this will be the same again. There is a complete ignoring and avoiding of the reality and enormity of the situation and the change due to take place. You may feel you have put everything into the relationship so it can't be over; the relationship has been your world, your life, so it can't be happening. Unfortunately, it is happening. Denial is often accompanied by a sense of fear. You cannot believe this is actually ending, even if the relationship was awful at times. You may feel overwhelmed and continue to be immobilised by fear. You start to experience the withdrawal from your husband or wife when you no longer receive replies to your texts or communications.

Pain and Guilt. It starts to unfold into a brutal process. You are likely to experience an additional step of pain and guilt. This often follows hot on the heels of denial as that temporary

41

buffer falls away and the pain of reality hits with ferocious intensity. You go back in time and think how you could have done things differently and you regret things you have done or said. This can lead to self-blame and thinking that the breakup is all your fault. Guilt is felt most keenly. The marriage breakdown brings real pain. You can be plunged into a seemingly never-ending abyss of pain and suffering.

Anger. Sometimes with denial, or after, or indeed at frequent times through the divorce process, anger is the emotion felt passionately by most. If it is your spouse that has made the decision, with anger often comes a sense of injustice; it is not fair what is happening and it is happening to you. You may question why, you may have suspicions, and continue to have fear. If you have made the decision to end the relationship, you may still feel anger. You may feel that you have been pushed to this point by your spouse's behaviour, either following a major event that may have occurred such as an affair, or a whole series of dissatisfactions that have now culminated through the course of the marriage to this point.

I would say that anger is the main emotion that needs to be tackled head on to make sure you do not get completely out of control and you don't say what you will later regret. Anger very much focuses on blaming someone or something and may also allow the continuation of denial to the situation.

Bargaining. An additional step was subsequently included in the Kubler-Ross grief curve – that of bargaining. This is particularly likely on the breakup of a relationship and can take place at any time, from the time of denial, to the pain of reality. Often you will offer to do anything, you will take the entire burden of responsibility, to make the relationship work. You are clinging onto any hope you have. Unfortunately, you are still under the illusion that you have control over the breakup. Sometimes it does work for a while, you may both try again and you are relieved the pain of withdrawal is over. Unfortunately, the relationship cannot just carry on with one person's efforts, and it inevitably falters again. Interestingly, if this happens, you may, rather than your spouse, then make the decision to break up. The process of breaking up and reconciling can happen several times before a final breakup, and divorce.

Depression. The lowest point often comes when denial and anger begin to wear off and there is a stark realisation that the relationship cannot be salvaged. Self-doubt and anxiety levels peak and it is possible to fall into depression. At this point, performance is often at its lowest and you may find it hard to take action. Your energy levels will be low and you are likely to feel demotivated. There is a tendency to fixate on small issues. Do be prepared that you may burst into tears without warning. You may find it difficult to cope with even the most mundane daily tasks. You may still carry on doing jobs for your spouse if you are in the same house, even though it will not change things. When going through this stage you can often feel sadness, fear – continued fear – but also regret, guilt and other negative emotions. You will have given up and now feel fully immersed in the dark. You feel pain. It is usual to show signs of indifference, or reclusiveness, pushing away support.

If you are feeling depressed, do be aware that it is not a definition of who you have become; it is just a phase you are going through. Through this period, you may feel loneliness and isolation. This is the time for self-reflection. As you think back to what has happened, you may start to lead yourself into the initial stages of acceptance. You get to understand why you are currently at this point and start opening up to the situation, whatever it is. Over time, you will start to see things more clearly. Please don't give up hope.

Acceptance. The final stage is acceptance and integration. You will get there even though it may not feel like it at the time of the breakup. You will become more optimistic, as you have survived the change, and open to new opportunities. Often, with acceptance, you may still need a good level of support for some time, and if the support is taken away you may lapse back into earlier stages. Sometimes, at the acceptance stage, you may become impatient for the change to be completed and are often held back by the practical side of selling the house and legal processes.

Integration. The final step is integration. Your situation has changed and has been fully replaced with the new reality. You have acceptance, hope and trust, going forwards. You have increased energy and your productivity is renewed. This is a great place to be! It will take time, but you will get here.

To recap, it is not a linear model with your emotions. Be prepared to be jolted backwards and forwards between different emotions over months or years. You may also experience several emotions in the same day. However, treat it like a piece of internal work, to process those emotions and get through stage by stage.

Tool for Processing Emotions

There is a direct connection between the brain's processing power and expressing emotions in writing. Psychologists have found that by writing about your feelings, you can overcome emotional upsets and feel happier as a result. You may wish to start a diary at this time. It can be cathartic to write down what is happening each day and how you are feeling. It is also particularly helpful to write at the end of each day, to let go of your feelings, rather than churning through them at 3 a.m.

By writing down our feelings, this reduces activity in the section of the brain known as the amygdala responsible for the intensity of our emotions, so it can help calm and release very strong emotions as well as process them over time. Studies have determined the therapeutic effects of writing overcoming symptoms of depression and anxiety. And it is fine to cry. Crying is a form of release. It releases the deep emotions.

Tool for Lifting Emotions

Sometimes it feels really hard to leap from a negative feeling state to a positive one. The Abraham-Hicks Emotional Guidance Scale is a helpful tool for lifting ourselves out of lower "vibrations". Vibrational energy is a complex topic but we know that there is more to our existence than what we simply perceive, or interpret, purely through our physical senses. Every form of matter, including our bodies, vibrates at a certain frequency.

Emotions can be broken down as e-motions. They are literally energy in motion – energy frequencies. We can choose which energetic frequencies we want to tune into and radiate, and these are known as vibrations. For instance, sadness and anger have low frequencies. Peace and joy have high frequencies, and you are operating at a high vibration when you experience these emotions.

The emotional guidance scale is a list of commonly felt emotions ranging from joy, appreciation, empowerment, freedom and love (the highest) to fear, grief, depression, despair and powerlessness (the lowest). There are many other emotions listed in between the top and the bottom of the grid. It is worth visiting the Abraham Hicks website, www.abraham-hicks.com

To gradually process your emotions, you identify which emotion you are feeling and take steps to get to the next one up on the scale, which is a better feeling one (even where it may still be negative). When we feel fearful or powerless, we are not going to make the leap to the top to love and joy. We have to gently guide ourselves back to better feeling emotions by taking one small step at a time. It is a matter of familiarising ourselves with the practice of reaching for a better-feeling thought and moving up the scale to a higher-vibration emotion.

We need to keep remembering that like attracts like. When we're low on the emotional scale, we're emitting negative energy which attracts people, situations and experiences that match that vibration. This is why often our day can go from bad to worse. As we lift ourselves out of a low vibration and move up the emotional scale, our point of attraction shifts.

There are several ways to move up to a higher-vibration emotion. They are all, in some respects, versions of the same methodology.

1. The next time you notice yourself at the bottom of the emotional scale, gently practise reaching for better-feeling

thoughts and emotions. Know that you can move up the scale step by step.

2. You can use the method of "acting as if". The As-If Principle was established by American philosopher William James in 1884. This principle suggests that when we act *as if* we already are, we become just that. Biologically, our body doesn't know the difference between the thought of an event happening and an event *actually* happening. It physiologically processes the thought exactly as it would the actual event. This is good news for us because it is an easy way to raise our vibration. You may think, what would the best version of myself do now, and how would I act? If you tell yourself to act more positively, whilst initially it may feel uncomfortable and even disingenuous, you will eventually become that way. You may go on to imagine that your divorce has now finished, and you feel a sense of relief; you are feeling more peaceful; everything has worked out just fine. Stay with those thoughts for some time. After a while, and if you practise this often, you will start to change how you feel and how you react.

3. There is a method you can include in your journaling. Move up the ladder to higher vibrations by writing at the top of your diary each day: "*I like the feeling of* ..." and see what flows out of your pen. No need to judge or edit.

There are also other, more subtle ways that work. Firstly, show appreciation for everything you have, and for the many small and large kindnesses that come your way through this process. You may have a friend who is listening to you or your parents are supporting you. Secondly, continue to be of service to someone else. You may have other friends you can support in different ways, or a family member or your local charity. See how you can help. Within minutes, you will be in a higher-vibration place because you'll no longer be focusing on yourself and your situation. Instead, you will have redirected your focus to others. The universe automatically supports this energy and reflects it back to you.

If all else fails, do something else you enjoy as a distraction, and try to add some lightness and laughter where you can. As you feel good, this will influence you feeling better generally.

Also, don't forget to recognise each small step that you take towards a better feeling thought and emotion, and quietly celebrate each action.

Mindfulness

Mindfulness is a technique where you pay attention to your present emotions, thoughts and body sensations, such as breathing, without passing judgment or reacting. Mindfulness is being aware. Mindfulness is about trying to be an observer each day of your thoughts and emotions, and the external situation – just witnessing what is happening. Mindfulness is about starting to live more consciously.

It can be practised at any time, wherever you are, whoever you are with, and whatever you are doing, by being fully engaged in the here and now. By doing so, you are free of both the past and future. This enables you to let go of questions and worries that are likely to arise at this time, such as "what if this happens?" You also become free of judgment of right or wrong, and the "I'm no good" or "this is hopeless" scenarios. This allows us to be totally present without distraction.

Labelling your Emotions

We, as individuals, can vary considerably in how we react to divorce and emotionally challenging events, to our life's slings and arrows. One way to practise mindfulness is to label your emotions by saying, for example, "I'm feeling angry at the moment" or "I'm feeling a lot of stress right now". Why does this help you? Just the labelling of what you are feeling brings in a small space between your thoughts. By creating this small space, you can bring in objectivity as the observer of your thoughts and reduce the grip of that emotion. As you become more practised at this, it has greater effect upon calming you down.

When you find your mind wandering and you get into negative thinking, firstly just feel and be present with the

47

thought and acknowledge the emotion. You have to be really aware and present to do this and pick up the negative emotion or thought as it arises. Whenever possible, check reactive thoughts and emotions. The part of the brain known as the amygdala is associated with experiencing strong emotions such as fear, and the fight or flight response. The more mindful you are, the less activation you have in this area of the brain, and so you can turn down the emotional response and improve your mood.

If you are finding that difficult, force yourself to do something else – preferably physical initially – and then in 10 minutes or so you will have forgotten what you were dwelling upon. The best way to break the cycle quickly is to get out of your head and concentrate on your bodily sensations. That is why doing something physical is good for you – even some stretching can help.

Our unconscious mind is known as the monkey mind as it jumps all over the place, from one thought to another, from one emotion to another. It is easy to follow negative emotions and continue with impulsive reactive thought patterns darting here and there. The easiest way to break the pattern is when an emotion such as anger starts, acknowledge that emotion and be mindful of it arising. Where is it arising in the body? Concentrate on the physical sensation and breathe into it and through it until it subsides. If it is a strong emotion, and still has a hold, go for a brisk walk or a run. If you break the cycle as soon as the emotion arises, then you will not feed it by thinking of what he or she has done, and past events, and end up in the cycle of anger and resentment.

One Day at a Time

To help you to become more mindful, consider deciding to live just one day at a time. Make a decision to limit your focus on this current day only. I have found in difficult times, just deciding I will only deal with anything that comes up for that day, and effectively stopping time, stops the worrying about the future or bringing up past fears. I steer myself away from past and future thinking. It is a good practice not to look back or forwards and stop the out-of-control mind patterns that keep you in the constant loop. Make the decision at the beginning of the day, respond to anything that crops up and then move on to the next task. You need to have the concentration of mind to stick to it. I have used this method in a number of situations. An example may be that you need to sort out your personal belongings ready to move out of the family home. Just take this as the task for the day, rather than ruminating about what this means to you. After time, you get into the habit of just doing what is necessary to get through the day, and a sense of ease naturally flows in.

One Moment at a Time

Moving onwards from taking each day at a time, try taking each moment at a time. Particularly when you are going through the pain of separation, the best place to be is in the present. If you dwell on the past, you suffer, and if you become anxious about the future, you suffer. Just do what you can do in this moment, as if it is all you have. Concentrate only on yourself and casually observe around you. Try to bring in a few minutes of space. Observe as you are simply breathing in and out, and how that happens effortlessly. It is not that easy initially, but with practice becomes easier, and it will transform your day as you go through each moment much lighter.

Mindfulness in Nature

It feels natural to be mindful in nature! Nature has a wonderful way of putting things in perspective, and whilst you can complete this exercise anywhere, it is really satisfying in a natural outdoor environment. In time you start to realise how insignificant you and your story really are in the scheme of the universe. You understand that you are simply akin to a small ant out in the world. If you were on the moon and looked down towards the Earth, you would not even be a speck in the enormity of the planet. And yet you are still part of it, and still able to make a contribution. You are also unconditionally supported by Mother Earth. You are helped and held.

I found sitting in the garden or the park where it was quiet and just observing the nature around me – seeing the beauty and stability of the trees, the colours and forms of the flowers, and looking up to the expanse of the sky – really helped me. Then I would listen – listen to the birds seemingly chatting away, the light wind rustling the leaves – and stop there for a while. Then I would engage my sense of smell; the light perfume or aromas of what was around me. Finally, I would feel my feet on the ground, my body on the chair or bench, and sit for a while, effortlessly sitting and breathing. Feeling calmer.

The method of engaging the senses brings you easily into a wider expanse, and you may get glimpses of, or a total feeling of, being at one with your environment, nature and the universe. The best way I found initially to become mindful, was engaging all the senses to bring some space into my mind.

Going with the Flow

These methods guide you towards fully experiencing the present moment. That is all there ever is. You slowly stop dwelling on the past or anticipating the future and you let it unfold. In challenging times, I have come to think this is how it is meant to be, and part of a greater plan. Even situations I have labelled in the past as unpleasant have, in hindsight, been great journeys for my growth. I like the analogy of peeling off layers of an onion at each life stage. Over the years I have come to believe that whatever is happening is for my highest and greatest good, and whilst I still find it hard not to label things good and bad, I go with the flow much more and am less resistant to change.

What is pleasant we often don't think about much; if it is nice we often enjoy it in the moment. However, what we view as unpleasant or bad, the mind grips onto with vigour and we cannot let go.

If you want an easy read on mindfulness, I recommend *Mindfulness on the Go* by the writer and psychotherapist

Padraig O'Morain. It is good for all aspects – relationships, work and home – and can be used when travelling. The great bonus is that it was written for us all on the go, so is in nice chunks and easily digestible. The chapter on Mindful Relationships is worth reading. This chapter outlines how our patterns become habits which our relationships fall into. There is also an interesting statement early on that, according to marriage research, most of the long-term differences between partners are never resolved. So, going over old issues is a waste of time. He outlines the importance of mindful listening and mindful speech in relationships which I would say is just as important going through a divorce, with the heightened emotions of a breakup. He also covers the mindfulness required to stop recycling resentments and this will help you to overcome the resentment triangle; of replaying a memory, feeling bitter or angry, and then reliving the scene again and again, as you tell yourself how rotten your spouse is.

Letting go of your Story

The more mindful you become, the less you will become embroiled in self-pity and your story. You can end up getting entangled only in the situation you are in and giving yourself various negative scenarios about what is happening or will happen. Try not to make it more of a story and exaggerate the situation. Ruminating and catastrophising is not going to change anything. The more you layer your story, the more difficult you will find to disengage from it. You will otherwise become overwhelmed and that is another stress on your already stressful life.

In *The Power of Now*, Eckhart Tolle outlines this perfectly. It is so easy for us to, as he says, become our story. So, for instance, we would probably say something like this: I am getting divorced, my spouse has left me or I have had to leave him or her as it was unbearable, he or she was disgraceful in their behaviour, and now this means that I ... And on and on. He asks a very poignant question. What is your problem right now? The same stuff is regurgitated automatically. He asks again, but what is your problem right now in this very moment? Well, there isn't really anything right now, but you know I have this and that going on ... Then it suddenly dawns – actually there is no problem right now. Stay in the present and there never will be. As he says, don't lose your sense of life, as what is going on is simply your life situation. If a moment comes where you have to take action regarding that life situation, take it and move on to the next moment. That's how life really is and should be. Don't live and relive the same old story. This is so important for anyone going through a relationship breakup. Get out of your head, so you don't lose your mind.

Create a new Reality

It is time to go inwards and create a new reality, as actually you have nothing now to lose. Joe Dispenza's book *You are the Placebo* is also as applicable to those, like himself, who suffered great physical trauma, to you in divorce experiencing a deep mental unrest. With effort and awareness, you can break those habitual thought and emotional patterns. You can also transform your life. From inner turmoil to tranquillity, get deeper into those layers to become more mindful and transform your thinking.

Case Scenario

Situation. Debra sits down. She has been married for 25 years and her husband Wayne is having an affair. He still expects her to do the cooking and cleaning and he does not want a divorce but wants to continue his relationship with his girlfriend. He is having his cake and eating it! Her three children are all adults and support her decision to divorce. But still she feels alone. She was looking forward to retirement and she reflects back into her marriage and bursts into tears. She finds it hard to cope with the reality the marriage is over, and that her life will change completely.

How we helped her. We assisted Debra with a referral to counselling and suggested she speak to her doctor.

By taking action only when she felt ready and talking through the next practical steps.

We advised she should first discuss and communicate her decision clearly to her husband and let him know that she has instructed solicitors.

After a few weeks, we phrased the first letter to her husband in a non-confrontational and sensitive way.

We then started divorce proceedings.

During the process, we encouraged Debra to spend more time with family and friends.

She was facing an uncertain and unknown future. We recommended that she kept a diary and start to process her emotions.

How she coped. She used courage to see a solicitor.

Strength to confront the issues with her husband.

Determination to stand up for herself and explore what she wanted.

With all these attributes we knew she would be fine, and she decided to let her husband know that she was starting off the divorce.

She sat down and started a journal to build up a picture of where she was currently, and what she would like to do in her life. Initially it was general, ready to fill in the gaps over time. Over the next few months, her friends then helped her write down her thoughts and fill in the gaps for her future life when they met up together.

Where she is now. Following her divorce, she decided to change her life around completely. She moved to be next to one of her daughters and enjoyed spending time with her young grandchildren. She joined various clubs, found a passion for painting, spent her summers in Europe on painting holidays, and met new friends. She also used these holidays as periods for reflection as it took a few years for her to feel comfortable and settled again. She became busier socially than she had ever been before and felt much more peaceful. She also became more aware to seize every moment of her life than ever before.

Evening Meditation

Evenings and weekends can be a difficult time, particularly if you are still in the same house. You may have had a busy day at work or with the children. You are now faced with the stony silence of your spouse, and your thoughts start to race again regarding your breakup. When you can, take a short walk. If you have children, speak to your spouse to look after them for just half an hour. You are going out to take some time for reflection. Find a safe quiet place near your house where you can go and sit and observe nature. Even if you do not have a park nearby, it may just be sitting on a bench near some grass or trees. This will be your spot. It is going to be where you can come and sit regularly without being disturbed. You are going to learn to engage all your senses on this regular outing.

- Breathing
- Seeing
- Hearing
- Smelling
- Tasting
- Feeling

Take a seat. Just sit and breathe. There may be times when you feel like crying. No judgment; express any emotion you need to. Then start to look around you. You may see some trees. What do you see? Is every leaf the same colour, the same size? Is there some breeze and movement as the leaves flutter? What do you see? That bird – where is the bird looking, where are they taking off to? How about the sky? Is it clouding over? Is that a bluey type of grey? Observe fully what you see, as it will not be the same the next time you sit on this seat. And those sounds, are there two birds or maybe more? Are they calling to each other? And what else can you hear? Cars nearby travelling along. By coming outside, what can you smell? Is that fresh vibrant air? Maybe you can detect some scents of flowers. Pause for a moment. Come to your taste. Can you taste what you had for dinner, maybe? Does your mouth feel dry? Now really feel into your sensations. The weight of your body on the bench; your feet lightly touching the ground. Engage all your senses now. What do you see, hear, smell, taste and touch? Just observe. Then take a few deep breaths. Really come into your environment, this moment. If your mind wanders, bring it back to this moment and observe your surroundings a little longer. You have become more mindful. Sit still for a while before you make the decision to get up and return to your house. As you walk back, decide when you will next return. And repeat. Each time you do this meditation it will be different. Enjoy each time without judgment.

| **Concluding Thought of the Day** |
| I let go of judgment. I appreciate what is around me. |

Chapter 3

PREPARING FOR DIVORCE, MEDIATION AND MEDITATION

Introduction

In this chapter we will discuss instructing your solicitor. You may decide to instruct a solicitor to deal with all aspects of your divorce, including negotiations on financial matters and discussions regarding your children. However, many couples seeking an amicable approach to these matters, may opt to attend an independent mediation process to help facilitate an agreement between them, whilst leaving the necessary drafting of legal documents and the court process to their solicitors. A less common, but growing approach is also to instruct solicitors who are collaboratively trained. In this process, issues are thrashed out with a view to reaching an agreement in a sequence of meetings attended by both sets of collaboratively trained solicitors, with you and your spouse. There are, therefore, several options as you prepare for your divorce. As we start to focus, we look at meditation in more detail, as a helpful tool at this time, to help you think clearly and calmly. There have been many studies on meditation and its benefits to both your wellbeing and mental faculties. We meet Paul and follow him through his journey through the mediation process. At this time, as your days may start with a sense of trepidation, we bring a simple breathing meditation into focus and stillness into your day.

Why you need a Solicitor

Of course, the question to start with is, do I need a solicitor? I often hear this: "It's all amicable. We have no children or assets and I think I can complete the divorce application". You may choose to deal with the divorce yourself but if there are other issues – finances or children considerations – it is better to engage a solicitor. The answer comes back to knowledge and support. You may have emotional and practical support from family and friends but you also need professional support. Your friends may have gone through a divorce or know someone that has, but no two situations are identical.

What if it is not all amicable? If your spouse is particularly hostile, the best route is definitely to engage solicitors to act for you. Also, where there are conflicting issues, ask yourself if these are minor matters that you think can be resolved, or major conflicts which need professional guidance to resolve them.

In any situation, at the very least I still recommend you have a fixed-fee meeting to check you have covered everything. Many divorcing couples later come unstuck, particularly with regards to financial matters, because they do not know the implications of the actions they are taking or failing to take. A couple of examples are as follows:

• I have had clients who, unrepresented at the time of divorce, decided they had nothing and so did not enter into a financial consent order only to find 10 years later, the former spouse decided to issue an application for finances, and they got a big shock. Their former spouse obtained a settlement based on the value and extent of their current assets; my client would have been much better off obtaining an order at the time of divorce.

• Also, clients who thought they had agreed finances between them at the time of the divorce and did not need a financial order. Their former spouse later changed their mind, or their circumstances changed, and an application could still be made to court, as they did not properly formalise the agreement at the time of divorce.

- I have also had clients who chose not to have legal advice on a financial order that was drafted by their spouse's solicitor and made when they divorced. Years later, when it came to drawing their pension on retirement, they realised the implications of having to continue to pay maintenance under the financial court order. It makes a huge impact, as you are just finishing work and looking forward to settling into retirement when you understand your former spouse still takes some benefit.

Therefore, it really is an important time to get proper legal advice. If you get advice at the time of your divorce, you can ensure everything is dealt with properly. It could cost you a lot more in the future if you do not. Whilst I understand that you want to minimise the steps you take and your legal costs, revisiting financial matters on divorce years later is always more expensive.

Finding a Solicitor

There are various ways to find a solicitor who can represent you. In all situations, do find a specialist family solicitor. Recommendation is generally the best way.

Ideally, an introduction may come from someone you know well, particularly, from a good friend or family member who has a similar outlook and expectations to your own. If you do not have a recommendation you can either complete a web search for local solicitors or go to the law society website – https://solicitors.lawsociety.org.uk/ – complete a search for "family and relationships" and put in your area or postcode for solicitors in your area. If you have international aspects, for instance, your spouse is abroad or you have dual citizenship and you have assets abroad, you may need to find a specialist solicitor with the right experience to deal with this.

If your matter is complex quality marks are important and look for whether the firm has Lexcel accreditation and whether they are in the top 500 legal firms. You may also want to check whether the individual solicitor has Law Society family law accreditation, or family law advanced accreditation. If there are major disputes regarding the children, then check whether the individual solicitor has children panel accreditation. I personally think that experience and practical application to your matter is more important than accreditations, although they do confirm a level of expertise.

It is important that you find a solicitor that has a flexible approach. They need to be both conciliatory and firm at times. You ought to have a good idea when you meet them whether your solicitor's approach is going to be in line with your outlook. You do not want a solicitor who is overly aggressive but, equally, they need to be strong enough if your spouse is going to be difficult.

"Resolution" are a membership organisation of over 6500 family lawyers and other professionals committed to the constructive resolution of family disputes. They also deal with training of collaborative lawyers. A search can be entered to find a solicitor in your area who is either a member of Resolution or also collaboratively trained. Solicitors who are members of Resolution, generally have a non-inflammatory and constructive approach due to their code of practice. You can search resolution members on their website.

http://www.resolution.org.uk

I would also recommend that you instruct a firm that either has a property (conveyancing) department or good links with a conveyancing firm. There will invariably be the sale or transfer of property to deal with, and this makes matters smoother as the departments can either liaise internally or at least easily if the conveyancers are used to dealing with the family firm. If a third firm has to be instructed, in my experience this complicates matters, and it can often be more expensive with the family solicitors liaising with another set of conveyancers.

Arranging an Initial Meeting

I would suggest that you phone the chosen firm and arrange an initial consultation. Most firms offer the initial meeting either free of charge or at a fixed fee. I suggest you arrange a 45 minute to 1 hour meeting if you can, as half an hour may be insufficient for the solicitor to take full instructions and give detailed advice and guidance on financial matters. However, you will be able to discuss the divorce and process, and perhaps an overview of your financial situation.

After the initial interview you will know:

- how you feel,
- how you connected with the solicitor,
- whether you understood the advice,
- whether you are comfortable with that person representing you.

If you are happy, stick with that solicitor for your divorce. If you are not sure, then arrange a fixed-fee meeting with another solicitor before you make up your mind. It is entirely your choice who you choose to instruct but it is better to make the right choice from the outset, rather than changing part way through the process. So, make a good decision early on.

You should have an idea of the experience and seniority of your solicitor from the first meeting but if you have any queries, just ask about their experience and they will be happy to share this with you. If you are dealing with a family department, often a more junior solicitor or paralegal can deal with the divorce procedure whilst financial matters are generally dealt with by more experienced solicitors. Children matters can often be dealt with by both.

Legal Fees

How much is your divorce likely to cost? Most firms will charge the divorce procedure only on a fixed-fee basis, so you should have full knowledge of this before you start, and you may also be asked to pay this fee up front. There will additionally be a court fee payable when your application is submitted.

Most of your legal costs will accumulate in resolving financial and children matters. These are both normally charged based on the time spent by the solicitor. They will inform you of their hourly charging rate and give you an overall estimate of likely fees. The general rule is that all communication is charged, from short emails to telephone calls. Do not underestimate your fees. Your solicitor will provide you with an initial estimate but if your spouse is contentious and you do not come to a swift agreement on matters, your legal fees will escalate considerably. Be mentally prepared for your initial estimate of fees at least to double or triple.

Understand from the outset that solicitors apply an hourly rate to your matter. Do not use your solicitor as a counsellor or send lots of emails unless you have a great deal of money. Generally, solicitors bill monthly so you will know how time is being expended. You will soon realise that it is better to keep communication to a minimum and only ask your solicitor to give overall guidance on side issues and continue to deal with the major matters.

How to meet Legal Fees

My suggestion is, if it is possible, save up for your legal fees before you start the process. This will take the pressure off you as you will know your legal fees are more or less covered. It will be one less thing to worry about. Please be very aware that law firms are strict on the retainer; if you do not pay their fees as interim bills are raised, they cannot be expected to continue to work for you. So, your delaying payment of fees will inevitably delay your proceedings. Do not expect your solicitor to drop everything for you, if your solicitor is also having to chase you for monies. Keep legal costs up-to-date and you should ensure that your service is not disrupted. Many firms will ask you to set up a monthly standing order arrangement so they have continued funds on account of legal costs.

If matters are very complex, it may be that your family will help you with your fees or you may need to look into borrowing from your bank. There are specific lenders that specialise in loans for financial proceedings. Ampla and Detach Lending are a couple of examples, although the interest rates can be high. They will liaise with your solicitor for case details to make sure they have the security of ensuring the loan can be repaid to them.

If you get a loan from your family this can be treated at a final financial hearing as a soft loan, i.e. not immediately repayable, which can be quite frustrating. Always get any loan documented and pass to your solicitor. Loans must be disclosed in financial proceedings.

If you have limited financial resources, how you are going to meet fees throughout the process is a difficult consideration. There is some possibility of help through public funding. Very few firms now have an arrangement with the government legal aid agency. Those firms can apply for public funding on your behalf. This is only available in very limited circumstances, normally where there has been domestic violence. This legal aid may also be available for mediation. Speak to your local Citizens Advice Bureau, who will have a list of local firms that may offer legal aid so that you can make enquiries.

Please note there are now "direct access barristers", i.e. counsel you can go straight to for advice and representation in court proceedings without going through solicitors. But it is better to have full representation throughout contested proceedings if you can afford it.

Confidentiality

Anything you say to your family solicitor is confidential so make sure that you cover everything. They have heard everything before so do not be worried about saying anything, and do not keep secrets. You must be as honest as possible so that they can guide you properly. Also, solicitors have a strict code of conduct with the Solicitors Regulation Authority and therefore, if you lie to them during your matter, they may not be able to act further for you.

Mediation

Mediation can be an aid to sorting out any issues between you both following your marriage breakdown, whilst still instructing solicitors to deal with the legal formalities.

What is Mediation?

Mediation is an alternative dispute resolution to help solve different types of issues and problems without going to court. Mediation is a means of resolving issues between you, with the help of an independent professional third person who does not take sides. You and your spouse remain the decision makers. The third person is called a mediator. You both meet through a series of private meetings with the neutral third person known as a mediator to resolve matters between you. An independent professionally trained person (the mediator, who may or may not also be a solicitor) helps you to come to an agreement regarding divorce, financial and children matters following your breakup. He or she helps you to come to a solution which works for both of you. The mediator is not there to counsel you or to help resolve marriage differences with a view to getting back together. Their approach is to see how you can move forwards independently with your lives.

Who are Mediators?

A mediator will have had previous experience in a relevant professional role, for instance legal, counselling or social work. Mediators are registered with the Family Mediation Council, to ensure certain professional standards and training is met. A registered family mediator may be either accredited, or working, under supervision, towards accreditation. You can have solicitors that are trained mediators. A solicitor mediator undertaking the mediation process with you cannot then advise either of you individually. Therefore, you will then need to instruct your own separate solicitors. A solicitor mediator is likely to be more expensive than other mediation services.

However, if you have really complex financial matters, I would recommend a solicitor mediator. Non-solicitor family mediators through their training generally have a good understanding of the court process and the orders a court could make in your situation. Even where they are not trained solicitors, they have the necessary background against which they can facilitate a suitable agreement.

Mediators will discuss the options available to both of you and they try to ensure that decisions are made jointly and fairly. They facilitate discussions between you, assist communication and encourage understanding. They focus the participants on their own and common interests with a view to arriving at a suitable outcome. They can also work hand-in-hand with your own solicitor through the process. If there are particularly complex issues, they will recommend you each take legal advice at various times in the process.

It is important to note that any agreement finally arrived at in mediation is not binding, and therefore you will still need to instruct your solicitors after the mediation process is complete to place the agreement, which is known as the memorandum of understanding, into an appropriate order.

When to use Mediation

You are not required to go through the mediation process. However, if you end up having to go to court to sort out your differences on financial or children issues, you normally need to show you have at least attended one introductory meeting known as Mediation Information and Assessment meeting (MIAM) which simply explains what mediation is and how it might help you.

Mediation, however, may be a more cost-effective option than dealing with all issues through your solicitors. If you come to a mutual set of terms, it will make the legal proceedings less costly, and they generally then move more quickly and with minimal hostility. Ideally, unless you have both agreed who will bring the divorce application, it is sometimes a good idea to discuss this first through mediation. Then move onto the issues such as financial matters, children issues and any side matters.

You can bring a divorce application without having attended mediation. If financial and children matters are agreed, there is no point in attending mediation. However, if you have tried to resolve these matters to no avail, and you are considering bringing either financial or children proceedings, you must have at least attended the initial appointment with the mediator (the MIAM – Mediation Information and Assessment meeting) before you bring a court application.

Exemptions

There are some exemptions when you don't need to attend mediation even if you are bringing a court application:

- If there was domestic violence supported by clear evidence, e.g. injunction/police investigation,
- If there are distance restrictions preventing you practically being able to attend,
- If there is urgency,
- If there is social services involvement,
- If there are several other specific exemptions.

Your solicitor or mediator will advise if any of these apply. You can also refer to the family mediation council website.

When to avoid Mediation

You do not need to see a mediator if everything is already agreed between you. I would not recommend mediation if there are any control issues between you and your partner or there has been any domestic violence. You must both come to mediation on an equal basis. If you do not feel comfortable seeing your spouse face-to-face, you may need your solicitor to deal with discussions and negotiations for you. It may be more expensive but it may be more comfortable for you. The mediator may otherwise propose that you sit in separate rooms whilst he or she is a go-between, or sessions take place by video link or telephone. This is possible. You will still need to engage in a one-off initial MIAM mediation appointment described above (unless any exemptions apply) if you want to bring financial or children proceedings.

Finding a Mediator

I would recommend you find a mediator in your area as this will make it easy for you to attend sessions, although many do now use Zoom or Skpe. Mediation services do vary according to my client's experiences. If it is not working for you early on, it may be worth considering changing mediator or stopping the process. I would still estimate 90% of my clients come out of mediation with a framework agreement, and I have often seen fairly complex children arrangements agreed in mediation which realistically would have taken a great deal of time and expense if agreed through solicitors. Contact arrangements and scheduling times for collecting and returning the children, and any further detail on arrangements, generally work well in mediation.

The Family Mediation Council is made up of national family mediation organisations in England and Wales and has a list of registered mediators who work within the standards and codes of practice set out by the council.

The website is:
https://www.familymediationcouncil.org.uk/

How to Afford costs of Mediation

There is normally a fixed cost for the first meeting and for each subsequent meeting payable by each of you. There will be further costs for time spent in preparation of documentation. You will each pay the mediator in advance of your sessions with them. Sometimes, your spouse will agree to meet both their own, and your costs of attending, if they have a much higher income, or as an incentive for you to choose this route to resolve issues between you. If you have a low income, you may be eligible for legal aid to meet your costs.

Working Together with your Solicitor and Mediator

In relation to financial issues, I would recommend that you take advice from your solicitors before putting forward any proposals in mediation. Quite often I have seen clients who have become very disgruntled when they think they have come to an agreement in mediation only to be told by their spouse that their solicitor has now advised against it, and they are back to square one. As a result, one party feels they have wasted all that time in mediation, and the other party should have obtained proper legal advice before or during the process to avoid this. Do not agree to anything in mediation unless you have had advice and are committed to it.

Procedure and Mediation Forms

One of you will make the first contact with the mediator. The mediator will then contact both of you to arrange an initial meeting known as the MIAM. The role of this meeting is as follows: to assess whether you are both suitable to proceed with the mediation process, and in general terms, what your aims and objectives are. The meeting is completely private and the mediator will assess whether your matter is suitable for mediation. If it is not, there will be no further sessions. If it is, a series of approximately three to six meetings are subsequently arranged. These are spread over a period of time with a view to resolving matters between you in the presence of the mediator.

Mediators often provide meetings out of hours but these are slightly more expensive than meetings within office hours. Sessions can be anything up to 90 minutes.

If you try Mediation and it does not Work

After the first mediation session (MIAM), if the mediator decides that it is not appropriate for you, they will complete form FM1 (Family Mediation Information and Assessment Form), confirming you have attended a MIAM. Also, if your spouse does not turn up, or the mediator determines that even an initial meeting is unsuitable, they will sign the form for you.

No enquiry by the court or your solicitors can be made as to why the mediator deemed it unsuitable.

If, after the MIAM, your mediator decides your matter is suitable for mediation but you do not want to continue, or after you have had a few sessions it is not getting anywhere, you can end the process. It is a completely voluntary process.

Provided you have at least attended the MIAM, the mediator will complete form FM1 which will allow you to make a financial application or children application to court.

This form will be valid for up to four months from the date of the MIAM. If you delay applying to court and you decide to bring your application to court after four months, you will need to attend another MIAM meeting and obtain a fresh form FM1. If any of the exemptions to attending a MIAM apply, your solicitor will sign the form.

If you try Mediation and come to an Agreement

Hopefully, matters will be agreed between you through mediation. There are documents the mediator can prepare for you at an additional charge. These are helpful to ensure that you both agree on the terms. I have also found these provide a framework for solicitors to convert the agreement into an order, and it avoids you having to spend a lot more time going over it with them. The documents a mediator will prepare if you achieve an agreement are as follows:

1. Preparation of a memorandum of understanding – the terms placed in this normally form the basis of a financial order and so aids your solicitor in covering all the agreed terms when they draft the financial order.

2. Preparation of an open statement of financial information. This sets out both your finances. As the court will require an accompanying financial statement (form D81) to be completed when asking for the court's approval on your financial order, this document normally gives all the information for your solicitor to prepare the form needed for court.

3. Preparation of a parenting plan – this forms the basis of children issues which, if agreed, do not need to be put into an order but can provide an agreed framework for the future. They can also be placed in an agreed order where matters may have started out being disputed and you both want to ask the court to define matters formally in a child arrangements order.

Collaborative Law

What is collaborative law?

The collaborative process involves the parties and their own collaboratively trained solicitors, again in a series of meetings, to try to resolve disputes without going to court.

How does this differ from mediation?

Although mediation and collaboration are both methods of resolving issues between divorcing couples without going to court, they differ considerably from each other. In the collaborative process, you are guided as a couple to reach an agreement with everyone working as a team. In mediation, the mediator cannot advise or represent either of you. All mediators are trained but some are lawyers and others are not. Collaboratively trained solicitors are lawyers first and foremost. Where otherwise there may be an imbalance of power between you, two skilled solicitors are able to go much further than a neutral mediator in seeing that the playing field is levelled.

Working Together with your Collaborative Law Solicitor

Collaborative law focuses on building a settlement around the needs of you, your spouse, and your children, rather than putting you each on opposing sides, to fight for your own position. The approach is considered useful for financial discussions and children issues. The collaborative process involves a binding agreement known as a Participation

Agreement between family solicitors and clients that there be no recourse to court proceedings (with a view to then submitting an agreed order on finances or children once matters are agreed). In this process, discussions take place face-to-face in four-way meetings, so you each have the benefit of a solicitor advising you and acting for you within those meetings. The advantage of this approach is that you can see what is happening at each stage of the process.

Is the Collaborative Law Process suitable for you?

The collaborative process needs a good level of communication and trust, and it is not possible in many breakups. It does ensure that there is not simply a stream of correspondence between solicitors over a long period of time, which can otherwise happen, and sometimes it is easier to thrash things out face-to-face. However, if negotiations were to break down and if either of you wished to instigate financial or children proceedings, then neither firm of solicitors could continue to act. So, you would each need to instruct new firms. As a result, many clients prefer the mediation route rather than the collaborative law route so they can retain the same legal advisors throughout. Also, whilst the collaborative approach can sometimes be cheaper and quicker than other alternatives, it can often be just as expensive as traditional negotiations between solicitors, as many meetings will often be required to resolve matters. Also, not all solicitors are collaborative lawyers and therefore this can also limit who is available to instruct.

Top Tips

DO

1. Arrange an initial consultation with your solicitor before you discuss anything with your spouse so you know the general principles that apply to your situation. Discuss with your solicitor whether mediation would be suitable. Also discuss

with them whether they are collaborative solicitors and whether this process may be an option.

2. Tell your solicitor if anything in your situation changes and seek guidance before taking action, i.e. keep them up to date.
3. If mediation is suitable, prepare a list of mediators in your area that your spouse can choose from.
4. Attend mediation (if you think it is suitable for you) as early as possible, ideally even before the divorce process starts.
5. Review whether to continue after three or four sessions. If there has been no progress then you may need to come away from mediation – it just does not work in all cases.

DO NOT

1. Make major decisions before consulting with your solicitor first. A few for instances where you should seek advice before taking action are: paying your spouse maintenance or giving them capital; selling or transferring property; making changes to joint bank accounts; or even booking your next wedding date if you intend to remarry.

Methods of Meditation

Meditation and Mediation

There is an affinity between meditation and mediation (and indeed the collaborative law process). Both meditation and mediation recognise the simultaneous nature of unity and opposition, and both seek a middle way. The two processes combine and complement each other; mediation being a practical way of resolving our external situation, whilst meditation concentrates on internal resolution to attain peace within. Both encourage us to transform our conflicts, allowing us to leave them behind.

What is Meditation?

Meditation is a technique for resting and stilling the mind, and attaining a state of consciousness that is different from our normal waking state. It is a means for experiencing the centre of consciousness, often labelled as "emptiness" or the "one-ness" within. In meditation, the mind is clear, relaxed, and inwardly focused. When you meditate, you are fully awake and alert, but your mind is not focused on the external world or on the events taking place around you. Meditation brings an inner state that is still, so that the mind becomes silent. When the mind is silent and no longer distracts you with mindless thoughts, knowledge of your inner self deepens. You find the peace and stillness within. Some say you find a space of vast freedom.

Meditation has ancient roots. It is widely accepted by archaeologists and scholars that it dates back to between 3500 to 5000 BCE. There are records in Indian scriptures known as Vedas in 1500 BCE that outline meditative practices. It has been adopted as a key practice in many religions and developed in recent times as a "new age" discovery. It has depth and history behind it.

Meditation and Mindfulness

Is there a difference between mindfulness and meditation? Mindfulness is the awareness of "some-thing" while meditation is the awareness of "no-thing". Whilst mindfulness can be applied to any situation throughout the day, meditation is usually practised for a specific amount of time. Meditation also goes hand in hand with mindfulness. In sitting for meditation, you apply concentrated effort in the "space" in your mind. Periods in between meditation during the day are known as "meditation breaks". This is where you bring mindfulness into your daily life and become aware of all around you. There is also a combination, known as mindfulness meditation. Here, you focus your meditation internally on an "object". Mindfulness supports and enriches meditation. Meditation also expands mindfulness.

When to Start

You will see that I have introduced meditation from the first chapter of this book. The earlier you are supported by meditation, the sooner you will reap the benefit. Now it is time to take that practice up a notch. As you start addressing the legal issues between you, and even during the mediation process, it is easy to feel debilitated and confused. If you have not meditated before, this is an opportune time to start. You may feel depressed and disillusioned at this time. Everything you believed to be true and comfortable has been turned upside down. If you regularly practise meditation, the benefits are long-lasting. It trains the mind and brings in awareness. I have found in my practice, and I have observed in others, that meditation will bring you ultimately from chaos to calm; chaos from your external world, to calm in your inner world.

Benefits of Meditation

Meditation is a science, which means that the process of meditation follows a particular order, has definite principles, and produces results that can be verified. There have been many scientific studies upon the benefits of meditation on the brain. It increases your cognitive abilities and promotes relaxation. It also promotes emotional wellbeing and aids with sleep. Sleep is necessary for any person's wellbeing and you particularly need plenty of rest when you are going through a divorce. Meditating regularly in the mornings brings a certain peace naturally through the day, and meditating before bedtime encourages a restful sleep. It has to be experienced to understand the peace and tranquillity that starts to underpin your mind, and so your life, and you let go a little more and cope better in stressful situations.

You will need to make many crucial decisions throughout your divorce. Your decisions will be better if they are thoughtful and intentional, rather than reactive. Meditation is one of the techniques you can use to ensure those decisions are coming from your conscious, rather than unconscious, mind. If you have inner quiet, you are more likely to make the right choices

73

and more helpful decisions. Otherwise, your past behavioural patterns will continue to play out, and you will be responding to what is happening with automated, and often unhelpful, responses. I remember spending time trying to rationalise, trying to gain perspective, and think about what had gone wrong, the choices made and what could have been done differently, to no avail. No amount of constant thinking actually helps. This is where meditation comes in – to break the loop of constant thinking.

How to sit in Meditation

Find a simple, uncluttered, quiet place where you will not be disturbed. You may have a few favourite places, or one space, that you can set aside for meditation practice. Learning how to be still is the method of meditation. The process of cultivating stillness begins with your body.

1. You can sit cross-legged on the floor with a cushion under you or simply sit on a chair with your feet on the ground. You keep your head, neck, and back straight while sitting in a meditative posture. Ensure that your back is upright but you do not need to hold it rigid.

2. Loosely place your hands in your lap. Often meditators will place their upturned right palm in their left palm, in the centre of their lap.

3. You can meditate with your eyes half closed, but I always find it easier to meditate with eyes fully closed.

4. You should let the tip of your tongue lightly touch the roof of your mouth, close your mouth, and keep this through the meditation. Whilst, practically, this helps against over salivating, you also ensure your energy flows in a circular motion through your body, and the tongue in this position forms the bodily connection.

Once you are comfortable, bring your awareness down through your body, allowing your muscles to fully relax except those that are supporting your head, neck, and back. Take your time and enjoy the process of letting go of the tension in your body. Meditation is the art and science of letting go, and this letting go begins with the body, and then progresses to thoughts.

You should initially practise regularly in the same posture to familiarise your body. To start building your meditation into a habit, it is also helpful to meditate at the same time and in the same place every day. Use this section as a template for sitting in the meditations we now continue through this book.

Forms of Meditation

A good place to begin for meditation is to become aware of the space between your thoughts. When you first start meditating, your thoughts will be racing; I have always been taught to view them as clouds in a clear sky that will eventually pass. As a result, you do not hold onto the thoughts and simply let them go. Just observe them and let them go. Do not become discouraged as thoughts will be prevalent with what you are going through, but their hold over you becomes less as you meditate more. Even if your mind is racing, do persevere. Like anything, with practice it becomes easier.

If you find this uncomfortable and you cannot settle, it is helpful to move on to concentrating on "an object". There are many forms of "object" meditation.

- Some are aimed at developing a clear and focused mind, known as "clear mind" meditations. Mindfulness meditation is a form of clear mind meditation. Attention is paid to the natural rhythm of the breath while sitting. The easiest meditation to begin with by way of concentrating on an object, is simply observing your breath. You are aware of your breath as it comes in and goes out. You do not control it; you simply observe it. It is still easy to lose yourself in other thoughts. To guide yourself back to your breath, you may want to name your breath internally to yourself as inhale and exhale, or just in and out. As you observe it, the breath automatically starts to slow down. Initially, simply sit for 10 minutes and practise this meditation.
- Other object meditations are aimed at developing altruistic states, such as love, loving kindness, compassion or

forgiveness, and gratitude, known as "open heart" meditations.

- Others use sound, as in chanting or intoning sacred words. If you have a special mantra, this may be beneficial.
- Another helpful meditation reflection through this particular part of your life is concentration on impermanence. If we reflect on the impermanence of all phenomena, it helps us to let go and we can really reflect deeply as to whether it was necessary to cling so tightly to this person or personal situation, and did our expectations ultimately just bring us suffering?

How often to Meditate

Just be gentle on yourself and start with 10 minutes a day, even initially only in the morning or in the evening if you do not feel you can fit in both. Then increase to 10 minutes in the morning, and the evening, or before you go to bed. If things become very stressful, add in another five minutes here and there during the day to centre yourself again. As you experience the benefits, start to extend these times. If you can, increase the time so you sit for around half an hour at each sitting. After a while, you will notice a subtle change in how you are able to deal with the pressures of the divorce and generally your life. Like any habit, it needs repetition to become part of your daily life. After some time, it should be an automatic part of your routine.

Guided Meditations

You may wish to find a class that you can join to help you become familiar with meditation practice. Guided meditations are also helpful. Use special guided meditations before bedtime if you find that your sleep has been disrupted through this difficult period.

There are many YouTube guided meditations and websites, so it is easy to find one, and often a voice that resonates with you.

A few examples are:

* https://tharpa.com/uk/ – they have various deeper meditations I would recommend for relaxation, a clear mind, and for a kind heart. Each audio consists of three short, guided meditations. Initially you may just sit for one of those, which is between 10 to 15 minutes on average. The meditation for a kind heart is to help improve our relationships by learning to cherish others. The first meditation reminds us that others are important and so is their happiness and freedom. The second is a wish to protect others from suffering. The third is an intention to give love and happiness to others. These meditations are particularly poignant at this time you're going through and can help transform your view.

* This leads on to the meditation known as metta bhavana or maitri bhavana which translates to loving kindness or friendliness meditation and encompasses loving kindness to all human beings. The meditation starts with the wish that we are well, happy, peaceful and free from suffering. We then extend this wish to our friends and family. It then progresses as we extend this wish further to those that challenge us, for instance our ex-spouse. We complete the meditation by extending the wish for peace and true happiness of all beings. There are many loving kindness meditations on you tube. This is one example: https://www.youtube.com/watch?v=sz7cpV7ERsM

* Meditation on gratitude is extremely important and I use this as my daily practice. When we are caught up with the woes of marriage breakdown, life often appears bleak. Gratitude reminds us of what we really have, not what we do not have; a cup brimming full not a cup half empty. We realise we are fortunate if we are well, we have water, food and shelter, we can see, hear, walk and breathe the very essence of life. When we are going through difficult periods a certain darkness consumes our outlook. We sometimes forget how fortunate we are, and to count our blessings. There are many in this world who do not have food, shelter,

and who are just surviving. A lovely dentist I know said that her husband refers to our problems as "champagne" problems. We still have a choice how to resolve them. The fact is that the majority of us have all our faculties, as well as having considerable comforts and good health. Life is already rich. I believe it is essential at this time and throughout life to make gratitude practice into a daily routine. My favourite is Deepak Chopra – Guided Meditation on Gratitude on YouTube.
https://m.youtube.com/watch?v=KSM6hVkYhIs

- I also like Deepak Chopra's guided YouTube meditation before bed which really helps to clear the day. At times of divorce, it is helpful to empty each day and start afresh the next. We want to stop the endless daily regurgitation of the same thoughts.
https://m.youtube.com/watch?v=7CaaHXjoRhA

- Guided Meditation by Mooji on YouTube is also very soothing and brings you into the present.
https://www.youtube.com/watch?v=2Ah88bK2V-A

- If you want to start going deeper, I have attended Sadhguru's inner engineering course and I completed his Isha Kriya meditation which increases awareness with the breath and eases us out of our identification with our mind and body.
https://www.youtube.com/watch?v=4nLv76RsouE

Once you have digested these meditations you may wish to liberate yourself in a retreat, perhaps on conclusion of your divorce and when your energy levels are high. Whilst both mentally and physically challenging, Vipassana meditation is a 10-day intensive retreat which can bring a whole new perspective to life. Very often the publicity surrounding this retreat is that it is austere as it is silent and there is no eye contact. However, we need to be silent to go within. Most people do not find this aspect difficult once you get used to withdrawing from the worldly noise. Vipassana means to see things as they really are and follows the practice of self-observation leading to transformation. It is not for the faint hearted, and you go very deep. It is ideal to have been able to sit in meditation for long periods as a preparation for this retreat, as it is physically demanding. For many of us, this experience can be one of the most gruelling and rewarding undertakings to complete. I particularly found it useful at a time I knew a relationship was at an end and I let it go far easier after this – it was an incredibly disciplined and soul searching experience and it put life firmly into perspective for me – https://www.dhamma.org/en/about/vipassana

My whole outlook and advice at this time is to be gentle on yourself, and just do what you can cope with it. It may be a few guided meditations, joining a class, or taking some time on a retreat. Perhaps look out for a local day course, or weekend meditation retreat at this time which can be a welcome break.

If there is one method I believe will help you to get through this time, it is meditation. Also, it is free. You will feel better not having spent money to temporarily make you feel good. It is often the case when people feel low – they go shopping either online or to the retail outlet. Whilst initially it may be a distraction, it can consume us. It is better to avoid having a temporary high, to simply receive the corresponding low of your credit card bill. This will put you under even more pressure. Do you really need that item, and the added financial stress the indulging will bring at this time?

The good payback for meditative practice is the longer lasting effects of meditation. Free financially, and free of thought. Freedom will truly help you to feel lighter, happier and more peaceful. If there is only one both scientific and spiritual practice I ask that you please adopt, it is meditation. It is amazing and will really transform your life like nothing else can possibly do that is out there. Whilst I came to yoga early in my 20s, meditation practice came much later in my 40s. How different I believe the choices I made would have been if I had meditated earlier. But equally, it is never too late. Meditation is a direct experience of the higher consciousness – it is bliss.

Case Scenario

Situation. We acted for Paul. He wanted to keep matters amicable with his wife Denise. They had been married for 16 years and had three children aged 7, 12 and 14. They both felt they had drifted apart and no longer had much in common apart from the children. They both agreed that Denise should keep the house until the children were independent but they did not know what Paul's share should be after that. Paul also had a good government pension which had to be factored into discussions. They wanted to achieve a financial compromise that was fair to both of them.

How we helped him. We suggested that Paul attend mediation with Denise and we set up the initial form of referral. They had five sessions in total. In the first meeting, the mediator explained the process to both of them and discussed what matters should be on the agenda for the next meeting. At the second appointment, they were able to define what time the children should spend with Paul and divide holidays to help balance out the childcare arrangements. At that session it was agreed that at the next meeting they would bring details of their finances. At the third meeting, they were able to exchange financial documents and subsequent to the meeting, the mediator prepared a joint summary of assets and liabilities for them to consider. They then needed to speak to their legal and financial advisers, and accountants, regarding tax implications, and consider proposals. At the fourth meeting, they were able to come to an agreement that Paul would have a legal charge over the marital home to be repaid to him when the youngest child was aged 21. The property was to be transferred into Denise's name and he was to be released from the mortgage. As Paul would be waiting for capital monies when the legal charge was repaid, it was agreed that Denise would have a slightly

80

lower percentage of Paul's pension by way of a pension sharing order. The only issue that remained was the level of maintenance that Paul needed to pay to Denise and for what period of time. They decided to go away and think about this for the next meeting. By the time they came to the fifth session, we had given Paul legal advice and Denise had taken legal advice upon the level of maintenance and length of term. They decided to compromise in the middle, agreed an amount payable and a term of four years.

Following the meeting, the agreement was put into a memorandum of understanding and a financial summary was prepared. Paul let us have a copy so that we could draw up the financial remedy order to be approved by Denise's solicitors and then filed at court. The court subsequently approved the order and matters were finalised for the future. The transfer of property and preparation of the legal charge was dealt with by conveyancers. Paul and Denise had an outline parenting agreement for the children and did not need to seek a court order to formalise these agreed arrangements.

How he coped. Paul was able to keep calm even through very stressful discussions in and out of mediation, as he retained his approach to concentrate on the children's best interests with Denise. He started to meditate at weekends to help him through.

Where he is now. He decided to increase his meditation practice to incorporate it into his routine more often after work. He occasionally attended a few courses. A further six months after their divorce, he started a small self-help group for men going through similar separations to help support each other. He found it particularly hard not being with his children every day so he could empathise with the other fathers and discuss the methods of communication he adopted.

He managed to retain a good friendship with Denise in the future, and often still went round to help her with a few house maintenance jobs. They sometimes had meals together with the children, and both felt much happier.

Morning Meditation

Find a quiet place where you will not be disturbed. Sit comfortably with your back erect, either on a chair with your feet on the floor or on a cushion sitting cross-legged. Place your hands loosely in your lap. Close your eyes. Tip of your tongue to the roof of your mouth, and your mouth closed. Take a couple of deep breaths. Then start to settle your breath. Start by simply observing your breath. Become aware of your breath as it comes in and goes out. Do not control it, just simply observe it. You may lose yourself in other thoughts or the sounds in the environment around you. Just guide yourself back to your breath. Say internally to yourself inhale and exhale, as you take each breath. As you observe it, the breath automatically starts to slow down. Sit for 10 minutes and observe your breath. You may wish to set a chime on your phone when 10 minutes is up so you don't feel the need to keep checking the clock. Take a final deep breath when you open your eyes and take the stillness into your day.

Opening Thought of the Day
I bring stillness and peace into my day.

Chapter 4

THE DIVORCE (AND HEALING) PROCESS

Introduction

In this chapter we discuss the divorce process which has changed since the introduction of no-fault divorce. We go through each stage of the proceedings, and an outline of the online divorce option. Once the divorce has started, the ball is rolling and it can be a time of great anguish. Don't put off the opportunity to heal yourself, particularly before any stress and negativity that you may carry unconsciously, starts to manifest itself physically. When the body is unable to eliminate stress, related biochemicals start localising in the tissues. Disorders and ultimately disease may develop. I have friends and clients that have had stressful marriages and break ups, who place their health conditions either fully down to this or are certain they were a major contributory factor. Please look after yourself, put any preconceived ideas aside and try any form of healing that resonates with you. I have given a few examples from reiki and theta healing, to nature itself. We also look at energy techniques that promote healing such as Qigong and Tai Chi. We meet Rita who, with two young children, had to develop confidence to go through her divorce. We end this chapter with a morning healing meditation, and affirmation that you are healed.

The Divorce Process

The divorce process is straightforward. It cannot be started until after one year has elapsed from the date of the marriage. You do not need to attend mediation prior to issuing divorce proceedings. There is only one ground for divorce and that is the marriage has broken down irretrievably. This is now simply evidenced by a statement that the marriage has broken down irretrievably. The court must take this to be conclusive evidence and do not require any further reasons or any period of separation to support this.

The person that starts the divorce is the Applicant and the other party, who receives the divorce application, is the Respondent. A joint divorce application can also be made to court, and both parties are Applicants. It is the same process for dissolution of civil partnerships (which I have therefore not made reference to). It is possible to apply on-line through the court digital service, or on paper using form D8. If the person applying is represented by a solicitor, the digital service must be used.

Divorce Process summary

Sole or Joint Application made by Applicant/s and issued by Court

28 days for Service on Respondent if Sole Application

14 days for Respondent to file acknowledgment of service

35 days for Respondent to file answer if disputing divorce

20 week period minimum before can apply for conditional order

Conditional Order application stage

Conditional Order

6 week and one day period before can apply for final order

Final order made on application

Sole and Joint applications

It is possible to apply for a divorce jointly or individually. A joint application can later be changed to a sole application at conditional or final order stage. But a sole application cannot be converted to a joint application.

If applied for individually, it is known as a "sole application" and the person applying as a "sole Applicant". As it is not possible to change the application to a joint application once it has been submitted, the decision must be made at the start.

If the application is made together, it is known as a "joint application" and the parties applying as "Applicant 1" and "Applicant 2." The parties are equally responsible for the application. It is possible to apply on-line through the court digital service, or on paper using form D8. If one or both joint Applicants have instructed a solicitor, the digital service must be used. However, if one solicitor acts for both parties paper forms must be used. In practice, I cannot envisage one solicitor being able to act, as with other questions over financial and children matters on divorce, the solicitor would have a conflict of interest.

If a joint application is made, both parties do not need to complete the application together for the digital service. Applicant 1 will provide all the necessary information, and Applicant 2 will receive an email asking them to review this information, and provide any additional information. Applicant 1 will then review Applicant 2's additions and submit the application to court.

If preparing the paper form the parties can easily prepare this together or post to each other before sending it off to the court. Whether the paper or digital form is used, both parties have to sign a statement of truth.

Jurisdiction

You are able to start divorce proceedings in England and Wales if you are *domiciled* or *habitually resident* in England and Wales. *Habitual residence* is the country where your centre of interest is, where you normally live or have your marital home. *Domicile* is a more complex term and can be a domicile of origin where you were born, or domicile of choice where you elect to reside. You can only be domiciled in one country. A domicile of choice can replace a domicile of origin if you decide to permanently relocate there. The application sets out the detail on these options as follows:

- both you and your spouse are habitually resident here
- the person receiving the divorce application is habitually resident here
- you were last habitually resident as a couple here, and one of you still lives here
- you are habitually resident in England and Wales and have been for 12 months
- you are domiciled here and have been habitually resident for six months
- or you are both domiciled here.

The online portal puts the question of jurisdiction simply and asks if you live your life mainly in England and Wales. If you are issuing a joint application for divorce, the form asks questions on residence to both Applicant 1 and Applicant 2. If other countries may also have jurisdiction for you to issue your divorce proceedings, you must get specialist legal advice as to which is the best jurisdiction for you to issue your application in.

Making the Application

The Applicant/s can apply for divorce online or by post. Online is generally easier to navigate and quicker. However, the information required and process remains the same. When the application is lodged at court, by post or online, the court will process the application and allocate a case number and it is then formally known as having been issued at court.

Applying Online

A digital service has been launched for no-fault divorce. The divorce procedure can now be accessed online at https://www.gov.uk/apply-for-divorce. There is also a digital divorce contact centre that can help with any queries by telephone 0300 303 0642. Their opening hours (as at July 2022) are Monday to Friday 8am to 8pm. Saturday 8am to 2pm.

The Divorce service also have a webchat.

 or email to contactdivorce@justice.gov.uk

If you do not feel confident using the internet or do not have access to a computer or smartphone there is also a dedicated digital support helpline telephone 0330 016 0051.

HMCTS have how to videos and on-line guidance for individuals and solicitors.

https://www.youtube.com/watch?v=ZJ7uEhKlb80
https://www.youtube.com/watch?v=ZqtDfqgJVts

Most solicitors are also now set up to issue divorce applications online and offer a fixed fee for completing the divorce process. They will know what to do if things go wrong. However, you can issue the divorce application online yourself if you prefer. The online forms are easy to follow and you respond to the questions. The online portal moves you along the form. You will simply upload your marriage certificate and official translation if applicable. On the portal one solicitor cannot act for both parties, a paper application will need to be made instead.

Online application

Users will first need to create an account or sign in to begin. You simply put in your email address and create a password. You then make the application. A digital version of the divorce application form D8 is completed. It is straightforward online as it takes you through each section and asks a series of questions.

- About your marriage. Who is applying to divorce, the date of your marriage and asks for confirmation that your marriage has broken down. The application goes on to ask whether you want to apply solely or jointly.
- Help with fees. If you have limited income and savings you may be able to seek help with fees. If you have already applied for an exemption from fees you will have a reference number you can insert. Otherwise the court fee will be payable, £593 (as at July 2022).
- Jurisdiction. It asks where you got married, and whether you live your life mainly in England and Wales.
- About you and your spouse. You need to confirm the names on your marriage certificate, and if you have since changed your name by deed poll this needs to be uploaded.
- How the court will contact you. Your contact details and confirmation as to whether you want to keep your details private from your spouse.
- How the court will contact your spouse. You need to provide the postal address and email if they have one.
- Whether there have been other court cases.
- Dividing your money and property. There will be an opportunity for you to confirm that you wish to apply for a financial order for yourself and your children. It does not mean that you need to proceed immediately with a financial application, and this is explained in detail on the court portal.

You next need to upload documents. This will be your marriage certificate, and translation if the certificate is not in English. If you have changed your name you will also upload a copy of your deed poll.

The court portal will summarise that you are applying for a divorce (and deciding how money and property is to be split if you have ticked that section). You then make a statement to confirm that you believe the facts stated are true, and this completes the application.

On a joint application if you are Applicant 1 you can select that Applicant 2 checks and then an email is generated to them to create an account and sign in. They have to confirm they agree as if they say no, the joint application will not be issued and Applicant 1 will then have to start again and issue a sole application.

If you are issuing a sole application and wish to keep your address confidential a link will automatically be generated giving information of domestic abuse support services, and further screens updating on financial orders available.

If you are unrepresented, information on financial consent orders and links to the government website on child maintenance will be given. An explanation will be provided that a separate application needs to be made for the court to deal with finances. If you select yes you wish to proceed it states you can apply at any time as long as your spouse is alive. If you tick no it makes it clear you can only apply for a financial order until you remarry but that you can apply at any time for a pension sharing/ compensation order.

Once the form has been completed

Once the form has been completed the portal will state that your application has been submitted and you will receive a 16 digit reference case number together with an email including this reference number. The email will confirm that your application will be checked and a date when you will hear whether the application has been accepted. Only once it has been accepted will a copy of the application be sent to your spouse.

Once the Court have checked and accepted the application it will issued. All parties will be given a reference number and an access code to enable them to sign in. Parties will need to agree to receive emails to use the digital service. They will be able to see documents and orders by accessing the service. It is also possible for parties to keep their contact details private from the other party.

Applying By Post

Paper applications are now sent to the following address (correct as of July 2022);

HMCTS Divorce and Dissolution Service, PO Box 13226, Harlow, CM20 9UG.

When received the court scan the documents into their electronic court system so the applications benefit from the courts digital case management system.

The Procedure by Post

Initial application

- An application for divorce (or dissolution of a civil partnership) is prepared (form D8). The form covers the same sections as for online divorce but is just set out and worded slightly differently. The applications are based upon irretrievable breakdown of marriage or civil partnership. A sole or joint application can be made. The application contains a statement from the Applicant or Applicants that the marriage has broken down irretrievably.
- The Applicant/s must give details if there are any existing or concluded proceedings in respect of the marriage, or which may have affected the validity or subsistence of the marriage. (If there are any, the court may give further directions as to how the divorce should proceed).
- You should always tick the boxes that you seek to raise all financial claims to protect your future position. Even if you have agreed matters, you will then formally seek a consent order later in your divorce, after the conditional order, dismissing those claims. By ticking the relevant boxes, you are not putting financial proceedings in motion; this is done separately.
- Whilst an application can be made for the other party to pay the costs, there is no provision in the form to do this, and a separate application needs to be made using form D11. Court fee of £167 (as at July 2022) as notice to Respondent is given. You may be able to apply for help with fees. The

application can be made at a later stage but must in any event be made before the conditional order is made final. The general position going forwards will be no costs are sought from the other party, but if the Applicant wishes to do so, they need to give reasons.

It is generally before the application is made that agreement is reached between the parties or their solicitors as to whether the Respondent will contribute towards the divorce costs.

If you have changed your name since you married you will need to attach your change of name deed or statutory declaration. You can choose to keep your contact details confidential on the form.

Marriage documents to lodge with the application by post are as follows:

- Original marriage certificate or registrar's official certified copy.
- Official translation if the marriage certificate is not in English.

The court will retain the documents sent, so keep a copy. If the Applicant wants them back, they will need to make an application for their return.

The certificate can also be uploaded online during the application process, or emailed if there are any issues with the online function. Then instructions are given to follow this by post.

If the marriage certificate is not available, a separate application to court can be made for the application to be lodged without it in form D11 with a supporting statement and there is an additional court fee payable of £53 (as at July 2022) without notice to the Respondent or £167 (as at July 2022) if notice is given. You may be able to apply for help with fees.

A certified copy of the marriage in the UK can be obtained from the Register of Births, Deaths, Marriages and Civil Partnerships in the district where the marriage took place. A fee will be payable. Or a certified copy can be obtained from the General Register Office, PO Box 2 Southport, Merseyside PR8

2JD by post or online at https://www.gov.uk/order-copy-birth-death-marriage-certificate

Court fees

Additionally, a court fee is payable by whoever brings the application, currently (July 2022) at £593. Joint Applicants can decide how they pay the fee on a paper application as either party can insert their details on the court fee page, but on the digital service Applicant 1 needs to pay. They can then decide between themselves who will meet the cost or whether they will divide it between them, but the court cannot deal with split fees. There are certain fee exemptions if either a sole Applicant or both joint Applicants have minimal savings and incomes are low or they are in receipt of certain state benefits. It is worth checking with your solicitor or the divorce centre as an application for exemption from fees can be made in that situation. Form EX160 Apply for help with fees form can be filed or go to the website https://www.gov.uk/get-help-with-court-fees

Various other general applications that may need to be made within the divorce are known as interim applications and these are applied for using form D11 and attract a court fee of £53 (as at July 2022) if either made by consent or without notice to the Respondent or £167 (as at July 2022) if notice is given. As above you can apply for help with fees if you are financially eligible.

After the court receive the application

Once the court receives the application, they give it a case reference number. If you apply online it may be processed more quickly, although there have been delays. If the Applicant has applied online an initial acknowledgment will be received confirming that it will be checked by court staff and then they will receive more information.

Joint application

On a joint application Applicant 1 will receive communications in the same way as for a sole Applicant as above. Applicant 2 will receive confirmation that the joint application has been checked and accepted and that a separate email has been sent to Applicant 1 confirming this. Both Applicant 1 and Applicant 2 are then asked to log in to acknowledge the application should proceed. If one party fails to complete this then the other party can proceed to make a sole application. The case screen will confirm the 20 week date to apply for a conditional order.

Sole application

On a sole application you will be informed as the Applicant by email when the application has been accepted and a copy sent to the Respondent. You will be told the date whereby they need to respond to the court. You do not need to do anything, and the court will let you know if they do or do not respond. The email will also include a link to track your progress on the divorce, and useful links to promote agreeing finances on divorce. Confirmation is given of the earliest date you are able to apply for a conditional order.

Respondent's Acknowledgment

The Respondent will be sent in the post, a copy of the application and details of how to create an online divorce account. They will be given the date by which they need to respond. If they cannot get online then they will need to contact the court to get a paper form of acknowledgement. If an email address has been provided for them, they will also receive email notification.

The Respondent has 14 days to complete an acknowledgement of service form (D 10) and return it to the court. The Respondent must give details of any existing or concluded proceedings in respect of the marriage or which may have affected the validity or subsistence of the marriage. If there are any, and the Respondent disputes the application for divorce, form D8B is also completed and when received by the court, the court may give further directions as to how the divorce should proceed. Otherwise the form is straightforward to complete, and provides contact details of the Respondent.

The Respondent can tick yes if they want the court to consider their financial position on divorce, but if they tick no it does not matter as it only states an intention. The Respondent can apply in all cases to delay the final divorce order to enable the court to consider finances. The Respondent should take specific legal advice prior to and once the conditional order stage has been reached, with regard to whether to issue their financial application and apply to delay the final divorce order.

Applicant/s apply for a conditional order

The Applicant/s can apply for a conditional order 20 weeks after their application has been issued by the court. They do this by completing an application for a conditional order (form D84) and send it to the court. This form is used by a sole Applicant, or joint Applicants, however a sole Applicant completes section A, and the joint Applicants complete section B. The remaining sections C and D are completed by both. (This form is also used to apply for judicial separation).

- Section A – Sole Applicant details and service information on the Respondent
- Section B – Joint Applicants details
- Section C – Statement supporting application and update if any changes
- Section D – Statement of truth

Sole Applicant additional steps

The sole Applicant will need to identify the Respondent's signature and attach the acknowledgement of service form confirming that the Respondent has received the application. If the Respondent has not filed an acknowledgement of service form then the following would need to be attached;

- A certificate of service form FP6
- A court order which dispenses with service or deems service
- Other evidence to show the Respondent has been served

Joint Applicants additional steps

The joint Applicants both complete the form, or at this stage it is possible to proceed as a sole Applicant by completing question 10, but once this election has been made, it cannot later be changed back to a joint application at final order stage. If one Applicant decides to proceed on a sole basis, the other Applicant must also be sent a copy of the application.

Change from Joint to Sole Application at Conditional Order Stage

The Applicant must send a copy of the conditional order application to the other party at the same time as the application is made. Upon the court's confirmation of entitlement to an order the other party becomes the Respondent for the remainder of proceedings. The sole Applicant then gives notice for the conditional order to be made final when they are able to do so under the required timescale ie after the 6 week period. The Respondent may apply 3 months after if the sole Applicant fails to apply.

Conditional order

The court dealing with an application for a conditional order must take the statement that the marriage has broken down irretrievably to be conclusive evidence, and provided service has been completed and make a divorce order. The court will send each party a Certificate of entitlement to a conditional order. This notice will certify that the Applicant/s are entitled to a conditional order on the ground that their divorce has broken down irretrievably and if the financial boxes have been ticked, to a financial order. The court will give a date for the hearing of the conditional order. Neither party will be in attendance.

Each party will receive the conditional order following the hearing date. The order confirms that it is not a final order and does not end the marriage. It will also state the date when the Applicant can apply for a final order. The order summarises how your legal rights and responsibilities will change after you are divorced so you can seek legal advice if you have any concerns about the implications. A divorce order is, in the first instance, a conditional order, and may not be made final before the end of the period of six weeks from the making of the conditional order.

The court may not make a conditional order unless:

- in the case of an application that is to proceed as an application by one party to the marriage only, that party has confirmed to the court that they wish the application to continue, or
- in the case of an application that is to proceed as an application by both parties to the marriage, those parties have confirmed to the court that they wish the application to continue.

A party may not give confirmation before the end of the period of 20 weeks from the start of proceedings.

The court may shorten or lengthen each part of the divorce procedure but must not lengthen for a total period exceeding 26 weeks.

The granting of a conditional order is an important stage in the divorce procedure as at any time after the order is made the court has the authority to make a final financial order. The court can still make interim orders such as interim maintenance, but the final order on finances can only be made after a conditional divorce order. Accordingly, it is good practice to enter into financial discussions as soon as the divorce application is issued so that hopefully the two matters will run in parallel, and as soon as you have the date for a conditional divorce order you will be in a position to file a financial consent order at court for the court's approval. If this is not possible, it can be filed at any time after. It can also be filed after the final divorce order, although I would ordinarily advise not applying for the final divorce order until financial matters have been concluded. There can be financial implications upon death benefits under pensions and policies in particular. Legal advice should be sought if you are considering applying for the final divorce order before having obtained a financial order. Also seek specific legal advice if you have remarriage plans.

A conditional divorce order can only be rescinded in limited situations where it would be contrary to justice – and specialist advice would be needed.

Final divorce order

A four-page application (form D36) is submitted to apply for a final divorce order. The form is completed where a sole Applicant started the divorce, or where both parties started jointly and continue to apply jointly. It is lodged at court by the Applicant/s at the earliest 6 weeks and one day ie 43 days after the conditional order is made. If more than one year has elapsed since the date of the conditional order, the application provides for reasons for the delay to be stated (normally the reason will be additional time spent to finalise financial matters and obtain a financial order). A statement of truth needs to be completed by the Applicant/s or the solicitor on their behalf.

Change from joint to Sole Application at Final Order Stage

If an application for the final order started jointly is made by a sole Applicant a two-page application (form D36 A) is signed and lodged at court by the Applicant at the earliest 6 weeks and one day ie 43 days after the conditional order is made. It is completed in the same way as the form D36, however, the form asks for confirmation that the other party has been given 14 days notice of their intention to apply, and that a certificate of service has been filed at court.

As previously mentioned, the Respondent can apply in all cases to delay the final order for the court to consider finances.

Only once the final divorce order is pronounced is the marriage at an end. Any financial order is subject to the final order being made. The final order recites that the conditional order has been made final, and that the marriage has legally ended. The order sets out how divorce affects inheritance under a will, and the appointment of a guardian.

Once the final order is received it will be a paper copy if it is a paper application, but a digital copy if it is an on-line application. The court have stated that the digital copy is to be acceptable as an original. However, if you are represented, it is a good idea for your solicitors to certify a few copies for you.

Timing

It is possible to apply using form D11 and requisite court fee to shorten the 20 week period and/or the 6 week period if there is any urgency in getting divorced. However, as divorces are now relatively quick, this is unlikely to be granted in other than most exceptional situations.

If a final order is applied for 12 months after the conditional order being made, the Applicant will have to explain the reason for this to the court.

If an urgent application needs to be made for a conditional or final order, a paper form must be used. A form D84 paper form is used for applying for a conditional order, and a form D36 for applying for a final order, in both cases accompanied by a form D11 Application Notice and requisite court fee seeking permission to make the urgent application, and giving reasons. It is likely that the procedure will only be expedited in limited situations, for instance terminal illness of one party, or perhaps imminent birth of a child to a party so they wish to remarry.

If a final order is applied for 12 months after the conditional order being made, the Applicant will have to explain the reason for this to the court.

Respondent applying for final order

If the Applicant does not apply for a divorce order, the Respondent can apply three months after the date the Applicant could have applied. However, the Respondent has to apply "on notice" to the Applicant using form D11 and a hearing date is then arranged. There is a court fee of £167 (as at July 2022). The costs of such an application, if matters are not resolved and attendance at court is required, may be expensive but it is useful for the Respondent to be able to do this if the Applicant is unreasonably delaying obtaining the final order.

Whilst it is usual to wait until the financial order is sealed before applying for a final order, in some situations you may want the final divorce order rather than waiting for finances to be completed. You should always obtain specific legal advice upon the implications for you before you consider making this application or if you have remarriage plans. You may be considering this course of action if financial matters cannot be resolved without financial proceedings which are taking time, and the situation is frustrating if you are a Respondent wanting the final order or if you are seeking to remarry.

If the court grant a final order on the Respondent's application before a financial order is made, they just want to safeguard the Applicant's position regarding any rights they would lose as a result of being divorced – this can simply be covered by the Respondent offering nominations on policies and pensions in favour of the Applicant and for an order and undertaking to remain in place until the final financial order. If there are limited assets and no pensions or policies, it is much more straightforward.

Should you Issue the Application or let your Spouse do so or apply jointly?

My view is that you should issue the divorce application if possible. This keeps you in control of the timing of the divorce procedure and, in particular, the two key dates – conditional order and final order. You can only have one application by either party at a time. The court would have to dismiss or determine an existing application or otherwise give permission.

Joint applications are encouraged by the court, however, one party could find themselves in a position where they are unable to continue jointly if the relationship deteriorates, or one party does not take the necessary action to progress the application. It is possible to then switch from joint to sole, but only at conditional and final order stage.

Disputing Proceedings

It is no longer possible to defend the reason for divorce. There are only limited situations now that your spouse can dispute the application. They can no longer dispute whether the marriage has irretrievably broken down. They can only dispute if they say

- England and Wales do not have jurisdiction.
- The marriage is not valid.
- The marriage has already been brought to an end (for instance by way of a previous divorce or proceedings in another country).

If they wish to dispute they need to do this by filing a paper form D8B, known as an answer, at court together with a court fee (£245 as at July 2022) unless they are eligible for Help with Fees. This needs to be filed within 21 days from the date the Respondent's acknowledgement was due to be filed, otherwise the Applicant can usually continue with their divorce.

Proceedings can also be challenged on the ground of fraud or procedural non-compliance.

If the Applicant is not pursuing their application, permission from the court will be required for the Respondent to pursue their own application.

Cost Applications

There is no provision on the divorce application itself to make a cost application. Cost orders are not to be expected to be made. An application, if made, would have to be separately applied for using form D11 and requisite court fee. It is difficult to envisage the reason for a cost application as of course the divorce is brought upon the basis of no-fault. An Applicant can make a cost application at the beginning of the procedure. However, an application should generally be made no later than the application for a conditional order, but has to be made before the date the order is made final. Grounds on which costs are sought need to be set out, and where costs are sought in a specified amount, a summary showing how the amount has been calculated. The application in form D11 and any written evidence in support must be served within 7 days of it being issued, and a certificate confirming it has been served filed at court within 7 days. If a Respondent disputes the application, they must file and serve a witness statement within 14 days of receiving the application setting out the grounds on which it is opposed. The court will normally deal with the issue of costs without a hearing.

Service of papers

By Court

Service of papers relates to the sending of papers to the other party. The documents to be served will comprise of the divorce application and form of acknowledgment for the Respondent to complete.

Sole Application

The general rule is that the court will send the divorce application to the Respondent, but an Applicant can request to do so. It is easier to let the court serve, however if the court is unsuccessful the Applicant must serve within a strict 28 day time limit of their application. The application will normally be served by court through email. The application will be served by court to the Respondent's email address giving them a link to the application if it was made on-line, or attaching a copy of the application if the Applicant applied by way of a paper application. The Respondent will additionally receive a letter by post notifying them of the application made, and that this has been sent to them by email. They will receive access details by way of a 16 digit reference number and an 8 character access code in the email and letter they receive.

If there is no postal address for the Respondent then an application using form D11 and requisite court fee for service by email only will have to be made.

The email address is provided by the Applicant, and if the Respondent has not provided an email address for service, it should be the Respondent's usual private email address actively used by them. Business email addresses are avoided where possible.

If the Respondent does not have an email address or the Applicant prefers they are not served by email, then they can be served by post. The court will serve by first class post.

The Applicant may ask the court to serve again at an alternative email/ postal address if service fails. If the court receives an undeliverable notice by Royal Mail the Applicant can provide an alternative address to which the papers can be sent. After a second attempt at service the Court will not try to serve the papers again. The Applicant may then need to take further steps to try to serve, for instance instructing a process server.

If the Applicant has also provided their own email address, they will be informed by email that their application has been served on the Respondent.

By the Applicant

The Applicant can opt to send papers to the Respondent themselves (which includes through their solicitors) within 28 days of the date the court issued the application. The Applicant must not personally serve the papers on their spouse.

If the Respondent is abroad, the court will not serve them, and it is up to the Applicant to ensure they are served abroad within 28 days of issue. To provide the correct mode of service the International laws of service in that country will apply.

28 day time limit for service

The Applicant must prove service of their divorce application on the Respondent. If the Respondent returns their acknowledgment form to court, by email or post, there is no requirement to prove service. However, if they fail to do so, other modes of service need to be considered. Where the Applicant serves the papers on the Respondent this must be completed within 28 days of the divorce application having been issued (Strictly prior to 12 midnight on the day 28 days after issue of the application).

The Applicant may apply for an order extending the time for compliance in serving the Respondent. The general rule is that the application to court to extend time must be made within the 28 day period. The application must be supported by evidence of reasonable steps taken to comply and the court will consider whether the Applicant has acted promptly. The Respondent does not need to be given notice of this application. However, ideally the Applicant should take all steps to try to serve within the 28 days.

Methods of Service

Postal

The easiest methods of service if email has not proved successful, are by first class post, document exchange or other service which provides for delivery the next business day. However, if the Respondent fails to respond, a signed for postal delivery of the application is worth considering. If sent recorded delivery, also keep the record of service. However if they have not responded when they have been served in this way the next step is normally personal service.

Personal service

Personal service must by someone other than the Applicant. Solicitors will have connections with enquiry agents/process servers to deal with personal service of the application on the Respondent. You will need to provide a photo of your spouse, if you have one, to aid identification, or a description and as much information as possible to help with service. It is generally avoided that the Respondent is served at work as this would cause embarrassment. It is also considered inappropriate to serve when the Respondent has contact with the child. If this method of service fails, your solicitor will help you apply to court for alternative methods of service such as substituted or deemed service. They will file a statement of service or other appropriate application at court for you so that the divorce can proceed.

Substituted service

This is where the Respondent is evading service and often a family member or friend in touch with them can be served. You specifically have to apply to the court first if you wish to attempt substituted service. You apply by using form D11 and a court fee of £53 (as at July 2022) without notice to the Respondent or £167 (as at July 2022) if notice is given.

Deemed service

The Respondent may have failed to file the form of acknowledgment but there is evidence they have been served, so you can ask for the service to be deemed. For instance, there may be communication from the Respondent or their solicitor which shows the Respondent received the application and this may be sufficient. You apply by using form D11 and a court fee of £53 (as at July 2022) without notice to the Respondent or £167 (as at July 2022) if notice is given.

Court Bailiff

Another option is an application for bailiff service by a court bailiff. A form, D89, needs to be completed and fee, currently (July 2022) £45, together with a photo if possible, and evidence that postal service has been attempted and failed or why it is not appropriate.

Dispensing with service

If it is impractical to serve the application by any of the above methods, the court does have power to dispense with service. You apply by using form D13B. However the court will not lightly make an order to dispense with service.

Joint application

In a joint application both parties will be served with notice of proceedings. In a sole application the Respondent only will be served.

Withdrawing the Application

The Applicant needs to complete form D11 with requisite court fee and send it to the court. A sole Applicant may withdraw at any time before service of the application on the Respondent by giving notice in writing to court. If it is a joint application, both Applicants need to complete a form and apply jointly. Whether the original application was on-line or a paper application the form needs to be completed and submitted.

Nullity

I will not cover nullity in detail, but nullity covers situations where the marriage is void or voidable. These proceedings can still be disputed. This area needs specialist advice, as the situations it can apply to are limited. Nullity applications must be made using the paper application process using form D8N. Joint applications are not available. Service of proceedings is the same as for divorce, including email service. If the Respondent wishes to dispute they need to do this by filing a paper form D8BN, known as an answer, at court together with a court fee (£245 as at July 2022) unless they are eligible for Help with Fees. This needs to be filed within 21 days from the date the acknowledgement was due to be filed, otherwise the Applicant can usually continue with their nullity application.

Top Tips

DO

1. Apply online for divorce if you can as it is easier. Make sure that you have your original/certified marriage certificate to hand to refer to as you make the application, and that you have scanned it to your computer ready to upload to your application. Also have your spouse's contact details ready to input.

2. If you need help with fees if you have a low income and limited savings make this application first as you will be given a reference number to insert into your divorce application.

3. If you are the Applicant it is a good idea to diarise the dates when the Respondent needs to respond taking early steps to serve your application within the 28 day period if they do not complete their acknowledgment form and diarise when you can apply for a conditional order.

4. If you are considering starting a joint application you ought to seek legal advice on whether it would be better to issue your own sole application.

5. You should tick the application to proceed with financial claims on a sole application and both tick financial claims on a joint application.

6. If you are the Respondent you should obtain specific legal advice at conditional order stage if you ought to apply to delay the making of a final order, and where there is a delay in proceedings making your own application for a final order.

7. Keep your final divorce order safely as you will invariably be asked for it in the future and you will need it if you decide to remarry. Also it will be relevant to other updates, such as

passport, driving licence. Ask your solicitor to prepare several certified copies for you, and ensure you update the tax office and other authorities of your newly changed status.

DO NOT

1. Issue the divorce application without having the discussion first with your spouse and getting their commitment to filing their acknowledgment of the papers as soon as your application is received by them. It is good practice to provide at least 7 days notice of intention to start divorce proceedings.

2. Issue a joint application if your spouse is likely to be unreliable in dealing with proceedings.

Healing

Going through a divorce or any breakup is painful. Even if blame is not allocated, you still feel devastated inside. This is an ideal time to consider healing so that whatever needs to heal is done now and you don't take that pain into your life and relationships in the future. As you go through the external divorce process, this is the right time to travel inwards towards the internal healing process. It has been shown in many scientific studies that if we go through a stressful time, or endure persistent negative emotions, these have an effect which is sometimes catastrophic on our mental and physical wellbeing. There are many forms of healing you may wish to try.

Reiki

What is reiki?

Reiki is an ancient method of energy healing uncovered by Dr Mikao Usui in Japan in the 1900s. The emphasis of his teaching was as much about spiritual awakening as physical healing. Reiki is a natural healing energy.

How does it work?

In Japanese, Rei means universal and Ki means energy similar to Chi, so Reiki is universal energy. This universal energy is channelled by the practitioner. Reiki differs from other forms of hands-on healing due to an attunement process, attuning the Reiki practitioner to a higher vibrational level to become a channel for Reiki. The healing works on all levels – emotional, mental and physical. It is a holistic system for balancing and harmonising the body, mind, emotions and spirit. As we know, when we go through emotional or mental disturbances this often affects our physical health. So that is why a treatment that heals on all levels is beneficial.

Reiki Treatment

I highly recommend trying a Reiki treatment; it is very relaxing. You are fully clothed and the practitioner does not need to place hands on you so it is a non-intrusive treatment. Some people love massages and some people do not like the idea. This is a nice treatment that suits most people. As you may be feeling a bit vulnerable or protective of your space, this is an ideal treatment.

You will normally lie down comfortably on a massage couch, fully clothed, sometimes with an additional blanket for warmth. There may be relaxing music. The practitioner will place their hands lightly on, or over, specific areas of your head, limbs, and torso, several minutes for each part. While the practitioner holds their hands lightly on or over the body, the transfer of healing energy takes place.

My Thoughts on Reiki

I actually came to learn about Reiki somewhere between my divorce and sorting out the finances. It was offered by chance on a yoga holiday. I took the first attunement and I remember my daily self-Reiki healing practice continued with a lovely feeling of peace, except for one day when tears started streaming down my face for no apparent reason. I have since developed my personal practice over 15 years as a Reiki master practitioner and for me, embracing the universal healing energies has become a way of life. We have become so distant from nature and the natural world that we have forgotten the natural way of life. Healing energy is in all of us. For instance, when a mother rubs the knee of her child following a fall, she is transferring magnetic energy.

One of my favourite publications on Reiki, is *The Joy of Reiki* by Nalin and Renoo Nirula. This was published in India. I read with interest the comment (p 48) that negative energies manifest in the energy body at least three years prior to the manifestation of disease by starting off as small functional disorders. Over time, we have warning signals and time to mend. Time goes quickly so don't ignore any signs or ailments which may have already crept up on you, and heal as quickly as possible.

Reiki Principles

Dr Mikao Usui also imparted the benefits of living a proper life and stated the following Reiki principles which myself and other practitioners follow. I have set these out below (there are several variations of translation but the message is the same and the one below is my favourite). I think they are useful to copy and frame and look at daily as an aid to good living.

Just for today (this reminds us that the present moment is all we have):
1. I will be slow to anger.
2. I release the need for worry.
3. I will work hard (including on myself) with integrity and honesty.
4. I will honour my parents, my teachers, my elders and every living being.
5. I will live with the attitude of gratitude.
6. I Respect the oneness of all life.

If you really concentrate on each line there is such deep meaning and poignancy to each statement. If we could live in this way, we would all live a simple and beautiful life.

To find a Reiki practitioner in your area try the Reiki Federation website.
http://www.reikifed.co.uk

Theta Healing

What is Theta Healing?

Another option for healing is Theta Healing. With Theta Healing you are brought into a very deep state of relaxation known as the Theta state. The brainwave of Theta becomes dominant in this state. We have several major brain frequencies – Gamma, Beta, Alpha, Theta and Delta. The Theta state is also used in hypnosis and so is an ideal state to access the subconscious. Once you are in the Theta state you can clear limiting beliefs.

Theta Healing Treatment

In a session, the practitioner sits near you and initially starts by listening and using probing questions. The technique then uses muscle testing to test any limiting beliefs that may be holding you back and clearing blockages. There is a sense of satisfaction after a treatment as the practitioner tests with you that the limiting beliefs have been cleared. Muscle testing is quite straightforward. A series of questions is asked, to which there is a yes or no answer. This can be done by standing up and lightly swaying forwards for yes and lightly swaying backwards for no. This can also be done with your arm held out to the side of you or by using your fingers as a circuit – normally your ring finger and thumb touching at the fingertips, which can be easily explained during the session. If it is a belief you have you will be able to hold your muscles or pose.

The scientific explanation behind how it works is that when your subconscious is holding onto a program, you test strongly with resistance and strength. When you are not holding on to a program or don't have that specific program, you will test weak by your arm moving easily downwards or your fingers coming easily undone.

It is now widely accepted that our thoughts can create our reality. You only have to speak to someone with an acute medical issue who talks of a stressful period of life leading up to their illness.

About Theta Healing

Theta Healing was founded by Vianna Stibal in 1995 when she was diagnosed with lymphatic cancer in the femur bone of her right leg and told she only had a few months to live. She developed healing using the meditative state of the Theta brain frequency to connect directly with the Source or Creator or God, or any other name depending on your spiritual and religious beliefs. She overcame her condition and went on to heal others.

My Thoughts on Theta Healing

Theta Healing is worth trying out at this time. It is a good chance to clear any limiting and negative beliefs and move forwards. We all have limiting and conditioned beliefs due to our experiences. I have had a few sessions and I was surprised to learn of my limiting beliefs. I found that some cleared more easily than others. One of my main ones, around approval, still comes up from time to time, but through the sessions, it helped me become aware of this. As the beliefs are deeply buried in the subconscious, what you think you believe, or outwardly project, may be at odds with your true beliefs. Some deep-rooted emotions may surface, but better to deal with them now rather than take them into your future.

Emotional Freedom Technique

Emotional freedom technique (EFT) is also popular to try to clear negative emotions. This works on the meridian points, similar to acupressure or acupuncture, but just uses the fingertips to tap an area to apply the pressure. By working on the points, it helps to balance the energy and restore balance, as well as release specific negative emotions. You may wish to find an EFT practitioner in your area to go through a simple routine you can apply yourself.

Energy Work

Eden Method

Working on your energy can be brought into a daily routine. Recently, I have been introduced to, and I have become more interested in, Donna Eden's energy work. After several serious illnesses in her youth, she turned her health and her life around with energy work. She has been teaching people since then how to work with the body's energy systems to reclaim their health and natural vitality.
https://edenmethod.com

During the coronavirus lockdown period I regularly used the seven-minute energy routine; it is really good when you need a boost.
https://www.youtube.com/watch?v=Di5Ua44iuXc

Qigong and Tai Chi

Qigong and Tai Chi are ancient practices widely used in China that both cultivate the Qi or Chi, which is the life energy that flows through the body's energy pathways by combining movement, breathing and meditation. They are both slow and relaxed methods of movement.

Qigong

Qigong is often spelt as Chi Kung. I have attended a few classes of this recently and really noticed a boost when my energy levels were low. I found it easy to learn and enjoyable to do. The aim of Qigong is to promote the movement of Qi or Chi in the body. This is done by opening the energy channels. The key points in Qigong practice are relaxation and deep breathing, both of which are prerequisites to allow Qi to flow. It is based on repetitions of a precise set of movements, specifically designed to benefit health on many different levels. Regular practice is designed to bring about a deep strengthening and healing effect for the whole body and all our systems, e.g. nervous and respiratory.

Tai Chi

Tai Chi is based in martial arts. It is a series of movements which are not repeated, as in Qigong. One movement is followed by another, with each movement an integral part of the next to make up a continuous flowing practice. Because each movement is connected, a 'pathway' is built and the Chi can flow in a continuous stream throughout the practice. Tai Chi takes considerably longer to learn and it takes time with a master practitioner to develop the art. However, its benefits are renowned to reduce stress, great to relax the mind, and may help with depression and other anxiety and cognitive disorders.

Other Holistic Treatments

I am in favour of any holistic treatment that relaxes you – if you do like a regular massage, reflexology, or any treatment that helps to rebalance your body from the tension it may be under, this is the time to treat and look after yourself. The body can store up a lot of tension at this time and this can manifest in both physical and mental ailments, so a regular treatment helps dissipate any negative impact on your system. Head and shoulder massages particularly work out those mental tensions that store in those parts of the body. A full body massage covers the whole system, as does reflexology and the use of pressure points. Aromatherapy oils can be tailored to your needs and lavender is a lovely one to have added to your massage oils to aid relaxation.

Nature

Try to spend some time in nature – nature is naturally healing for us as living beings – even if it is just a short walk in the evening or at the weekend. It is really important to get out

– it is very easy to become insular at this time and even just a smile to or from a stranger can give you a lift. I find that in stressful times I do not feel like going out at all. I really have to push myself. But I find it so important to get fresh air; it helps you energise and dispel those negative energies. Nature replenishes with positive energy.

Go for a brisk walk, a run or a cycle ride. Any form of physical exercise, particularly outside, literally throws out any negative energy from the body and replaces it with energy from the environment.

Nutrition

Eat and drink well and healthily – try organic foods and plenty of water. Do not be tempted to seek regular solace in a glass of wine or whisky – or a bottle. It is not good for the body, dehydrates you, will affect your mood and give you highs and lows. I have only recently really understood how important water is. I always thought healthy food and plenty of fruit and vegetables were the most important. But I notice when I am drinking plenty of water, I crave sweet and junk foods much less. Studies have shown that even mild dehydration has an effect and will add to stress – 1% to 3% can affect your brain function and physical energy levels.

You need a diet that keeps you both healthy and calm. It is worth looking into ayurvedic diets and vegan plant-based foods at this time. It may also be worth adding daily vitamin and mineral supplements. Check with your doctor for any recommended supplements if your energy levels are low. Most of us in the West are woefully lacking vitamin D, and I find that B vitamins really help the nervous system in times of stress.

I personally think this is the time for your soul and your karma to avoid meat products if you can. The vegan diet is growing globally for many reasons. This is a compassionate time to look after yourself and other living beings.

Case Scenario

Situation. Rita came to see me. She had been married for seven years to Patrick and had two young children, but a month prior she had found out that her husband was phoning escort services. He tried to cover it up saying he was seeing them to have a massage and he was not aware of what else they did. He accused her of not trusting him and that there was nothing more to it.

How we helped her. The initial meeting enabled her to go through in detail what had happened and as her story unfolded, Rita realised that she knew the truth of the situation and could no longer trust her husband. She recounted how he spent their cash savings, and how he had suddenly become interested in his appearance. She also knew that there were several telephone numbers that he had phoned over quite a period of time, and she had no doubt that he had been sleeping with many women.

We advised her strategically that Rita should ask her husband to leave so that she could have some space and that when he was renting somewhere else, she could then consider discussing matters further with him and starting off the divorce procedure. Otherwise, there was a good chance that he would refuse to leave and make things very difficult for her going through the divorce.

In the meantime, she would leave all her financial paperwork with her mother so that no paperwork was kept in the house.

We started divorce proceedings after her husband moved out and she was then able to discuss the situation objectively with him.

We also discussed financial matters and what options there were for her to financially be able to look after the children by working part time and receiving some help from the state, and with support of maintenance from her husband.

She felt very low and lost her self-esteem so we suggested that she try to take some time out for herself to recuperate and heal.

How she coped. Resilience and resolve: She realised that her husband was lying but already felt worn down by his comments. She now had to resolve to see the divorce through and change her life.

Knowledge: She processed all the facts before her and had the necessary information to make her decision.

Confidence: She spent time with friends to seek more support and help her regain her confidence. Her mum looked after the children for a week whilst she took some days out for herself. She found some discounted treatments and got her hair and nails done. She booked in a massage and Reiki treatment. She decided to start studying in the evenings when the children were in bed. After six months, she returned to her previous nursing career and was able to work part-time hours to fit in with the children, which also entitled her to receive further assistance by way of state benefits.

Where she is now. She is relieved that they divorced. We obtained a financial order transferring the property to her and she lives in the house with her two children. Although she does not have a great deal of disposable income, with the help of additional state benefits, she makes ends meet. Her ex-husband pays the mortgage and maintenance. Her husband is now in a new relationship. They discuss amicably his arrangements to see the children. Rita looks and feels much more confident and happier. Every Easter and Summer holiday when her ex-husband has the children for a few weeks, she still takes time out for herself and books in several of her favourite treatments. She has now started a reflexology course in her spare time.

Evening Meditation

Have a nice relaxing bath or shower and do this meditation before bedtime. Find a quiet place where you will not be disturbed. Sit comfortably with your back erect, either on a chair with your feet on the floor or on a cushion sitting cross-legged. Place your hands loosely in your lap. Close your eyes. Take a couple of deep breaths. Then start to settle into your breath. Inhale fully through your nose, and then take a few sighing breaths as you exhale through your mouth. Let everything go. Do this as many times as you need to until you feel more centred. Then inhale and exhale naturally through your nostrils with your mouth closed. Concentrate on your breath. After a few breaths, imagine a beautiful violet light shining down from over you, through the top of your head, your crown centre, and cascading down through every cell of your body, bringing with it healing energy. That healing energy goes through every organ, each muscle and every cell of your body. That light continues to radiate through you. Feel that healing energy as it keeps pouring over you, and through you. Get a sense of the power and enormity of the universe you are in. Keep breathing and healing, and when you are ready to rise, take a few final breaths before opening your eyes. Thank the vast universe for being a part of it, and for helping you to heal yourself. Take your time as you rise from meditation and prepare for a good night's sleep.

Concluding Thought of the Day
I am healed.

Chapter 5

SEPARATION AND SELF-ISOLATION

Introduction

If you are adamant your marriage is over, it is better to go straight to divorce. Otherwise, you are invariably adding another step and more time. This can have a frustrating effect on you when you just want to move on. However, another option is to separate formally and enter into a separation deed. If there are religious reasons why you do not wish to divorce, an application for a judicial separation order may also be an option but is more rarely used. We also look into the isolation or loneliness you may feel if you separate. We look at how to view this and a few possibilities to give you a lift, learnt from our lessons through the pandemic lockdown. We also reflect on whether this may still have lasting effects in your relationship, as it has for many others. From isolation, we also look at how we may reconnect in simple ways with others and the spouse we have separated from. We meet Robert who thought financial matters were agreed with his spouse when he separated, only to find that this had changed when they eventually divorced. We end this chapter with a morning meditation and look forward to embracing a new future.

Separation Deeds

Some couples opt to separate for several years and postpone their decision of whether they really want a divorce. This is a good option if you are not really sure you want a divorce and there is a possibility the marriage may be salvaged. It allows time for you both to come to terms with the relationship being over without it resulting in a shock for one or both of you. This step may provide a transition period for the family as a whole to adjust, particularly if there are children. If you go down this route and you are separating, you should arrange to see a solicitor and enter into a legal separation deed with your spouse.

What is a Legal Separation Deed?

A legal separation deed, also known as a separation agreement, is a written agreement setting out how you want to deal with finances, particularly property, payment of bills, maintenance and other practical issues on your separation. The agreement outlines the details of any agreed financial division on your future divorce. Unless there is any material change of circumstances, if you subsequently divorce, this gives you the security of having already agreed financial matters which can simply be updated to place into an agreed order on divorce. It is also a clear marker that you have formally separated.

The term "maintenance agreement" and "separation agreement" are often used interchangeably – a maintenance agreement does not set out an agreement to live apart but covers agreed financial provision between spouses.

What the Separation Agreement Includes

The separation deed sets out your agreement to live apart, the distribution of assets, and in particular, how you will deal with the family home, maintenance and arrangements for the children. You can, in fact, deal with any agreed matters in the deed but not all will be legally enforceable so a solicitor is required to advise on this. The deed normally focuses on financial matters.

The agreement should ensure that each of your housing and income needs are met; it is useful to have these discussions early on. Of course, you can only deal with what there is enough of to go around and it is often an eye opener how much of a stretch it may become to cover the expenses of two separate households.

A separation deed will often cover the following (the list is not exhaustive):

- The date you have separated, when you will divorce and who will issue the application. It will also cover which country you will issue in and where finances will be heard, particularly if there are other jurisdictions involved.
- How the marital home will be dealt with, who will occupy it and who will pay the bills.
- How other properties will be dealt with, and whether these will be regarded as matrimonial, or non-matrimonial assets.
- How inheritances you have already received or may be expecting in the future, and trusts will be dealt with, and will these be ring fenced so the other will not claim against these.
- How other assets and bank accounts are to be dealt with, and whether, for instance, they are to be transferred or cashed in and divided, and in what shares.
- How pensions are to be dealt with on divorce.
- Payment of maintenance, both spousal and child maintenance, and general payment of bills can all be covered.
- If there are any debts, who will take responsibility for these, and whether, if joint, one party is to be released.
- The contents of the home and possessions are also covered.
- Also, importantly, what the provision is going to be if either of you die whilst you are separated, and whether new wills should be made.

- Often children arrangements are set out so it is clear where your children will live and when they will see each of you, as well as maintenance provision and school fees. A parent cannot contract out of providing support for their child in the agreement, and it is still possible to bring financial claims relating to children, notwithstanding the agreement.

Reviewing the Deed

You can also provide for the agreement to be reviewed on some specific event, but separation deeds are much less likely to be reviewed than pre and post-nuptial agreements, as if circumstances do not change, the next inevitable step is divorce. However, it is a good idea to review the agreement if there is a subsequent specific change in circumstances. This ensures that when you proceed to divorce, the most recent agreement takes into account any significant change so it can still be held to be fair. Changes in circumstances may include, for example, where a party may have lost their job, or the children may now primarily be living with the other parent, as opposed to the parent originally envisaged.

Reasons to use a Separation Agreement

1. A separation agreement is particularly useful if you have not yet been married for one year and have decided to divorce but are not yet able to.
2. Most couples opt to enter into separation agreements where they want the early certainty of an agreement covering financial matters.
3. It is an effective way to protect assets and identify on divorce what will be regarded as "non-matrimonial" property including assets that may be acquired post separation, which, particularly if you are the financially stronger partner, you will not want to divide with your spouse in the event of future divorce.
4. The written agreement covers how you want to deal with financial issues currently on separation and eventual

divorce. It can also cover other practical issues including the children. It therefore gives both immediate clarity to your situation and outlines what you may divide now, and the security of knowing how you will deal with financial matters on divorce.

Criteria to give the Best Chance of being upheld on Divorce

1. Full financial disclosure. This means all your financial information and key documents are produced. Therefore, you each have sufficient information upon which to base your decision to enter into the agreement and a comprehensive understanding of the implications.

2. It is also imperative that you have both received your own legal advice and engaged independent solicitors. If, as often happens, one person asks whether they can use the same solicitor, unfortunately they cannot, as this is a conflict of interest (not even different offices in the same firm). So, if your ex refuses to engage solicitors, I have often advised my client to pay for at least a one-off meeting for them, with an independent solicitor of their choice, so it can be shown they obtained legal advice. If the finances are complex, the alternative is to meet their solicitor's costs up to a set limit. If they have had the opportunity of obtaining legal advice but still will not do so, go ahead and complete the agreement but there is more risk of it not being upheld at divorce (although it could still well be if the agreement is fair).

3. The terms of the agreement must be substantially fair – there are no defined parameters as to what constitutes fairness but in section 25 Matrimonial Causes Act 1973, factors are applied (as explained later in chapter 7 dealing with financial matters on divorce) and fairness can often be determined as equality depending on the weight given to relevant factors. At the very least, start with considering that it meets both your, the children's housing and your ex's needs. Really look objectively at what is fair. If it is clearly unjust to one person, there is no

point in either of you entering into an agreement that will have no chance of being upheld by the court.

4. Finally, you must have both entered into the agreement freely, so there must be no duress or pressure on the other person to enter into the agreement. It is also imperative that there has been no fraud or misrepresentation as it will not be upheld in that situation.

5. Contractual requirements need to be followed including confirmation by way of a statement in the deed that you both intend to create legal relations. The agreement is executed in a certain way as a deed and must be signed before independent witnesses. The agreement can also annex a draft of the financial order that is intended to be submitted on divorce. This will save some time and cost later.

6. If you have dealt with all the requirements, there has to be some significant change in your finances between separation and divorce for you both not subsequently being held to the terms on future divorce. Therefore, be alert to any significant change that happens in the intervening period, and review the deed if necessary.

The courts have said that they should give effect on divorce to an agreement that is freely entered into by each party with a full appreciation of its implications unless, in the circumstances, it would not be fair to hold the parties to that agreement. You cannot oust the court's jurisdiction to consider finances on divorce within the separation deed.

Whilst the separation deed is a contractual agreement if entered into properly, it is still not strictly binding in the event of a later divorce in England and Wales. However, the terms may be decisive on divorce even if one of you later changes your mind and no longer wants to be bound by it, and there has been no significant change in your respective situations. As long as the agreement was fair, the court can be asked by a party to place the terms into a final financial order on divorce. The court can also place some parts of the agreement into an order even if they decide other parts are unfair. A separation deed is definitely worth proceeding with, but equally, only proceed on the basis you fully accept being bound by it on a future divorce.

If other countries are involved regarding your domicile or residence or where you have assets, an agreement should also be drafted in that jurisdiction. The separation deed also usually confirms in which jurisdiction you will subsequently commence the divorce proceedings. If you do have assets abroad, or either of you are resident or domiciled in another jurisdiction, it is important to take legal advice in that country. Your solicitor in England and Wales should liaise with your legal advisor abroad, regarding the divorce laws in that country. A similar separation agreement in other countries may be binding on divorce, so it may be prudent to have an agreement in that jurisdiction and reflect that the subsequent divorce will commence there.

Top Tips

DO

1. Realise that many of us have gone through this and come out the other side; that you are not alone however unbearable your current situation appears to you. Be gentle on yourself as you move forwards with the separation and take it a step at a time.

2. Get legal advice even if you decide to separate rather than divorce, so you are aware of any implications.

DO NOT

1. Save costs by writing out your own financial arrangement for the future. You are not going to be able to hold your spouse to it later even if you have both signed it before a witness. It has to be done properly. There needs to be an exchange of financial information and documents to back up that information, known as disclosure, and you should each have your own legal advisors, or the opportunity to obtain that advice. It is a formal legal agreement prepared by solicitors and they can advise on its fairness.

2. Separate only, and later regret the delay to divorce. It is easy to procrastinate even when you know deep down what you need to do. Try to move away from a place of fear to one of expectation that it will all work out. Do not delay at all if your spouse is likely to move abroad. This means you need to sort things out quickly and be able to serve proceedings whilst your spouse is still in England and Wales. It becomes much more difficult if your spouse moves abroad or doesn't tell you where they are going!

(Judicial) Separation Order

What is a separation order?

This a court order, confirming that you have both separated judicially due to irretrievable marriage breakdown.

Why obtain a (Judicial) Separation Order?

Most couples opt to divorce (or enter into a separation deed), rather than proceed with an application for a judicial separation order as this does not end the marriage. It is rare in practice and generally arises where you have strong religious or cultural reasons for not wanting a divorce. I can only recall dealing with one of these during my career. You still have to issue divorce proceedings if you subsequently decide to end the marriage, and therefore this can duplicate the costs. However, you do not need to wait one year after you have married before issuing these proceedings. It is also worth bearing in mind that the court's powers regarding finances are more restricted, and the court cannot make a pension sharing order.

Effect of a Judicial Separation Order

A judicial separation order relieves the Applicant of the need to cohabit with the Respondent. So, it is a formal separation. If either party dies without having made a will, their estate will not pass to the other (the same as for parties that divorce) and the party will be treated as having predeceased on the date of the separation order. This is also the case for provision in an existing will. The spouse can no longer take benefit unless a new will is made, specifically stating that following the separation order they are still to benefit. It is very important to make a will in addition to agreeing financial matters on a separation order. The court do not have to consider whether the marriage has irretrievably broken down for a separation order.

Procedure

Either or both parties may apply for a judicial separation order. The application is made by a statement from one, or both, that they wish to be judicially separated. Again, as for the divorce procedure, the statement is definitive evidence and no factors need to be relied on. The court must make a judicial separation order. The same procedure is used for civil partners to obtain a separation order.

Applications for judicial separation must be made using a paper application, and cannot be made on-line. The application asks one party, if a sole application, or both parties if a joint application, if they would like to be separated. The process is basically the same as for divorce but there are a few differences from the divorce procedure:

Even if an order of judicial separation has been granted it does not prevent either party issuing a divorce application.

There is currently (July 2022) a court fee of £365 for filing a judicial separation application.

The initial application is made using form D8S.

The subsequent application for the final judicial separation order is made using form D84.

Otherwise, save as to seeking a judicial separation order, all documents that need to be filed and served are the same as for the divorce procedure. If it is a sole application, service on the Respondent takes place in the same way as for divorce. Respondents can also dispute the separation application in the same limited circumstances as for divorce. Similarly, for Applicants that have started a joint application but are unable to continue either because the relationship has deteriorated or the other party is not taking action to progress the application, they can switch from joint to sole, but only when applying for the judicial separation order.

However, just one order of judicial separation is obtained. Applications for financial remedies are made in the usual way (excluding pension sharing orders which are unavailable on judicial separation).

Physical Separation and Isolation

Physical separation is a massive adjustment for both of you. From being together as a couple, you are now apart. You no longer have the sense of presence of your spouse. You may not have even been talking much by the end, but that person, and therefore, their presence, was still around. We were used to doing everything with our husband or wife, even if it was just watching television, or routinely making the dinner, doing the dishes or going to the shops. Suddenly, we are torn away from that presence.

It is not unusual to feel unsettled, as if you have lost a part of you. In a way, this has happened. Your husband or wife became part of your identity. Part of your story. You are now alone. You may have a feeling of not being whole, adding to your feeling of loss.

It is hard to sever those invisible strings that bind you. It is not unusual in separation for one party to still crave seeing the other, and wanting communication with the other, and trying to actively pursue this. This can be part of non-acceptance. It takes time to release all the strings, although one by one over time, they do get released. It is almost as if over time we are able to morph ourselves back together again.

Self-isolation

Space created from a separation brings an element of personal isolation. We are forced to keep our distance from our spouse by virtue of separation. This may also have a knock-on effect on the interaction that we had with common friends and extended family. The structure and familiarity of what we knew has changed. Sometimes this change can happen dramatically, and we can almost feel cut off. We may also choose not to socialise as much as we may just not feel like it. Initially, friends and family may try to take us out to get our minds off the situation. But after a while, this may quieten down, and we are left with longer periods of being alone.

Self-isolation was thrust upon us with the sad outbreak of coronavirus. When we were specifically told by our respective governments not to interact, and to socially distance ourselves, how difficult it was for us to be effectively quarantined away from loved ones, and even to be unable to say hello to a fellow human being in your vicinity. No hugs, and even smiles were tentative, for the fear of catching something. It is hard not to feel that warmth of another when you are separated.

The times of the pandemic and financial upheaval may have also affected our relationship. Significant periods of hardship make us question how we live, and indeed for many couples who have endured such a testing time, who we live with. We reflect upon how we live and who we love. How difficult was it too, to be confined with only our loved ones? The external and material world shrunk in one fell swoop with the onset of the coronavirus. For couples in such close quarters, the stress of children at home, additional home duties, dealing with the weekly shopping needs and financial pressures on business and jobs, pushed relationships to the threshold. Also, current generations that were not before affected by the severity of war conditions, had not built up the resilience of previous generations. The shock and fear of the situation, the financial ramifications on jobs and businesses which followed months after, took its toll on relationships. Financial hardship and recessionary periods often have ramifications for relationships.

Like shockwaves, sometimes breakups follow months after. However, the effect may still have an influence years afterwards.

Separation can follow quickly where the strain is too much. With a long period of self-isolation during the coronavirus outbreak, it also made us question our very existence, our purpose. Our relationship may no longer have been consistent with our changed outlook, and we may have outgrown it without realising. We may feel our relationship is no longer consistent with our contribution to the world, and we may have a complete turnaround of our life. This makes us dwell more on the question – who am I, and what do I want?

Tools to Lift the Loneliness

If you start to feel lonely when you are separated and find the whole area of self- isolation a challenge, then walking in nature and meditation are helpful remedies. Both meditation and walking in nature keep your body and mind well and grounded.

You may also need to challenge yourself to join clubs or a course and meet new friends. It may be the time to develop a new, or existing interest. You may not feel like attending a club or a course initially, but it will give you a refreshing distraction and the opportunity to meet people that just know you, and not you as part of a "couple". It will be an opportunity to learn about something you may have always wanted to know about so with that interest, you will inject enthusiasm and positive energy. It will also help you as your mind becomes absorbed by something other than your breakup. Small steps will help you feel better.

Periods of reflection. With a period of isolation, it is an opportunity to have time well spent. It is only by being alone that we can really get to think about who we are, who we have become, and who we would like to be. Whilst we have many entertainments in this world, sometimes it is really good to be alone. As my mum always said, we come into this world alone and leave the world alone. Separation is inevitable. Separation teaches us this. We are alone with our thoughts and who we really are. We can decide what really matters, both now, and what we should take forward from the past to the future. Why is it that monks and nuns go on silent retreat? Retreating from the world, and the business of the world, is good. It provides a better perspective of the whole and true picture of our existence.

Connection and Compliments

If you are struggling with isolation from the separation, you could develop your connections with others at this time. It may be with those you know well, your neighbours or even strangers. An instant way to develop connection is through a smile. As you smile at the person at your supermarket checkout and they smile back, there is an instant connection. You also may have lit up their day. You have shared a sweet experience. As we get older, very often our outer circle retracts and sometimes the time spent to say hello or smile, keeps us connected. Do not forget your elderly relatives or neighbours, or even your local care home. Some people do not see anyone they can spend time with day to day, not out of choice. If you can spare a few minutes to make someone smile, it is a lovely feeling of connection. You may start to feel more connected. Think about those further away too, who you could pick up the phone with, or better still, see them on a video call. As you share your connection outwards in a positive way, you will feel more connected to yourself.

Following on from giving a smile, I would like you to try at least one day a week (if not every day) giving a compliment to anyone you meet. It may be a lovely dress your friend is wearing or something they said that was really helpful. It may be a work colleague who does a piece of work you think is great. Appreciation for the little things goes a long way. It is also a much better habit to get into than criticism. We are so good at criticism, criticising each other, the traffic, the weather, the government. Do we step back from the grey clouds and look at the rainbow in the sky, rather than taking it for granted and ignoring its beauty?

It is particularly so with your estranged spouse. Have you got into the habit of criticising every single thing they do wrong? We ignore the fact that they may offer to pick up the children when we have to work late, or just want some time away with our friends. Do we take it for granted, or do we say thank you? Do we ignore all their good qualities and take them and their efforts for granted, so that we have an unbalanced view of the villain or villainess? On your next interaction, give them a genuine compliment. See how it breaks the ice, the tension between you. Build on this every time you meet up. This will repay you dividends in the long run. With time who knows, they may cooperate with you more. This is not the goal, but often arises naturally as a result of more positive interactions.

Our human tendency is still to seek love and recognition from others. Why not make another happy for just a moment, and join the joy of the feeling you both have as a result?

Case Scenario

Situation. Robert instructed us. Julie and Robert had been married for 12 years and decided to separate amicably but Julie blamed Robert for their financial position. They had severe financial difficulties and neither could afford to buy out the other from the family home. Julie said she would go and live in rented accommodation with their two children, and it was agreed she would receive a small lump sum once equity could be released from the family home. When they separated, they agreed financial matters between them and both signed a statement of their agreed terms. They did not divorce until two years later. When they came to divorce, Robert wanted to put their agreement into an agreed financial order. Julie changed her mind and said she wanted to return to the house with the children. A battle started that neither could afford and as a result, trying to agree the finances on divorce became long and drawn out. As neither wanted nor could afford the cost of financial proceedings, nothing was resolved financially for some time. Julie's claims remained open.

How we helped him. If Robert had taken legal advice when he separated, we could have placed their written agreement between them in a formal deed of separation, and his wife would not have been easily able to change the terms unless there had been a material change in their situations.

We discussed with him options for loan funding of legal costs. We gave initial information so he could make his own enquiries from a few companies at the time. This enabled him to fund financial proceedings to resolve matters.

How he coped. He learnt that he simply had to let go as the contested financial process is very costly. He had to develop considerable patience as his wife refused to engage with him. He found it difficult to communicate with Julie, as she refused to discuss matters or meet with him. He found the lack of communication frustrating. He had to find different ways to interact with her.

Where he is now. Eventually, Julie's position changed as she met someone else, and then she engaged fully in the court process and discussions for settlement. Part way through financial proceedings, a financial consent order was drawn up in the previous agreed terms. Robert felt disgruntled for a while but over time, he accepted his own responsibilities and he had to work on his negative emotions. Eventually, he did manage to buy out Julie's share and change around his financial position. Their communication also improved once financial matters were resolved.

Morning Meditation

When you wake, you will probably be waking up alone. Or, possibly still next to your spouse, knowing that the inevitable breakup is upon you. Just take a few moments this morning as you shower, feel the warm water wash over your body, and decide just for today, you are going to let the past go and embrace your future. The water, as it cascades down, washes away any tears you may have had overnight or you feel able to express now. The water heals and purifies you. You are starting afresh. You may feel alone, but you are not alone. You are whole. Each droplet of water soothes you. Just breathe and enjoy the sensation of the water trickling down. Really feel into the warmth of each drop as it pours over you. Anything today is possible. You are whole. You will keep that thought as you move into your day.

Opening Thought of the Day
I am whole and I embrace my future with open arms.

Chapter 6

IMPACT ON CHILDREN, COUNSELLING AND CREATIVITY

Introduction

Most couples are primarily concerned about the effect of separation and divorce on their children. When you start divorce proceedings you do not need to define what the arrangements are for the children. The court do not ask you what the child arrangements are, or whether or not they are agreed, at any time throughout your divorce. Most couples try to resolve matters between themselves, or with the help of a mediator. If the parents cannot agree and resolve issues, a separate court application asking the court to decide children matters must be made. The couples that successfully navigate the path through the breakup with their children are those that put the children's needs as first priority. Those couples have open communication between them and maintain consistent approaches. They avoid making negative remarks about the other spouse to the children. Sometimes, a little help is needed. Child counselling is specialised and can be helpful, if you feel your child is finding it difficult to cope. I also bring in the creative tool of drawing and journaling for children. It is important to maintain playfulness. I have brought in a suggestion for laughing yoga which you can do with your children and will be a good release for you too! Music can also be relaxing as well as therapeutic. We follow Donald's experience of how his breakup affected the children, and how he finally resolved matters. Our evening meditation is a nice, fun one to ask your younger children to participate in. I invite you to recall our innate childlike nature as much as possible, which just makes everything you are going through that bit lighter.

Communicating with and about your Children

We have all been told communication is fundamental to relationships. This is key to your relationship with your child at this time. They can feel anxious, quite vulnerable and can have mixed emotions. They may blame themselves if they do not understand, or feel angry at you or your spouse, often the parent wanting to leave. Or they may just feel sad and bewildered at the family unit breaking up. They may withdraw inwards at this time or possibly go off the rails a bit.

Breaking the news

I really advise you to try to be open with them and give them the news together if you can, in a natural and non-emotional way. You will both have to make a decision whether the children will primarily live with one of you, or you will try to divide their time as equally as is possible between you. There are no hard and fast rules, as what may work for one couple and their children, may not be suitable for another. You should have thought this through together before you discuss this with your children.

It often comes down to practical and logistical decisions, particularly if one of you is moving out of the area. It may be appropriate for the parent the children are not living with to see the children at weekends. Every other weekend is often considered where both parents are working, and each may want to spend quality time with the children at weekends. It also depends on the ages of the children; younger children may need more frequent intervals with each parent. Decisions may also be influenced by the children's wishes, particularly if they are older. It is good to adopt a regular routine as soon as you are able to.

Children are adaptable but will seek reassurance at this time. You should both try to say the same about the situation and the decisions you are making, and not contradict each other. The most destructive breakups impact badly on the children. Try to keep your dignity and do not badmouth your spouse in front of the children, or directly in private to the children. Emotions may be volatile but your children will soak up the remarks made, and it will be unpleasant for them. Also, do not manipulate your children into taking sides. I have seen this far too often. You may not agree with your spouse's decisions or behaviour, but the relationship they have with their children is different, and it is not your place to put a slant on that.

How may your child react?

The degree of upset a child can feel will depend on their sensitivities. It is important for every child that the situation is handled carefully. The chats with them need to be tailored to the age of the child and their understanding. A very sensitive child will need constant reassurance from both parents. They may also need this reassurance over a long period of time. Children can feel a huge sense of loss at no longer having both parents in the family unit they have felt secure in. They will feel as if they are losing the parent they may be spending less time with as a result of the marriage breakdown, as well as the impact from a possible change of home. For any new house, make it a priority to get their room decorated first and make them comfortable with their favourite items. Try to make it more of an adventure than a loss for them.

If they are younger children, you will be giving them more general and less information, as they do not have an understanding of time. So perhaps say, in two sleeps time you will be having two sleeps with your father or mother. However, it may still be necessary to provide repetition so they understand the situation.

For older children, you will be much more open and communicative about the situation and they are likely to ask reasons why and details of what has gone wrong. They do not need to have all the minute details but it is important to be honest with them. They may need to be reassured that it is nothing to do with them, as children can also feel guilt and blame, and often anger at the parent who wants to bring the divorce, or the other parent if they perceive that parent as having caused the breakup. They may also need help to respond to their friend's questions about changing home and schools. For older children particularly, also keep an eye on their schooling and any tendency to withdraw –keep up constant emotional support.

Teachers and other family members

I would highly recommend you put your children's schoolteachers in the picture so they can also look out for any issues that may start to manifest at school. Also, grandparents and aunts and uncles can be involved for support, as sometimes children will confide in them and take comfort from being with them. This is also a time when one set of the spouse's parents or extended family often become ostracised. Grandparents have a different relationship with their grandchildren. Whatever you think of your spouse's parents, do not use this as an excuse to control their contact with the children.

Agreeing a Future Framework

The court only become involved when matters cannot be resolved and a separate court application needs to be made. Ideally, you want to agree a structure of child arrangements between you but if this proves difficult and you need some assistance, mediation is often a helpful way to define the future arrangements.

I recommend at the outset of divorce, seeking a mediator to assist you. They will often help you to arrive at a framework for future arrangements. This is known as a parenting plan. If you arrive at this plan, you can avoid making an application to court. Please also note that whilst there may be a pattern of arrangements that have worked for most couples, there is no "norm", and an arrangement that may be in a friend's court order or in their parenting plan may not be your experience. It is always better to try to thrash out an agreement between you based on your situation and both of your and the children's needs.

Matters I would suggest you cover (non–exhaustive) are:

- Who the children will primarily live with, or will you share care?
- How can the children's needs be covered? What is practical and economical?
- What contact time is spent with the other parent; collection times to be agreed and flexibility on travel arrangements. Consider whether it will be overnight contact (it may depend on accommodation). Include contact with extended family.
- In what circumstances is a change to agreed arrangements acceptable? What notice needs to be given?
- Frequency of phone calls to the children.
- Will each of you take responsibility for homework, activities, school pickups and drop offs.
- Holiday arrangements and special occasions, such as the children's and your birthdays and religious days or events.
- Taking the children abroad and who will hold their passports.
- Introduction of new partners (this is always a sore point but must be anticipated).
- Will you both attend parent's evenings and other school functions together?
- Financial considerations to support the agreed arrangements.

An agreed framework can be a helpful document you can each refer to and be guided by, but the arrangements are not set in stone and you should be flexible as arrangements evolve and the children get older as the arrangements will inevitably change. You can also perhaps agree when the plan or certain aspects of the plan will be reviewed.

Starting Proceedings and MIAM's

If you get to the point of attending mediation and being unable to agree arrangements, or the agreement breaks down, then the next step is starting children proceedings. It does not matter who brought the divorce. It is open to either of you to apply to court. Attendance at mediation, the first mediation information and assessment meeting (MIAM) is compulsory before an application is made to the court, unless an exemption applies. There is a long list of exemptions so it is worth checking first if you have to embark upon mediation. Exemptions include domestic violence and geographical limitations. If you have an emergency situation, you may not have to attend a MIAM.

After attending a MIAM, and at any stage through the course of mediation, if agreement has not been reached, the mediator will sign for you the Family Mediation Information and Assessment Form (FM 1) confirming you have attended mediation, and you will be able to start children proceedings to enable the court to determine children matters between you.

Children Proceedings

Orders That can be Made

The main order that is likely to be sought by you or your spouse is a Child Arrangements Order. This order decides the arrangements for whom a child is to live with, spend time with or otherwise have contact with, and when a child is to live, spend time or otherwise have contact with any person.

There are two additional orders that may be applied for.

1. A "specific issue order" for the purpose of determining a specific question which has arisen, or which may arise, in connection with any aspect of *parental responsibility* for a child.

2. A "prohibited steps order" that can be granted by the court to stop one parent from exercising their *parental responsibility* in a way that is not in the child's best interests.

Either of you can apply for a child arrangements order and the court can ultimately make any order they determine suitable, even if you have not specifically asked for a particular order. The old terminology of "custody orders, separate residence orders and contact orders" is no longer used. A single "child arrangements order" is now made.

What is Parental Responsibility?

Parental responsibility means the legal rights, duties, powers, responsibilities and authority a parent has for a child. It is focused on a parent's responsibilities, rather than any right to see their child. A person who has parental responsibility for a child has the right to make decisions about their care and upbringing. Important decisions in a child's life must be agreed with any other person who has parental responsibility. The mother of the child will automatically have parental responsibility. A father will automatically have parental responsibility if you are married, or if he is registered on the birth certificate. You will therefore both have the right to be involved in major decisions such as where the child should live, schooling, medical treatment and religion to be practised. You cannot change the surname of the child without the other's consent or leave of the court. So, if any of these matters need to be resolved, a specific issue application is applied for.

Application for Child Arrangements Order

A court form, C100, is the application for a child arrangements order. The same application form is used if you wish to apply for a specific issue order or prohibited steps order. It is completed by the person bringing the application, or their solicitor, and is filed at court. The form outlines what you are seeking. In divorce, it is most likely to be an application for a child arrangements order outlining with whom the child is to live or when they will spend time with them.

If you are bringing an application for the court to determine children matters, you are the Applicant and the other parent is the Respondent, regardless of which of you brought the divorce. You must each attend every hearing unless the court specifically direct that you do not need to attend.

You only need to give a very brief background of current arrangements for the children in the form, and why you are seeking the orders you are asking for. It is not necessary to, nor is there any provision to enable you to file statements. This will be directed by the court later after the first court hearing if matters have not been resolved.

The child arrangements order determining where a child will live lasts until the child is aged 18, but the order can be varied or dismissed by future application. Contact arrangements to see a child will end when the child is age 16 but this order can last until age 18 in exceptional cases. If the child does not want to see the parent by age 16 the court are unlikely to get involved except in limited situations as, by then, the court takes the view the child can decide themselves whether to see their parent further. If you and your spouse happen to reconcile, the order will cease to have effect if you live together for more than six months.

A court fee is payable to court when you file your application form C100 (currently £ 232 as at July 2022). You also need to provide two copies of your form C100 for the court.

The form C100 can be downloaded from the government website:
https://assets.publishing.service.gov.uk/government/uploads/system/uploads/attachment_data/file/874364/C100_eng_0818.pdf

Matters that may be covered in the Application

The matters to be covered in a child arrangements application may be as extensive as those I suggested that you try to agree in a parenting plan between you. Or they may be set out in broad categories as follows:

You can apply that your child lives with you, or the other parent and you have time with your child, or this may be shared.

You can apply for contact with your child if you are happy that they live with your spouse. If you want them to live with you, you can ask for contact arrangements with your spouse to be defined.

Contact between the child and a parent can be direct, i.e. face-to-face or telephone contact, or indirect, for instance by letters or cards. Contact can also take place in several ways, perhaps for a few hours, a full day, overnight or staying contact, and contact can also be supervised. Conditions may also be placed on contact arrangements, for instance the requirement to take the child to pre-arranged activities. In extreme situations the court can also order there be no contact with the child.

Specific Issue Orders

There are circumstances where you may wish to apply for a specific issue order if there is any issue relating to parental responsibility. The most common application is when a couple cannot agree which school their child should attend.

Prohibited Steps Orders

You can apply for a prohibited steps order to ensure that a parent cannot take certain steps without the consent of the court. The most common application is to seek that the parent does not take the child out of the UK where there is a concern a parent may wish to reside abroad.

Cases with Domestic Violence

If there have been any incidents of domestic violence, abuse or harm between you both, or between your spouse and your child, then another supplemental form (Form C1A) needs to be completed which outlines your main areas of concern. It is not necessary that any complaint has previously been filed with the police.

In this form you tell the court about harm that you, a child or children have suffered, or are at risk of suffering. You also use this form to respond to any allegations made by the other person in their application.

The form C1A is lodged at court with your child arrangements application form C100. When filing the application at court you will send two further copies so the court can then send a copy to your spouse.

This form can also be downloaded from the government website.
https://assets.publishing.service.gov.uk/government/uploads/system/uploads/attachment_data/file/866131/c1a-eng.pdf

Once your application form has been processed by the court, your spouse, the Respondent, will be asked to complete an acknowledgment of the application form C7 and state briefly their position. They may themselves also file a form C1A if harm to the child is alleged.

First Hearing Dispute Resolution Appointment

The court will then notify you and the other parent of the first court appointment which is a first hearing dispute resolution appointment, known as a FHDRA. The court apply a stricter timetable in children matters and try to deal with matters without delay. The hearing should be listed within five to six weeks of the application being lodged.

CAFCASS

Prior to the hearing, the Children and Family Court Advisory and Support Service, known as CAFCASS, will have already carried out various risk checks with the police and social services upon safety issues of the child, known as safeguarding checks. CAFCASS investigates and reports any issues to the court concerning the children's welfare and is an organisation responsible for safeguarding the interests of children involved in court proceedings.

At the first court appointment, you will generally arrive one hour prior to the allotted court time and meet with your representatives to try to resolve matters. Your solicitor may represent you at court, or you may have a barrister, and in complex cases your barrister and solicitor will both be present with you at court. Your solicitor or barrister (known as Counsel) will do all the talking in the hearing. A court welfare officer will also be present at the appointment and is appointed by the court. If it is not possible to come to an agreement, the court will give various directions for the matter to proceed:

- The court may suggest you both file statements.
- The court may ask that the court welfare service prepare a report. The court welfare service aim to have an understanding of any welfare issues that either of you are raising. The court welfare officer will make an assertion based on these initial investigations as to whether they feel they should be involved further to prepare a report. The court welfare service officer assists the judge by making findings and recommendations in their report which the judge can subsequently follow or give appropriate weight to when making a final order. The court welfare report may involve the officer speaking to both parents, and often the children depending on their ages, to ascertain their wishes and feelings, and also observing contact.
- The court may also consider if it is necessary to have evidence from other experts, e.g. medical experts.
- The court can also order, at any stage of proceedings prior to a final order, that a party undergo an activity, for instance, counselling or classes that may assist in improving involvement in the child's life.
- They can also send you to, or back to mediation if they think that will assist.

The court must consider the wishes and feelings of the child, taking into account the child's age and level of understanding in the circumstances. This will normally be determined by CAFCASS or social services and reported to the court. In some cases, a judge may speak directly with a child to determine their wishes and feelings if this is thought to be necessary. This tends to be with older children. This is only one of the factors the court will consider from the welfare checklist, and therefore, particularly with younger children rather than teenagers, their wishes may not necessarily govern the outcome.

Dispute Resolution Appointment

The court will then normally list a further review hearing known as a DRA, dispute resolution appointment, once all the evidence is together, to see if matters can be agreed or to narrow down the issues. Again, you will be present at court with your representatives. Only then if matters are not agreed, will they list the matter for a final hearing and possibly give further directions to be complied with.

Final Hearing

At a final hearing, your representatives will set out the issues. Both you and your spouse will give oral evidence, may be cross-examined together with the other experts, including the court welfare officer, before the judge makes a final order.

If there are allegations of violence, often the hearing will be split. First, there is a fact-finding hearing and the judge will make a decision as to whether all or some of the allegations are accepted, by applying the test of a balance of probabilities. It is necessary for the court to address issues of harm or domestic violence, as these would have a bearing on any order they are considering making. The court will then look at the remaining evidence and arguments.

The court will always be looking to make orders in the best interests of the child. They will take into account their needs and often, particularly if they are older, their wishes. Normally the court will view that it is in the best interests of the child to have contact with, and spend time with, each parent but not where the child is at risk of suffering harm.

Factors the Court take into Account

In family proceedings involving children, the courts must consider the welfare of a child of paramount concern. The welfare checklist consists of seven statutory criteria that the courts must consider under section 1(3) Children Act 1989 when reaching its decision in cases involving children.

The criteria set out in the welfare checklist are:

a. The ascertainable wishes and feelings of the child concerned.
b. The child's physical, emotional and educational needs.
c. The likely effect on the child if circumstances change as a result of the court's decision.
d. The child's age, sex, backgrounds and any other characteristics which will be relevant to the court's decision.
e. Any harm the child has suffered or maybe at risk of suffering.
f. The capability of the child's parents (or any other person the court finds relevant) at meeting the child's needs.
g. The powers available to the court in the given proceedings.

Final Order

The court will make a final order determining the issues, normally clarifying with whom the child or children are to live and spend time with. They may define all arrangements and add further conditions on contact or exercise of parental rights. When the court makes a final order, they will attach a notice warning of the consequences of non- compliance. Despite the court now being able to order various sanctions if your spouse fails to comply with the order, it still takes an effort to go back to court and seek enforcement. The court have various options open to them to enforce the order ranging from varying contact, fines, compensation orders, and even committal to prison.

Top Tips

DO

1. If possible, try to keep communicating for the benefit of the children. It is both costly and arduous to keep going backwards and forwards to court on children matters.
2. Attend mediation early if you cannot agree children issues between you.
3. Keep a diary where there are more major issues, for instance, domestic violence, or if your spouse fails to bring your child back or refuses to let them come to you on pre-arranged dates.

DO NOT

1. Write reams of information in your application to the court. Keep to the point; you can write a statement later if directed by the court after the first hearing.
2. Keep perspective. Do not nit-pick – courts are not interested if your spouse is 10 minutes late to collect your child.

Counselling and Creativity

This is a really hard time for children. Their dream of the family unit has been shattered. They often feel they are somehow to blame, not understanding why they are living with one parent and often seeing fractious interchanges between parents on contact. They may also have to accept that you or your spouse now has another partner and they may find that difficult to accept. I have even seen adult children being unable to come to terms with this.

They may find it difficult to sleep, have problems with schoolwork, and lose concentration generally. Children do not always have the emotional maturity and verbal skills to express how they feel to others.

Do consider with children that are struggling to understand or even cope, consulting with their doctor and the school as to whether they should see an independent child counsellor. You must make a joint decision with your spouse, but the school may be supportive in speaking to both parents if they think this may help. Your child may also speak to the teachers, but they may not be sure who to turn to and their performance at school may be affected. Extended family may also be too close to the individual parent for them to be able to confide fully.

The most important approach is to nurture and protect the children. Communicate effectively with them as often as possible so they are not keeping their emotions buried deep, to avoid future issues for them. Explain and help them understand. Just to recap, do not use words of blame or encourage them to take sides. Short term, I have seen parents who feel they have some victory with this control but who knows what long-term effect it has on the child.

As you are going inwards at this time, do also give your children space to go inwards too. They need to process their feelings, and depending on their age, especially coming up to teen years, they may also prefer to do this alone initially. Just look out for signs of struggle and be there to counsel. Seek independent counsellors for them if required.

Relate offers children and young people counselling. You can also find a registered counsellor through the counselling directory.

https://www.counselling-directory.org.uk/childrelatedissues.html?gclid=EAIaIQobChMI29fizZbp4QIVp5PtCh3alwrtEAAYASAAEgLcY_D_BwE

Play

Non-verbal therapy and activities such as art, music, and play, provide children with the opportunity to express themselves more easily. It is important for children to know that it is safe to be honest about how they are feeling and that they can learn ways to express and cope with their current situation.

Art and Play

Child counselling often uses art and play, particularly with younger children, to help them express their emotions more fully. In art therapy, children can draw, paint or create a sculpture that tells a story. They are encouraged, with the therapist's help, to talk about the different parts of what they created. You can also do some of these projects with your child, but if they have withdrawn from you, a therapist may be better to start off the process. The therapy may be one to one, or in a group with other families or children. The children will normally be placed in similar age groups. This helps them realise that others are going through the same situation and may have similar emotions. They may not feel as alone, or unusual, compared to friends whose parents are together. It can be a good supportive network.

Therapists may ask your children to draw the following:
- their family or part of the family
- any new family or new home
- how you act with each other
- how you act with them
- leaving one house to go to the other parent.

There are many art projects that children can be encouraged to create.
1. An angry painting. Children are encouraged to use thick paint and to press hard on paintbrushes to create a painting that helps them to release their feelings. They may then be encouraged to start talking about how they feel.
2. A journal that they take between homes. They can draw or write different activities and feelings to keep in the book and they can decide whether or not they want to share their book with others.
3. Making a clay object. They can use clay that dries quickly to create a small object that can fit in their pocket and can travel with them between homes. This becomes an object of

security and comfort and can help them adjust from one household to another.

4. A feelings box. Normally a shoebox, with stickers, pictures and drawings, your child decorates the outside of the box. They are encouraged to whisper into the box their current feelings. They can also add pictures to keep in the box when they want to express what is happening. They may like to keep their favourite toy in it each time they come and go.

Music

Music is an underestimated help for all age groups. Encourage your children to listen to their favourite music; the lyrics may sometimes resonate with what they are going through. Particularly for teenagers, and if your child has special needs, they may want to get lost in another world for a while. Music can help release strong emotions. Melodic and classical music can also help to calm down difficult emotions and soothe the soul. Perhaps have this on sometimes in the home. Choose music you all like to listen to in common areas of the home.

There is also music therapy available if you think your child would perhaps benefit from this, rather than, or in addition to, arts and play. The therapist may encourage listening to music, or playing together on several instruments, and maybe singing to lyrics. It may start a passion for learning a new instrument.

Laughing yoga

What is this?

When I first heard of laughing yoga (through my parents) when I was already past middle age, the first thing I thought was: is it a gimmick? I added it into my yoga practice, did more of it, and read more about the founder, Dr Madan Kataria who started a "laughter yoga" practice in India in 1995. I wondered why we did not do this earlier as a family. One of the most interesting points Dr Kataria made was that as children, we used to laugh around 300 to 400 times a day, and as adults, on average 15 times a day. What a sad fact.

So why is laughing yoga in this section? It is something really easily done together with children, although teenagers may need some persuasion. Younger children in particular will love it. They may start laughing more than you, or even at you, but the bond is indescribable. It will also loosen things up between you and take the seriousness out of the situation.

Laughing yoga shows us life does not have to be so serious all the time. However, it does have a serious side – the benefits have helped people cope with stress and depression. It oxygenates the lungs with deep belly laughing to promote better health. Laughing yoga allows adults and children to open up to express themselves freely. Science has found that our body does not know whether it is simulated or natural laughter, although laughter may naturally occur as you get into the session. It is great to increase those endorphins.

It would be good if you could encourage your children to sit in meditation but children often have a short attention span. We ourselves often find it difficult to sit in meditation and to put in the concerted effort to detach ourselves from the external goings on to attain peace and harmony. While laughing, we do not have any conscious thought process and therefore, effortlessly, we can take our mind away from distracting thoughts and feel joy and harmony.

Our brain is made up of the right and left hemispheres. With laughing yoga, we start to develop the playfulness of the right side of the brain. The left side of our brain tends towards more logical and analytical tasks. The right hemisphere deals with the imagination, creativity and healing. The right side can be stimulated by playfulness and can give freedom to emotions and creativity.

You don't have to spend money to do this with the children, and they will enjoy the time spent with you without distraction.

How to do Laughing Yoga

Laughing yoga sessions start with:

- gentle warm-up movements. These include stretching, whilst chanting ho,ho,ho, ha,ha,ha, and clapping. These initial exercises reduce inhibitions and help cultivate playfulness.
- Breathing exercises are also used to prepare the lungs. There is deep belly breathing.
- A series of laughter exercises follow that combine acting and visualisation techniques, with childlike playfulness.
- The deep belly laughs last for at least 10 to 15 minutes to get the full benefits of oxygen into the lungs.

No one compares themselves to anyone else and there is no competition. You are free to interpret what your teacher suggests you act out however you choose. Sometimes, the exercises go over tough times we may have had in the week and you just laugh at them, which takes the heat out of what may have happened and helps to dissipate any negative feelings and our sense of seriousness over the situation.

Dr Kataria shares his theory behind laughter yoga and introduces many of the laughter exercises you can choose from on YouTube.

https://www.youtube.com/watch?v=5hf2umYCKr8
https://www.youtube.com/watch?v=Fq4kTZuLops

Case Scenario

Situation. Donald was a lovely mild mannered man who worked hard in his business. His wife Kylie was often highly strung when he got home from work. They had been married for 15 years and had two boys aged 7 and 10. The elder boy could understand more about the marriage breakup and was close to his father. When he saw his mother shouting at Donald, he did not want to be near her and asked to live with his father when they sold the house and bought their own properties. The seven year old was impressionable and Kylie spoke to him about the divorce and about Donald in a derogatory manner. As a result, the seven year old often questioned his father about why he was making his mother unhappy. The situation worsened and once the sale finally went through, the situation concluded with each boy spending more time with the parent they could understand more or wanted to support (even as children).

How we helped him. We advised Donald that he could seek a child arrangement order from court setting out the times the boys were to live with him or spend time with him. The order could also include conditions that Kylie did not talk about him to the boys in a derogatory manner, and also provide for additional telephone contact in between visits. They eventually agreed a parenting plan after proceedings were issued.

How he coped. He had the resolve to start the children proceedings to ensure that whatever it took, both sons lived with him on an equal basis.

He had the tenacity and flexibility to face his future, making time for the children.

Where he is now. He reduced some of his business hours to fit around the children and changed his outlook. He met a lovely lady a few years later who also had children, and they decided to live together. It took a bit of time for the children to adjust, but with effort it all worked out well, and Donald and his partner understood and supported each other.

Evening Meditation

You can do this meditation alone or with your child. Put aside 15 minutes before your child's bedtime to do this together. It is a nice one to do if your child is tucked up in bed, or you may sit comfortably together, maybe cross-legged on some comfy cushions. Take several deep breaths together. Put your hands on your belly to really feel into that breath. Breathe in and out until you feel calm and relaxed. Close your eyes.

Now, imagine that you are breathing in light from a beautiful big rainbow and breathing out different coloured bubbles. You can have as many of the same or different coloured bubbles as you like. Imagine all those bubbles simply floating in front of you. As they float, a worry, a thought, or feeling may come to you. Imagine putting it into a bubble. You choose the coloured bubble it goes into. Let it float around in the bubble.

When you are ready, let it go, drifting away into the distance. As you do this, another or the same thought or feeling may come to you. Put it inside another bubble. Let it float in front of you for a while, until you are ready to let it go. Keep doing this for as long as you need to and your thoughts start to subside, and you or your child start to feel sleepy. Finally, have a cuddle (with your child or hug yourself). Go to sleep knowing all troubles, thoughts and emotions have floated away.

| **Concluding Thought of the Day** |
| I will bring laughter and playfulness into my life. |

Chapter 7

FINANCES, FINANCIAL FREEDOM AND PHYSICAL YOGA

Introduction

You are likely to spend most of your time resolving financial issues on divorce, and most of your solicitor's fees will be incurred in this area. Therefore, it is worth trying to agree matters early on. As financial matters are complex, I have covered this over two chapters. In this chapter I cover the most common approaches to resolving financial matters outside court proceedings, and the factors the court take into account when deciding what order is fair, so you can consider these before you try to agree matters between you. Your solicitor is likely to mention these factors known as section 25 factors. I also cover the consent order which will be sent to court for approval once you have reached an agreement. In the next chapter I cover financial remedy proceedings. I go on to reflect on financial freedom, and what this may mean for you. It is a stressful time, you may face an uncertain financial future and a lot of energy is spent in dealing with finances. I conclude with yoga exercises to help you physically dissipate some of that stress and remain centred. We meet Miranda who decided to come to a "kitchen table" agreement with her husband and take her chances as to whether the court would approve an order. We then meet Lubka who moved to England from Poland and entered into a civil partnership. We look at what specific steps we needed to take in her situation. We conclude with a morning meditation known as the black smoke meditation, breathing out any negativity and breathing in a new positive energy. We finish positive and energised.

Reaching an Agreement

I always suggest that you start addressing financial matters simultaneously with making the decision to divorce. Financial matters are dealt with separately from the divorce procedure. You can reach a financial agreement between you through mediation or directly through solicitors. You may also use more formal forums for resolution outside the court process such as arbitration or private financial resolution appointments (FDR's). Once matters are agreed, the agreement is then placed in a formal financial remedy order known as a "consent order" by your solicitors, signed by both of you and your representatives, and sent to court for approval. The court can only approve the financial remedy order once the conditional divorce order has been granted.

If you cannot reach an agreement, financial proceedings will need to be issued. Ideally, you want to be at the conditional order stage for no-fault divorce, with financial matters already agreed and the financial consent order drawn up ready to file. To achieve this, it is important to start reciprocating financial disclosure and try to agree financial matters at the outset of the divorce.

Applications for finances and interim applications can be made any time after you have applied for a divorce order. The court have jurisdiction to deal with final orders by consent, or contested proceedings once the conditional order for divorce has been made, and ideally prior to a final divorce order.

Form D81 (to be completed with consent order)

Even where agreement has been reached through negotiation, financial statements must be completed for the court. The court require a prescribed Statement of Information form D81 to be filed together with the draft consent order, so that the judge has a basic level of financial information with which to adjudicate the fairness of any proposed settlement. Thus, financial disclosure is unavoidable. If the judge feels the agreement is fair, he/she approves the consent order, which is then dated and sealed by the court. This form is explained in greater detail when I explain the financial order.

There are various possible approaches to try to achieve an agreement.

Voluntary Disclosure

I would say that voluntary financial disclosure is always necessary. You should enter into any agreement with full knowledge and understanding of what its terms are based on, so disclosure of finances is an essential pre-requisite. When done voluntarily, there are no sanctions for non-compliance. Although it can, where the disclosure is in some significant way misleading or dishonest, mean that any court order made could potentially be subject to being set aside.

Form E (in-depth financial statement)

Solicitors recommend that full financial disclosure is done by way of completion of a form E. This is a standard court prescribed form which is completed in financial proceedings but also widely used by solicitors and mediators before entering into voluntary discussions. The form contains sections to be completed for every type of asset, so nothing is missed out. Every section also identifies the required supporting documentation to be produced which must accompany the completed form. Therefore, it is easier to check whether information on the form is correct or not.

However, it is important to keep to a broad timetable as otherwise time elapses and no agreement is reached. In these cases, it would be better to simply issue financial proceedings early. Voluntary disclosure is always best exchanged through solicitors or in mediation rather than directly, as solicitors and mediators are familiar with the form E and required documents and know what to look out for or what may have been missed.

By way of disclosure, be prepared to obtain:

- valuations for the marital home and any other property.
- valuations for other assets (for pensions it is a cash equivalent fund valuation).
- an up to date mortgage redemption statement.
- gather twelve months bank and other account statements.
- collate statements showing your liabilities.
- payslips and Form P60, or year-end accounts if you are self-employed.
- Also prepare a breakdown of your expenditure needs.

Please note that you must make full disclosure of your assets, known as full and frank disclosure. If you fail to disclose true values of all assets held by you or in which you have an interest, or any material information such as you are living together with a third party or are shortly due an inheritance, your spouse could re-open matters in the future. So be truthful and be careful to provide accurate disclosure.

Once financial disclosure has taken place, normally solicitors would negotiate on your behalf in correspondence and discussions over the phone to try to reach an agreement to conclude a financial settlement between you.

Round Table Meeting

A round table meeting can be arranged once you have exchanged disclosure with both sets of solicitors, and you and your spouse. If matters drag on in correspondence, or you want to try to settle matters quickly, a constructive way to bring matters to a conclusion can be by way of a round table meeting. Although such meetings can be intensive and will be expensive, as both sets of solicitors will be attending for at least half a day, they are an effective way of bringing matters to a head and usually do result in an amicable resolution. If you do not reach an agreement, you will at least have narrowed down the issues between you.

Mediation

Mediation is growing in popularity if the parties' relationship remains amicable as they can attempt to resolve matters by visiting an independent mediator. This gives some formality, but also objectivity, to the process. It is less likely to be emotional or confrontational when discussions are with a mediator. As mentioned earlier, an agreement reached in mediation is not binding and I have seen many couples spend months of time and money to reach an agreement, for one party to change their mind. It is also not unusual for one party to delay making appointments with the mediator or be tardy in providing their disclosure through this process. This means that the timetable can easily drift, as it depends on everyone's availability for the sessions to take place.

If you both attend mediation, you can let the mediation process guide the exchange of financial documents and facilitate an agreement. If you reach an agreement you will then need your solicitor to draw up the financial order and assist you with the content of the short financial statement form D81 to be filed at court with the consent order.

Any agreement arrived at in mediation, or even signed between you and witnessed, is not binding, so it is imperative that a financial order is entered into. If you arrive at an agreement in mediation, the mediator will prepare several documents for you.

- The first is known as a memorandum of understanding and it outlines what you have agreed.
- The second is an open financial statement that supports it, outlining your disclosed financial information.

You should pass copies to your solicitor as these documents will assist them in preparing the financial order and accompanying form D81 financial statement. It is imperative that you instruct a solicitor to prepare the financial order. It ensures the correct legal terminology is used and that you do not leave yourself open in the future. Normally one solicitor will prepare the draft financial order and then send it to your spouse's solicitor for approval or for any changes.

The Solicitor's Role through Mediation

It is always advisable to have a meeting for guidance on your potential settlement from your solicitor before you either attend mediation or discuss matters with your spouse so you know in general terms what you are entitled to. Throughout mediation as issues come up you may need to refer to your solicitors for guidance. Clients are more likely to ask their solicitors to attend a mediation meeting when it may be critical to achieve settlement. Sessions between couples involving their solicitors can be useful. It is never helpful for an agreement to later be undone because your solicitor advises it is unfair, and the court are unlikely to approve it. This loses any goodwill with your spouse who won't trust you if you renege on an agreement, even though you should probably not have agreed to it in the first place.

Negotiations Through Solicitors

You can ask solicitors to guide you through the financial process from the outset. This is useful where there is no real hope of sitting down with your ex and coming to any agreement directly, or where you feel you may be bullied or at a disadvantage in mediation. You can let your solicitor deal directly with your ex or their solicitor, so you have some distance from your legal matters, which can be a good thing. But do be careful that correspondence does not result in dealing with lots of issues along the way, or small points, as costs can quickly escalate. This is easier said than done if your spouse is being difficult.

Kitchen Table Agreement

Some couples still favour trying to sort finances directly between them, known as a Kitchen Table Agreement. If you are both financially aware, you could try to sit down and discuss matters between you. This is not my preferred route as you have to be absolutely certain that you know your spouse will divulge everything, and you also need to be aware of what is reasonable for settlement. However, from a costs perspective, this is the cheapest option. Generally, clients will have first each have received legal advice, and then sit down with their spouse and discuss matters face-to-face with a view to agreeing terms. Once terms are agreed, solicitors would be instructed to prepare the draft financial consent order and other necessary paperwork. Be prepared for the solicitors to ask you to sign disclaimers if they have not seen your disclosure or advised on the terms of settlement. Also be prepared that the solicitors are unlikely to agree that their name should be included on the financial consent order setting out any terms of agreement reached in the absence of full financial disclosure.

A kitchen table agreement is very risky. It is always advisable to have full and frank disclosure as then your solicitors can advise you properly and negotiate an order that is reasonable, with the best chance of being approved by the court.

Private FDRs

Couples can opt to go further and choose more formal forums to thrash out a settlement, particularly if there are a lot of assets and parties wish to ensure that they reach an agreement with the view and opinion of an independent judge. They are known as Private Financial Dispute Resolution Hearings (FDR's) and are expensive. They are appropriate where there are complex issues or legal arguments, and there is a lot of money. These can be an effective way of bringing a dispute to a prompt conclusion. A private FDR can take place before court proceedings are started, or at any stage during ongoing proceedings. A private FDR can take place wherever you both choose, such as at the solicitors' office, or barristers' chambers. The advocates can be solicitors or they can instruct barristers, and the judge is chosen by the parties. The FDR can deal with all or some of the issues, as the parties so choose. The parties will pay for the judge whose fee is agreed in advance. Those judges suitable to conduct private FDRs may be barristers or experienced solicitors. Very often, both your barrister and your solicitor will be present to represent you. If settlement is not reached, then normally you and your spouse are back to the court process, but you may possibly avoid a court directed FDR hearing and get listed quicker to final hearing.

The Financial Remedies Court encourages the use of Private FDR's. If one is arranged, the date should be given to court, as they will then list a short mention hearing after this to review next steps, which will be vacated if the parties file a final consent order and forms D81 and this is approved by the Judge.

Collaborative Law

Collaborative Law still remains an option, very often as an alternative to mediation but it is not used as much. Discussions take place face-to-face in four-way meetings, you and your spouse, and your respective solicitors. Accordingly, you will have the benefit of a solicitor advising you and acting for you within those meetings. All parties and their solicitors would need to sign a Participation Agreement binding them to the process. Normally no proceedings for finances are brought during this process. If negotiations were to break down, then neither firm of solicitors could act in proceedings.

Collaborative law can be neither a cheap or quick alternative and it is often just as expensive as traditional solicitor negotiations. The advantage of this approach is that clients can see what is happening in the process and that can sometimes make for more amicable and transparent discussions.

Arbitration

Since February 2012 it has been possible to resolve family financial disputes by way of arbitration. The scheme is run by the Institute of Family Law Arbitrators (IFLA) and operates under the Family Law Arbitration Scheme Arbitration Rules 2014. Arbitration can only be used if both parties agree. The arbitrator is agreed between the parties, or alternatively the IFLA may appoint an arbitrator. The arbitrator's decision is final and binding on the parties regarding any financial and property disputes. The same arbitrator will deal with all stages of the case from start to finish and their decision (known as the "award") is produced, to then be drawn up into a court order. An arbitrator can deal with the whole financial case or they can be engaged just to deal with specific aspects of a dispute. Solicitors assisting clients through arbitration can agree the timetable and work around the needs of the clients involved, more readily than through a court process. Arbitration has been very little used to date but is a growth area of law. The main advantages are the speed of the process, choice of arbitrator and venue, and costs savings inherent in a more efficient process. It is also worth noting that arbitration proceedings are private – there is no risk of court reporters or the press becoming involved at any stage. It will be interesting to see if this takes off in the future. Resolution are encouraging the group connectivity which is trying to bring solicitors, mediators and arbitrators together in a collaborative process to settle disputes in a timely way without going through court proceedings.

Factors Considered by the Court in Determining a Financial Order

Financial claims against one another are not concluded until there has been an approved financial court order. If there are contested financial proceedings resulting in a determination at court, your representatives and the court will prepare the final order. If overall agreement is reached on finances out of court, the draft order is sent to court for approval. A judge can consider the fairness or otherwise of any proposed settlement by considering the summary financial statements filed at the same time by you or your solicitor. Even if matters are agreed between you, the proposed consent order still has to be "fair and reasonable" to be approved by the court. It is therefore important you consider the factors the court would take into consideration ahead of your discussions.

With regard to financial claims, divorce courts have very wide powers to deal with any assets in a case. Both parties in a divorce have identical claims in law for maintenance, a lump sum, property adjustment and pension claims. However, these are still subject to the application of section 25 factors.

If no agreement is reached and financial proceedings are commenced in the divorce proceedings, the judge deciding the case will have to consider Section 25 of the Matrimonial Causes Act 1973. This sets out the criteria that the judge has to consider in deciding what would be "fair". We therefore have to bear these factors in mind throughout our negotiations to achieve a settlement, as ultimately only the court can approve any settlement and ratify it by way of a court order. The section 25 factors are set out as follows:

1. *The Court will have regard to all the circumstances of the case, first consideration being given to the welfare of any child of the family who has not attained the age of eighteen.*
2. *The income, earning capacity, property and other financial resources which each of the parties to the marriage has or is likely to have in the foreseeable future, including in the case of earning capacity any increase in that capacity which it would in the opinion of the court be reasonable to expect a party to the marriage to take steps to acquire* (this may include likely inheritances).
3. *The financial needs, obligations and responsibilities which each of the parties to the marriage has or is likely to have in the foreseeable future* (particularly relevant where children).
4. *The standard of living enjoyed by the family before the breakdown of the marriage* (generally looked at in big money cases as in most situations the practical position is there is not enough to go around so this becomes almost irrelevant).
5. *The age of each party to the marriage and the duration of the marriage* (most arguments for departure from equality are where there are short marriages).

6. *Any physical or mental disability of either of the parties to the marriage.*
7. *The contributions which each of the parties has made or is likely in the foreseeable future to make to the welfare of the family, including any contribution by looking after the home or caring for the family* (if one party has been a breadwinner and the other a homemaker caring for children, the court will take the view that both have contributed).
8. *The conduct of each of the parties, if that conduct is such that it would in the opinion of the court be inequitable to disregard it* (this has to be significant conduct not general behaviour through the marriage).
9. *The value to each of the parties to the marriage of any benefit which, by reason of the dissolution or annulment of the marriage, that party will lose the chance of acquiring* (for instance widows pension benefits).

The court can decide to consider some factors as relevant but not others and decide what weight to give to each factor. The court also have a duty in all cases to decide whether a clean break can be achieved.

There are many decided contested financial cases which serve as precedents, against which your case is likely to be considered. These cases have often gone to the higher courts such as the Court of Appeal, and therefore their decisions influence how the judge looks at your case. They are often known as big money cases as the cases that are decided in the higher courts invariably involve a great deal of money, normally millions of pounds, but the principles are then applied to future cases.

The court has to consider the case law including, in particular, the House of Lords case of White v White in 2000, which gave us the "yardstick of equality" and "sharing principle", whereby the court must consider whether a settlement is fair when compared with an equal division of the assets. If it is not felt to be fair, "good reasons" must be provided for departing from equality. (Good reasons may for instance be that there is limited capital to cover accommodation needs, the needs of children of the family, or possibly contributions made by one party). Subsequent case law has continued to emphasise the principle of "sharing".

Your solicitor is likely to use terms such as fairness which in most cases means equality, but not all, as fairness can cover various aspects of:

- needs
- sharing
- compensation

The needs of the parties come first. Where there are children, the needs of the parent with the children living with them is considered practically as a priority. Depending on the available assets both parents should be housed similarly. If there are sufficient assets the sharing principle is applied, particularly to assets accrued during the marriage. The court can consider the principle of compensation but these cases are far and few between. The claim in these cases is that there is a *relationship generated disadvantage* which should provide additional compensation. For instance, where a spouse has given up a very lucrative career opportunity to look after the children, they may seek additional compensation. However, many of these situations still fall in the sharing principle, and the compensatory element is the exception rather than the norm.

Matrimonial and Non-matrimonial property

There is currently a distinction between matrimonial and non-matrimonial property. Matrimonial assets have been accrued between the couple during the marriage. Non-matrimonial assets are not the financial product of, or generated by the parties' endeavours, during the marriage.

So, if a party brings property (other than the marital home) or other assets into the marriage, or those acquired by inheritance or gift during the marriage, they are generally treated as non-matrimonial property.

The "sharing" principle applies to assets treated as matrimonial property. Sharing normally means an equal division of assets and is often the same, however long or short the marriages are. To the extent that property is non-matrimonial property, there is more likely to be a departure from equality. There will be cases where it would be fair for there to be a lesser or no award of non-matrimonial property to the other spouse. However, if each party cannot be rehoused without recourse to those assets and it is a "needs" case, the non-matrimonial property is also likely to be shared.

Marital Home

The marital home, even if brought into the marriage at the outset by one person, is looked at specifically, as the house is viewed as taking a central place in the marriage. So, it is normally treated as matrimonial property to be shared. In respect of the marital home, an argument may be raised that the net equity accrued before the marriage should at least be reflected in the award for the benefit of the party that brought in the property to the marriage.

The Assets

When looking at the period in which assets accrued, the court will consider the span of the partnership from when the parties permanently started to cohabit pre-marriage to either separation, or up to the date when the finances are now being determined by the court.

The court will put all assets into the "pot" to be considered. The court can make an order against any asset of the parties, regardless of whose name it is held in. They can order a sale or transfer of any property or asset. They can even order property to continue to be held even if in joint names, the most usual scenario of a family home being held until the children attain majority, or until they complete first degree-level education. The court can also order one party to pay the other a lump sum or series of lump sums.

For **pensions**, the court will look at the up-to-date cash value of the funds, and an argument is normally made for only the proportion accrued during the relationship to be taken into account. If there is a "needs" situation pension value accrued outside of the period of the relationship may also be considered. The court can make a pension sharing order, which is the most common order made these days, which effectively takes out a portion of the pension fund from one scheme, and puts it into another new, or existing scheme for the spouse. Pensions are extremely complex and need specialist pension actuary reports to be commissioned to decide what are the correct assumptions and divisions to achieve fairness (often equality). Pension actuaries can also determine what lump sum could be given to the other party to "offset" their pension claims. They can also recommend earmarking a pension sum similar to a maintenance order that could be paid, but this has disadvantages for the recipient if the payer dies, and as it can be varied.

Spousal maintenance is often down to the individual case and normally based on needs. It is therefore usually only considered in situations where there are children or it has been a long marriage and one spouse has very limited earnings and earning capacity. As the court have moved towards an outlook of a clean break where possible, even where there are children, more increasingly where the parent with care has some earnings, and the children are in secondary school, be prepared for a possible clean break.

Otherwise, maintenance periods that may be made can be for a fixed term, extendable or non-extendable, or in increasingly limited circumstances, for joint lives. Maintenance is always reviewable by future applications to court by either party where there has been a change of financial circumstances, upwards or downwards. Maintenance automatically ceases on the recipient's remarriage. Provision in the order can also be included for it to cease on other events such as the children reaching a certain age, or the recipient's cohabitation normally termed for a continuous period of at least six months in the past

12-month period, to allow time to ensure the relationship is secure.

Overall, the court still has an ultimate and wide discretion regarding what to award, and they take what is known as a "broad brush approach". The court can apply a broad assessment to the division of assets, as the court determines any proposed award as a fair outcome having regard to all the section 25 factors.

Financial Remedy Order

When you have both reached an agreement, I have often been asked in the past whether the same solicitor can deal with matters for both of you. As mentioned before, a solicitor cannot represent both of you. Whilst it is possible that one solicitor prepares the consent order and you sign it, I still recommend you get your own independent legal advice. Often your advisor will seek some minor and major changes in the draft order to protect your position. Also, where one party does not have representation, the court sometimes arranges a short court hearing to ensure the order is understood before approving it.

The order is generally outlined in a set format:
- Definitions cover parties and properties and salient information.
- Recitals which cover background information.
- Declarations, which may include a declaration of solvency. This is important where your spouse is transferring property to you, particularly if you have been separated for some time and he or she may have debt.
- Agreements cover matters agreed between you. Very often this includes the division of contents of the house.
- Undertakings which cover matters that the court cannot order but you want to be enforceable, which is particularly useful for businesses and indemnities on tax. Undertakings to the court help to protect your position on your spouse's compliance.

- Then the main part of the order itself outlines a series of orders. The orders range from property, lump sums, pension, maintenance, and end with dismissal of claims clauses and costs.
- **Property** orders can include sale or transfer of property.
- **Pension** sharing or attachment orders will have a separate form of annex giving full details of the pension being shared or earmarked.
- **Maintenance** orders will confirm the term of maintenance, and whether or not it can be extended, and may provide for annual increases or reviews.
- **Lump sum** orders may provide for interest due if not paid by a certain date. They have to be carefully drafted if there is a series of lump sums or payment by instalments to ensure enforcement, and whether or not the amount/s and timing are variable.
- **Dismissal clauses** provide for the dismissal of claims between you both during your lifetime, and also your respective estates on death. Dismissal may be dependent upon agreed terms having been complied with, or there may be a deferred dismissal of claims if there is any agreed ongoing provision (usually maintenance).
- **Liberty to apply** to the court, which provides if there is any issue on timing and implementation an application can be made to court for guidance.
- **No order as to costs** means that you each pay your own solicitor costs unless a contribution has been agreed, normally limited to any divorce proceeding costs.

If there is provision on pensions or release from an existing mortgage (unless a remortgage where the mortgage will be repaid), you will need the pension trustee's or mortgagee's consent. So, the order cannot be finalised to send to court until they have approved the same.

Often pension providers require specific detail on the pension plan name and number to be included in the order. If there is a pension sharing or attachment order, the pension provider will need to be asked to approve the draft order and the accompanying pension sharing or attachment annex.

If you or your spouse also reside abroad or have assets abroad, your solicitor should ensure that the order covers those assets. If a clean break of further claims is agreed then it is subject to those assets being dealt with first so as to avoid enforcement issues abroad. The order should also ensure neither of you can make further claims in any other jurisdiction thereafter.

Maintenance

Do check the order carefully regarding spousal maintenance and the stated term. Be certain of all specified triggering events where it is agreed maintenance will stop, usually when the children reach a certain age or complete full-time education, or if the spouse receiving maintenance cohabits over a certain period of time or remarries. The order will clearly define when you or your spouse cannot make further claims or can no longer apply to extend any maintenance term.

The level of maintenance, once set in the order, is the level to be paid unless the maintenance is varied by agreement or subsequent court order. You cannot prevent a future application for variation of maintenance if spousal maintenance is included in the order. However, sometimes it is appropriate to insert a further recital to limit the circumstances you expect maintenance to be varied. For instance, it may only be if you or your spouse loses their job and fail, despite sincere attempts, to obtain another position, or in the event of disability. The order may already provide for a reduction in maintenance on some triggering event, for instance, a child leaving home.

It used to be widely accepted that in all cases where there are children, there should also be spousal maintenance, even at a nominal level if the spouse with care was earning well. However, increasingly, the courts are promoting a clean break outlook and are much less likely to add the safety net of a nominal maintenance order which would keep the door open for a future upwards variation of spousal maintenance. It will depend on your particular circumstances and how case law is being applied. But I have settled cases more recently where either substantive or nominal spousal maintenance does not continue beyond children starting in secondary education.

Child Maintenance

The overall authority for child maintenance is held by the government department known as the child maintenance service, formerly the child support agency, and not the court, where the parents are both habitually resident in the UK. Regarding child maintenance, this can be agreed between you and the amount can be stated in the order but currently, one year after the date of the order, either party can apply to the child maintenance service, https://www.gov.uk/child-maintenance, for an assessment and this will oust the child maintenance level set out in the order. So, it is always best to agree child maintenance along the lines of the likely assessment even if you state it in the order. You can reflect in the order that neither of you intend to apply to the child maintenance service but it does not stop you from subsequently doing so.

Please note that where the child maintenance service does not have jurisdiction, any agreement must be put into an order.

- This covers top-up orders where the paying party of maintenance has a high salary, over the child maintenance service limit.
- Also, payment of school fees and university fees and expenses for disability.
- Additionally, for children, once they are over the age of 16 and after they have completed A-level equivalent full-time education, the child maintenance service no longer has jurisdiction, so it is usual to see child maintenance continuing under the court order to the child completing first degree university education.
- For stepchildren treated as children of the family during the marriage, it is possible to seek child maintenance.

- In cases where the receiving parent is not in the UK or the paying parent is abroad and not working for a British based organisation.

Form D81

To accompany the order, the court will require sight of a financial statement as previously summarised. You will both complete a financial statement form D81 totalling your assets into categories and outlining your income positions. There are two parts of the form that need to be signed: page 5, confirming you agree your spouse's disclosure; and page 6, confirming your disclosure is true and accurate.

- As mentioned before, please ensure you disclose financial information on all your assets and any foreseeable changes.
- My clients have sometimes struggled with the capital section. The form needs to be completed, outlining the current financial position and not what assets you will have when the order has been put into effect.
- For property, the net equity figures are inserted.
- I find it useful to do a separate sheet showing how you have arrived at the property and capital figures where you have various assets, and even the same with pensions and debts if there are several, to accompany the form to go to your spouse's solicitor, so it is clear what has been covered. This also helps you/your solicitor not to forget anything. The accompanying sheet will not go to court but is useful for disclosure purposes so it can be clear what information your form was based upon, if any issue is raised later on.
- You also need to cover a few additional sections. You will need to confirm where you will live and whether you have cohabitation or remarriage plans.
- Regarding notice to the mortgagee, this is not necessary if you are remortgaging with another lender and repaying the existing mortgage.

- If there is pension sharing or attachment, the trustees should already have been given notice and have approved the draft order.

The consent order in triplicate and form/s D81 and court fee of £53 (as at July 2022) are filed at court by your solicitor. A form A is also usually filed for each party.

Form A

Most courts will also require a form A to be filed by your solicitor which details financial claims being raised by a party, and then effectively closed by being dealt with in the consent order. This is the form used to start off financial proceedings and proceed with a party's claims. But here it is used as a formal mechanism to simply raise, and then deal, with your respective claims against the other in accordance with the terms of the consent order. Your solicitor completes the first page of the form and confirms the order is by consent. It is then usual for your solicitor to write on the top of the first page "for dismissal purposes only", so the court note you are not bringing separate financial proceedings. Each party's representatives will complete a separate form.

The judge can only consider the draft order once a conditional divorce order has been made. Sometimes the judge will have queries –it is not simply a "rubber stamping exercise" even if matters are agreed. So, particularly if the assets are not being divided equally, we give any further information that will assist the judge in making an agreed order within the order, or form D81. Once the order is approved, a sealed financial order will be received from the court. Your spouse will also receive a sealed order directly from the court.

Ensure you comply with all matters stated in the order and then you can be sure there will be no issues later on. Also, if there are any ongoing obligations, for instance, maintenance, keep the order safely.

Top Tips

DO

1. Write off for your pension valuation as soon as the divorce starts. This takes months to arrive so the sooner you can apply the better.

2. Start getting your financial paperwork together as early as possible.

DO NOT

1. Discuss financial matters without having received legal advice on your likely settlement.

Financial Freedom

If we apply our rationale, let's face it, no one comes out of a divorce financially richer. It is a division. There can only be a division of the available assets. However, it is possible to come out of the divorce with a sense of financial freedom. Whatever your settlement is or what you are "left with", it is yours and you can make the decision how you will use it. If finances are tight, you may have no option but to buy a smaller house but you can make it your home and your space. I had a poignant message once from a friend who said if we allow our primitive minds to take over, we can be unhappy even if we live in a palace. So, if you were a prisoner metaphorically in your home, it does not matter how nice it was and it is better to be free and at peace wherever you have to go.

In reality, there is no such thing as security – being protected from danger or threat. Financial security or comforts can be taken away from us at any time. There are many wealthy business people who make a final deal and lose everything, or those who have carefully invested money over time to lose it in one fell swoop with a rogue investment or a failing pension scheme. Health, we all hope, will be good throughout our lives but there is never any guarantee as illness or accidents can befall us at any time. Security of a relationship is the same. After thinking you have invested many years, a relationship can suddenly hit a crunch point and be over before you have time to take it all in. Security is not truly to be found in either money, health or a relationship.

Yoga

Yoga means union and is derived from the Sanskrit word yuj which means to join. The meaning of yoga is the union of body, mind, and spirit. According to the philosophy of yoga, we suffer because of not knowing our true self, due to the illusion of separation of our individual consciousness from the universal consciousness. Yoga is a group of physical, mental, and spiritual practices which originated in ancient India. Yoga is a discipline. Most people in the Western world think of yoga as hatha yoga, which is a generic term and refers to any type of yoga that teaches physical postures. Yoga in fact originated as a spiritual discipline. Around 400 BCE, the sage Patanjali compiled yoga sutras or discourses (which were likely to be oral teachings given in those times) into texts on the ancient practice and philosophy of yoga. These sutras are viewed as one of the foundations of classical yoga. Patanjali defines yoga as the settling of the thought waves in the mind.

In modern day we have moved further towards the physical aspects of yoga. Physical yoga is undertaken not just for the flexibility and strength it brings to the body, but the effect that has on settling down the body and mind. When we are practising physical yoga, it prevents us from thinking of other things and the constant turning of the mind. The asanas or postures bring health benefits to the nervous system and provide other internal benefits to the body and its organs. The physical asanas do not only bring balance into the body but also to the mind.

There are now many styles taught. These are a few examples:

- Vinyasa and Ashtanga yoga. Rigorous styles of yoga following a specific sequence of postures, as each style links every movement to a breath. The difference is that Ashtanga performs the same poses in the exact same order.
- Iyengar. Attention is paid to finding the proper alignment in a pose.
- Bikram and hot yoga. Both classes, slightly different sequences, in hot yoga studios!
- Restorative and yin yoga. The class often uses bolsters and cushions to help you relax into poses and let go rather than take action. A great one to feel relaxed and rejuvenated afterwards, for any frazzled nerves.
- Anusara and Dru yoga, which is heart-centred yoga, more gentle and flowing practices.

If you are a beginner to yoga, I recommend that you start with a traditional Hatha yoga class, so you learn the main postures, which are adopted by the various styles. Ideally, join a small class so your teacher can check you are in the correct position. You do not want to get into bad habits which are more difficult to undo later on.

The beauty of yoga is that it is not competitive; you can go at your own pace and within the constraints of your body. It is suitable for all ages and does not matter what weight you are. It is important to keep hydrated throughout the yoga routine as it is easy to underestimate the physical workout to your body. There are then various variations of yoga you can try once you have a good understanding of Hatha yoga. I have a few favourites. Dru yoga, which is gentle, looks for the still point within us and has a lovely flow to it. Yin yoga is a restorative where you stay supported in postures and is a great class for letting go and relaxation. I have never seen such a rapid effect on my strength than I had from a few sessions of Iyengar yoga, which emphasises precision and alignment.

The yoga I would recommend when going through a divorce are the more restorative types such as yin yoga. If you need a physical boost, and overall vitality, try other classes. You may complete a few daily cycles of surya namaskar, popularly known as the sun salutation. If you do this regularly it will keep up your vitality. Make sure you attend a class to get into the right postures as it is easy to overexert yourself and the last thing you want at this time is an injury!

Whichever routines you choose to do, I recommend longer time in the relaxation poses as you are going through a stressful and challenging time. There are two particular poses – balasana; child's pose and savasana; corpse posture. Check with your teacher whether these are suitable for you.

Balasana (child's pose)

Balasana or child's pose is a restful pose. You start by kneeling on the floor. Touch your big toes together and sit back on your heels, then separate your knees about as wide as your hips. This can also be done without separating your knees, keeping them together. Exhale and bring your upper body forwards, folding over and laying your torso down between your thighs, or over your thighs if you have kept your knees together. Your arms can fall by your side behind you or are extended forwards. You then just take a few breaths. This is a really good stress reliever. Generally avoided if you have any knee issues or you are pregnant.

Savasana (corpse pose)

Savasana, or corpse posture, to relax your body fully. Lie on your back, elongating your spine before relaxing it to the floor. Have your legs falling naturally out to the sides, each the same distance away from your centre. Make sure your shoulders are relaxed and your neck is nicely lengthened from your body. Your arms should be loosely beside your body, with palms facing upwards. Close your eyes and breathe. Then take your attention to each part of the body, starting with your toes, and relax every part up to your head. Feel each part sinking into the floor and finally relax the muscles of your face and calm your mind. It is beneficial to take five to ten minutes to really relax;

you may even fall asleep if you haven't been getting enough rest. To come out of the posture, you gently roll to one side and then sit up. This pose relieves stress and relaxes the body and mind. It is good for almost everyone to do. Exceptions may be if you have had a back injury or have a disability preventing you from lying on your back.

Retreats

If you have the opportunity go to a yoga retreat, there are so many to choose from either nearby or go further afield if you need a getaway – I visited Carlingford Yoga retreat which concentrates on Iyengar yoga. You have wholesome home-cooked vegetarian food and yoga that will push you quite a bit! Although I went with a friend, the lovely benefit with yoga retreats is that they are equally comfortable to go to on your own.

https://www.carlingfordyoga.ie/category/yoga/

I also visited the Snowdonia Lodge in Wales for a Dru yoga weekend retreat. This was some time ago but was really chilled and the scenery was amazing.

https://druyoga.com

I made a very good friend by attending yoga retreats in Greece and Morocco. They are great for a real getaway and easy to make friends if you are on your own.

Case Scenario 1

Situation. Miranda and Rajiv had been married for eight years. Miranda had a daughter from her previous relationship, age 13. They decided that they would sit down together and look at their finances to try to come to an agreement between them. Miranda came to us prior to this, stating that she was aware her husband had property abroad in Sri Lanka but that he stated that due to property issues with the title to the land, it did not have a value. We advised Miranda of the importance of full and frank disclosure, and that in the event she entered into a kitchen

179

table agreement, we would need her to sign a form of disclaimer. We advised her that a settlement on divorce is a once and for all order, and that she should not make a quick decision now, only to regret it in the future.

How we helped her. We were happy to prepare a financial consent order for her, or consider an order prepared by her husband's solicitor. Rajiv's solicitor prepared the order for her signature. It referred to the completion of full financial disclosure, which there had not been, and we advised that the clause be removed. She knew that she was taking a relatively small lump sum of £50,000, which would enable her to move out and rent initially, and the balance could be held towards a deposit on a future property. Our advice was that even on the limited financial summary of information, she could be entitled to significantly more.

We also advised her that the judge must approve any consent order. Miranda decided that, as she was receiving the lump sum upon the signature of the order and that she had to move out of the property, if the judge later did not accept the reasonableness of the order, she may then reconsider her position at that time. Whilst that was risky and we advised that she should not sign an order unless she felt it was going to be approved by the judge, she decided to go ahead and see how the process unfolded.

As we had advised, the judge considered the terms of the order and did not feel that it was fair. This enabled her to reopen negotiations with her husband's solicitors. So, she had the £50,000 which set her up initially and she was fortunate that as the judge wasn't willing to make the terms into an approved order, she was able to reopen the negotiations. She received a further £100,000 lump sum, and a clean break order was subsequently sealed by the court. She was lucky, however, to get this result.

How she coped. She learnt a great deal of independence through this period. She started to manage her finances and decided she would not look for financial support if she met another partner in the future.

Where she is now. She decided to move with her daughter to a more affordable area and used some of her settlement to open up her own small coffee shop, which subsequently thrived and she was able to employ a few members of staff. Her daughter took a little time to adjust to her new school but she soon made friends.

Case Scenario 2

Situation. Tania and Lubka met in Poland and lived together for five years before moving to England, which was Tania's home. They then entered into a civil partnership and lived together in England for a further two years, until Tania decided that the relationship was over and filed for the dissolution of the civil partnership. Lubka instructed us as she was worried about her rights. During the period of their civil partnership, Lubka had also received an inheritance and put some of the capital into Tania's home to renovate it. She had the remainder in her own bank account. However, what she had left would not be enough to purchase a home for herself. Tania had higher earnings whereas Lubka had only done odd jobs since she moved.

How we helped her. We immediately put Lubka in touch with an immigration specialist to advise her regarding her residence in the UK.

We advised Lubka of the "section 25" factors that would be considered by the court in deciding a financial order, and which factors the court would in all likelihood give weight to. We informed her that although she had only been in a civil partnership for two years, the court would consider that the length of the relationship was in total seven years, and the court would also consider her contributions towards the home and foreseeable income resources. We advised that the court would view Tania's property as a marital home, and accordingly it would be treated as matrimonial property. We also advised that Lubka was likely to be able to retain her remaining inheritance money, and a share in Tania's property. Tania had other assets in her sole name which she had built up prior to their relationship which she would most likely keep. They would both have their housing needs met and a fair division of the overall assets.

We entered into negotiations with Tania's solicitor and an agreement was arrived at whereby Lubka would retain her inheritance and receive a half share of the marital home, which would enable her to purchase a mortgage-free property, and there would be a clean break of all further claims between them.

How she coped. Lubka had the flexibility to adjust to her circumstances and make a new home having moved to a new country. Despite the breakdown of the civil partnership, she saw this move as an opportunity.

Lubka learnt what it was like to be completely self-reliant, as her family and friends were all in Poland, and she managed to settle matters without family or other support.

Where she is now. Lubka moved area from the south to the north of England and found a carer's position in a lovely residential home. She also met members of her Polish community and enjoyed her leisure time. She was pleased she had moved to England and now began a new adventure by herself, increasing her network of friends.

Morning Meditation

When you wake, have a good stretch and stand up, shaking your body like a dog or a cat when they want to get rid of excess or negative energy. Take a seat in your meditation area on your cushion or sit on a chair. Back erect, but not held rigid, hands loosely in your lap, right palm in your left palm, palms facing upwards. Close your eyes and take a few deep breaths. Take your attention to your nostrils and next time you inhale, imagine you are drawing in white light through your nostrils and down into your body; energising and positive energy. As you exhale, gather up all the negative thoughts and emotions you have been feeling, and exhale out, in the aspect of thick black smoke, all that negativity. Alternate for five to ten minutes with your breath, breathing in pure white energising white light, and breathing out black smoke. Once you feel you have dispelled your negative thoughts and emotions, settle back into your breath before you open your eyes. As you rise from meditation, have a final shake of the body and stretch out, energised to start the day.

Opening Thought of the Day
I am positive and I am energised.

Chapter 8

FINANCIAL PROCEEDINGS, FORGIVENESS, TAKE A BREATH AND REDUCE STRESS

Introduction

We all hope matters can be resolved. Unfortunately, sometimes this is not possible. If you cannot reach an agreement, financial matters may be the subject of financial remedy proceedings, separate from the divorce procedure. It does not matter who brought the divorce. You or your spouse have to specifically apply to court for financial matters to be concluded through a court process. The financial remedy proceedings have several stages, which I will explain in this chapter, so there are still opportunities to resolve matters. However, if this does not happen, then a judge at a final hearing will determine the outcome. Financial proceedings can be very stressful, and we touch on forgiveness, which you may need in bucket loads through this time. We also move on from the physical yoga postures of the last chapter, to yogic and other breathing techniques to reduce levels of stress. We meet Harry who had a short marriage with his husband and how we came to an agreement part way through his proceedings. We then meet Nadeem whose case went to a final hearing. You finish this chapter with a much needed evening smile meditation, and a gentle reminder to smile regardless of what may be happening in proceedings.

When to Issue your Financial Application?

This is a difficult one. You or your spouse must have already issued your divorce application at court. You must attend the first mediation appointment before you apply to court for a financial remedy, unless any of the mediation exemptions apply, so it is worth exploring mediation. But give yourself a time limit to try to resolve matters. It is very frustrating to have either spent months and months in mediation, or directly through solicitors providing voluntary financial disclosure and trying to achieve a settlement, for you to get nowhere. I would give an upper limit of three or four months as time easily passes by. In many instances where we have decided to issue proceedings, we make it clear that we are issuing to provide a framework and timetable to matters, but that we are still open to resolving matters amicably. There is an expectation by the court that you will have attempted mediation and voluntary disclosure before court proceedings are issued.

A court application for financial remedy can be the best or only option available where there is excessive delay, where voluntary discussions break down, or one party refuses to engage in mediation or arrive at any compromise. The issue of proceedings is sometimes the only way to break the deadlock in negotiation and drive the case towards an effective resolution. Also, if one party fails to disclose assets, or deals with their assets in such a way as to try to avoid claims, court is unavoidable. The court's wrath is required to obtain court orders to make the other party disclose the full extent of their assets or stop them from taking action to thwart your claims.

Please note that financial proceedings can be applied for at any time during the divorce process or after the divorce has finished (providing the other party is still alive). However, if you remarry you are precluded from making certain financial claims, so it is better to always deal with financial resolution at the time of the divorce.

Benefit of Financial Proceedings

The principal benefit of financial remedy proceedings is a fixed court timetable, requiring progress even where one party is determined to delay or frustrate matters. When financial proceedings are issued, the court will set fairly strict timelines which must be adhered to. The judge can also give penalties including cost orders for non-compliance, and they may issue penal notices so if they are in contempt of court they may go to prison if they fail to comply with court directions.

The costs of contested financial remedy proceedings are invariably higher than the other options to settle matters, although sometimes the very issue of proceedings often has the effect of focusing attention and getting people to engage with the negotiations. Financial proceedings are expensive and not for the fainthearted. It is the exception that ultimately proceeds to a final hearing as most matters settle earlier in the process. Often, if it does continue to a final hearing, neither party generally comes out feeling they have won, and each has incurred a great deal of stress and cost.

Starting Proceedings

The following main stages are involved in most financial proceedings:
1. Filing the financial application at court.
2. Receiving a standard court order giving directions to be complied with, and a timetable.
3. First appointment (initial court hearing).
4. Financial dispute resolution hearing (second court hearing).
5. Final court hearing.

1. Filing the Financial Application at Court

To file the financial application at court, a form A (notice of intention to proceed with an application for a financial order) has to be completed and filed at court, in triplicate, with a court fee (as at July 2022) of £275. If your matter is highly complex with considerable legal issues in addition to high net worth assets, a certificate can be lodged detailing the complexities with your application, and sent directly to the Financial Remedies Unit which is at the Central Family Court in London for consideration to start your application in that court.

Solicitors are able to file the application on-line. But Applicants who are not represented need to file a paper application and pay an additional fee.

The form A is accompanied by a form FM1 (Family Mediation Information and Assessment Form), signed by the mediator to show you have attempted mediation which needs to be included unless any of the exemptions apply.

The form A states all the financial claims you are raising.

- In the first part of the form, it is better to tick all claims at the outset to avoid having to amend the form later on, apart from maintenance pending suit unless you are seeking an interim order for maintenance, as then the court will immediately list the application for a hearing.

- The second half of the form is only relevant if you are seeking provision for the children. The child maintenance service deal with maintenance for the children if you are both resident in the UK, so it is only appropriate to tick if you are seeking further provision not covered by them. For instance, top-up orders, medical expenses and, most commonly, school fees.

There is a fast-track procedure if the application is for periodical payments (maintenance) only, in which case a form A1 is used, otherwise a standard procedure applies.

Allocation Questionnaire

In order for cases to be appropriately allocated, the Applicant must file an allocation questionnaire. The majority of cases will automatically be dealt with by the Financial Remedies Court. Only if the overall assets exceed £15m or net annual income £1m will the matter likely be transferred to the High Court. Most cases are non-complex cases and referred to a

District Judge and allocated to a standard list. A Circuit Judge will only hear complex cases. A complex case will likely include substantial assets held offshore, or in trusts or unquoted corporate entities. There are additional questions to be answered and an explanation required if it is to be added to a Complexity List of the court. The Respondent will need to be consulted for the purposes of completing the questionnaire.

The court will serve the proceedings directly on your spouse within four days of your application being processed and having been given a case number. If there are any mortgagees, they should be served with the application by your solicitors who will have filed extra copies of the form A if they require further sealed court copies for service.

2. Receiving a Standard Court Order giving Directions to be Complied with and a Timetable

If, as is likely, your matter is listed for the standard procedure, the court will provide you or your solicitors and your spouse with a notice of proceedings in form C. This form will set out a first hearing date and give directions to be complied with before that date. This date should be set by the court 12–16 weeks after the issue of form A (notice of intention to proceed with financial claims), and forms E (financial statements in a prescribed format) should be exchanged four weeks prior to that hearing.

Form E

Thirty-five days before the first appointment, each of you must file at court a full financial statement known as form E and serve a copy on the other party. There should be simultaneous exchange of your respective completed forms. This is an in-depth financial statement of your assets, income, liabilities and other relevant circumstances. The form E has a requisite list of documents that must be filed with it and you must be careful to ensure you include all documents so you are not later accused of inadequate financial disclosure. It is absolutely essential that you include all relevant financial information on the form. You will sign a statement of truth to confirm that you are making full and frank, and clear and accurate, disclosure of your finances and all other circumstances. Also, in signing, you understand proceedings for contempt of court could be brought against you if you do not provide this.

Other Standard Court Directions

The additional standard directions include filing 14 days before the hearing:

- a concise statement of issues – which is prepared, highlighting the main areas of dispute and agreed matters, and outlining your position and if possible, the order you are seeking.
- a chronology – giving key dates – and this should not include disputed or inflammatory information.
- a questionnaire setting out further information and documents required from the other party. This sometimes covers items missing from the form E and where it does, it is important to make it clear further queries may need to be raised on sight of that information. In addition, you may be raising questions as a result of what has already been disclosed. The court does not like either party to embark on a "fishing expedition" so do not seek unnecessary information –concentrate only on the important information needed so a settlement or order can be fairly arrived at. NB this questionnaire does not need to be replied to before the court appointment as it is finalised before the judge at the first hearing. The questionnaire must not exceed four pages of A4 in length, using not smaller than a 12-point font with 1.5 spacing. The court are only likely to approve longer questionnaires in complexity cases.
- a form G – this confirms whether or not you will be in a position to treat the first hearing as an FDR (financial dispute resolution) hearing as mentioned later in this

chapter. This is a hearing listed with the purpose of trying to settle matters between you. If you have enough disclosure so you have the full picture of your spouse's financial position, you should be able to, but if the disclosure is materially lacking then it will not be possible.

A date will be given within the standard directions order in readiness for the hearing when these documents should be filed and exchanged simultaneously. Sometimes, if you have been able to exchange forms E earlier, you will be able to exchange these documents also in advance of the court direction deadline. You should do what you can to comply with the dates as if you do not, your failure to do so can be construed as conduct in financial proceedings and there can be cost penalties.

If your spouse is not complying, normally a letter outlining the position to the court will result in the court, of their own volition, attaching a penal notice to the order so that your spouse will be in contempt of court if they still fail to comply. The court may then make it clear that they will make adverse inferences, or refuse further evidence from your spouse if the non-compliance continues.

Your legal advisor will also file at court a few days before the first appointment a form H cost estimate. This details what your legal costs are to date and includes the likely costs of the first hearing. It is also necessary for your solicitors to prepare a cost estimate for the subsequent hearing and certify to the court that you have seen the same. This form H, is filed and served prior to each hearing, and must be included in the bundle. Prior to final hearing a more detailed cost form H1 is used.

Additional Court Directions

On 11th (amended 12th) January 2022 a statement was issued by senior judges on the efficient conduct of financial remedy proceedings (FRC Efficiency Statement), which came in with immediate effect. This adds further requirements in addition to the standard directions, that must be complied with.

- 14 days before the first appointment the parties are to file a joint market appraisal of the marital home. If a joint appraisal cannot be agreed then separate appraisals need to be filed.

- 14 days before the first appointment the parties should use their best endeavours to file no more than 3 sets of property particulars and joint (or if impossible separate) details as to mortgage capacity.
- Questionnaires should not exceed 4 pages, and longer questionnaires only likely to be approved in complexity cases.
- 1 day before the first appointment the Applicant must file a composite case summary and schedule of assets. There are approved templates Es1 and Es2 that must be used for this purpose. Any items that are not agreed must be clearly denoted. The composite schedule of assets sets out each parties value they state for an asset, and it does not need to be agreed for the purpose of the hearing.
- Position statements (normally prepared by Counsel) must be no longer than 6 pages, in numbered paragraphs, A4 paper not less than 12 font size and 1.5 spacing. The statement will cross reference any documents in the bundle and not include any extensive quotes from documents. This sets out your position, defines and confines the areas of controversy. If any case is mentioned, the proposition of law must first be stated and then the parts that support the proposition. Also short details of any open offers made are included. It is sent to the Judge by 11am on the working day before the hearing and exchanged no later than one hour after it has been sent to the Judge. A position statement is filed for subsequent hearings and must be self-contained ie not incorporate reference to previous filed position statements.
- As best practice, after the court hearing, the order must be agreed and lodged before leaving court (if at least one party is legally represented). The order should accurately reflect the result of the hearing. Recitals in the order should not summarise what happened in the hearing, just record neutrally essential background matters which are not part

of the main body of the order. If it was a remote hearing the order should be lodged the day of the hearing. If not possible, the order must be lodged within two working days of hearing.

- The date for the next hearing should be fixed and stated in the order before the parties leave court

There is a possibility if your case is straightforward that your and your spouse's solicitors can agree a directions order and avoid the first appointment, which must be filed by email at least 14 days prior to hearing, and only once approved by the District Judge will the hearing be vacated. If you have not heard within 7 days of the hearing your solicitors will send a reminder marked "Accelerated First Appointment Second Request". All prescribed documents namely, statement of issues, chronology, and questionnaire must have also been filed prior to 14 days, or when the agreed order is submitted for approval. Your case will then be listed for a financial dispute resolution (FDR) hearing.

If the parties are sufficiently prepared to ask the court to use the first appointment as an FDR hearing then it is mandatory that the directions in relation to housing particulars, mortgage information and questionnaires have been complied with.

A court bundle of "essential reading" for the Judge will need to be filed at court by the Applicant's solicitor several days in advance of the hearing. A court bundle is a ring binder of the papers needed for your case put in a specific order and paginated so it can be easily referenced by the judge. In some instances bundles can be sent electronically. This will generally be all documents, apart from enclosures to forms E. The bundle index will be sent to the Respondent' solicitor for approval prior to the bundle being prepared. If the Applicant does not have solicitors acting for them, the Respondent's solicitor will prepare the court bundle.

Remote Hearings and Attendance at Court

The hearing date listed may require you to attend court in person, or increasingly post pandemic, hearings may take place "remotely" by video link or telephone. All parties and their representatives will all join remotely to the hearing before the Judge. If the hearing is a video hearing, your representatives will provide their email contact details to court and be given details of the video link prior to hearing which they will pass to you. If it is a telephone hearing, your number will be forwarded to court in advance of the hearing by your representatives and you will be dialled into the hearing by the court if it takes place by telephone. The telephone hearings are more difficult to follow than hearings you attend in person, but you will normally have a debrief call with your advisors after the hearing.

Whilst going to court in person may be a daunting prospect, there is nothing to worry about. Don't forget, the judge has also had life experience, may have been or be married or divorced, and probably have a family. They are in a position of authority and whilst they may come across formally, their position is to uphold the law and make fair decisions. At the hearing your barrister or solicitor will speak on your behalf. If at any stage the Judge asks you a question directly you just need to address them politely, and it is common protocol to use Sir or Madam.

Every case will now be allocated to an individual Judge at the earliest opportunity. The allocated judge will either conduct the first two hearings ie first appointment and FDR hearing, or the first appointment and all hearings except the FDR including the final hearing.

3. First Appointment

You will normally have to attend an hour before each court hearing, which will provide an opportunity to talk to your representatives. You will have a conference in a separate room before the court hearing with them. If you are represented, you will not need to say anything at the first appointment. Your solicitor, or a barrister (known as Counsel), will do all the talking in the hearing. You can ask your solicitor only to represent you at this hearing but if there is little chance of early agreement and there are complex issues, it is better to instruct a barrister to be your advocate at this hearing. This also has the benefit of you being able to feedback to your solicitor whether you are happy to retain the barrister for future hearings. Whilst you will need to meet the costs of a barrister and solicitor, it is often helpful if both are present with you at court. Your solicitor will have instructed Counsel and has an in-depth knowledge of your matter so can often support both you and the barrister at court. A barrister and solicitor have complementary roles.

The objective of the first appointment or directions hearing is to define and narrow, if possible, the issues and give further necessary directions for the matter to proceed as effectively as possible and, thereby, save costs. It is at this hearing that your representative will go through the other side's questionnaire and raise any objections to the questions raised. The judge will make a final decision regarding both questionnaires, which questions are to be answered and which are not required, and also confirm a date by which the answers are to be provided.

The judge may then also give other directions, the most common being the instruction of an expert where the value of an asset, very often a property, cannot be agreed. A chartered surveyor or estate agent would be jointly instructed by the parties. There is a specific format for the letter of instruction and formalities to ensure the expert is independently instructed. It is important you are happy with the choice of expert as you are committed to accept the joint report unless there are clear flaws. If this is the case, queries can be raised and the expert called to court at a final hearing to give evidence. There may be other expert evidence required in complex cases, for instance, a forensic accountant. The further directions are timetabled to be dealt with.

The matter is listed for an FDR (financial dispute resolution) hearing. As mentioned, in some cases, you can opt to use the first directions hearing as an FDR (if you and your spouse file a form G confirming so) as you are hopeful you can settle matters and there has been sufficient disclosure. If you are both happy to treat the hearing as an FDR, it is important that the court office is also separately updated in advance of the hearing date so you can ensure that adequate time is allocated.

4. FDR Financial Dispute Resolution Hearing

An FDR (financial dispute resolution) hearing is a forum for Without Prejudice discussions. The aim is to try to settle matters on the day. "Without Prejudice" is a legal term which means "without detriment to any right or claim". This means that whatever is said on a Without Prejudice basis cannot later be used against you to your disadvantage.

This means that any proposals and negotiations discussed on the day cannot be referred to later in evidence if you do not agree and the proceedings continue. This enables free discussion to take place without a party feeling they are compromising their position if matters do not settle. You will have both exchanged Without Prejudice proposals prior to this hearing, so you have a starting point for discussions.

For this hearing, your representative, either your solicitor or barrister, will have also prepared and filed at court a position statement setting out your position, and to define and confine the areas of controversy. Also, an up-to-date form H showing the up-to-date costs position including the costs of this hearing, and estimating the costs to final hearing which your solicitor will need to certify they have shown you. Additional court directions as set out below will need to be complied with. Again, a court bundle is filed at court by the Applicant's solicitor, once the Respondent's solicitor has approved the bundle index.

Additional Court Directions

Under the FRC Efficiency Statement the court also require that additional directions are complied with in advance of the FDR as follows;

- 7 days before the FDR appointment the Applicant must file an updated composite case summary and composite schedule of assets and income. (The same templates used for the first appointment are updated).
- 7 days before the FDR appointment the Applicant must file a composite and "neutral" chronology.

- Position statements (normally prepared by Counsel) must be no longer than 12 pages.
- The order must be agreed and lodged before leaving court (if at least one party is legally represented)
- The date for the next hearing should be fixed and stated in the order before the parties leave court

The hearing will be listed with a time estimate of 1 and ½ hours. If matters are complicated your solicitor will need to ask in advance if more time is required.

If the hearing takes place remotely as a video hearing, your representatives will provide their email contact details to court and be given details of the video link prior to hearing which they will pass to you.

However, many FDR's are still taking place with you attending court in person. At this appointment you must also attend court an hour before the allotted time and your representative will speak to the opposing barrister/solicitor and try to settle matters. A lot of time will be spent in a conference room with your representative going between the other side and reporting back to you. Often, a few matters are listed before the judge at the same time, so whoever is ready, either confirming their negotiations are getting nowhere or that they have reached settlement, will go in first. So be prepared not to go in at your allotted time and to spend many hours in court. Always leave the full day free and make childcare arrangements until the evening. It is helpful to have both your solicitor and barrister at these hearings. As Counsel undertakes the negotiations in another conference room with your spouse's barrister or representative, sometimes you can then discuss matters in between with your solicitor, and as you are instructing your solicitor throughout, they can ensure nothing is missed.

If you reach an agreement, you will go before the judge with your representative who will outline the agreement. It is usual practice for them to prepare and then present a draft financial order for the judge to approve. You will be waiting around whilst this is drafted and then your barrister or solicitor will go through this to check you understand it and everything is covered correctly. You and your representatives will sign, and so will your spouse and their representative. You must be happy with what you are signing as there will be no going back. If in doubt, ask that the matter is adjourned to allow for an agreed order to be filed at court within a few weeks if you need more time to consider. Your representatives may still advise that further directions and listing for final hearing are agreed at court in default of an agreed order so as to avoid a further directions hearing. Also, be prepared that a good offer could come off the table from your spouse after time for reflection, so often it is better to wrap things up at court if you are advised it is a good offer, even if you feel there a few things you may have given in on.

If you cannot reach an agreement, you will all go before the judge. The judge will give an indication of the likely order he or she would make if the matter continued to a final hearing. You will then maybe have the opportunity of further discussions to see if you can settle matters, or if not, then the court will give directions for the matter to go to a final hearing. A timetable for the final hearing must be made at the FDR hearing if it has not resulted in a settlement. It is important to note that an FDR is a Without Prejudice court appointment so you cannot refer to the judge's indication at final hearing, nor the discussions that took place. Also, the judge at an FDR will not hear the matter at final hearing so you will always be listed before a different judge.

5. Final Hearing

Before the Final Hearing

- If the matter proceeds to a final hearing the court will seek a time estimate at the FDR hearing from your and your spouse's representatives of how long is needed before it is listed.
- The court may give further directions, including, for instance, any expert witnesses that need to be called.

- Court bundles. The court will direct that court bundles are agreed and filed at court by a certain date, normally no later than five days before hearing. Copies are prepared for all parties and representatives. The judge will not want unnecessary documents to be included in the bundles. Therefore do not be alarmed to find that not all documents are presented at final hearing nor the letters that have been exchanged between solicitors. But any documents upon which your case relies should be included. A bundle index will be prepared by the Applicant's solicitor to be agreed.
- Also, a case summary and up-to-date chronology and schedule of assets will be included at the start of the bundle. Prior to hearing, each representative will also outline (with reference to case law) each party's case.
- The court will direct for the Applicant to file open proposals for settlement 14 days before the final hearing and the Respondent to reply not less than seven days before final hearing. So, these proposals will be open to the judge at the final hearing so they can see what you are each seeking. Very often these proposals will be a bit less than what you are prepared to settle on to allow for some further compromise at the hearing.
- A much fuller form outlining legal costs and disbursements, Form H1, is filed at court, together with a detailed schedule of costs if costs are being sought from your spouse.

Additional Court Directions

Under the FRC Efficiency Statement the court also require that additional directions are complied with in advance of the final hearing as follows;
- 7 days before the final hearing the Applicant must file an updated composite case summary and composite schedule of assets and income. (The same templates used for the FDR appointment are updated).
- 7 days before the final hearing the Applicant must file an updated chronology.

- If directions have been given to file a section 25 statement this should be limited to 15 pages excluding exhibits.
- Court bundles to be limited to 350 pages unless the court have given a specific direction for this to be exceeded and whilst they must be filed not less than 2 days before final hearing the FDR order normally provides for filing 5 days prior. The Respondent must be served with a copy at the same time. Often now, e-bundles are sent to court. Correspondence (including with experts), bank, credit card statements and other financial records must not be included unless a specific prior court direction has been made. A separate bundle of authorities ie cases relied upon will be prepared by the advocates and must contain no more than 10 authorities.
- Position statements (normally prepared by Counsel) must be no longer than 15 pages.

You must attend the final hearing. It is particularly helpful to have continuity with the solicitor and barrister who represented you at the FDR to final hearing. Early continuity of a barrister is helpful even from the first appointment so you have a representative fully familiar with your case throughout. When the matter is listed for final hearing, your solicitor will be able to give dates to avoid if your barrister is on another hearing, in advance of the final hearing date being listed.

If you do have a change of representative, it is a good idea to have a separate conference in advance of the final hearing date so you can go over any evidence.

What happens at Final Hearing

- At the final hearing the Applicant's representative will give a summary first and then the Respondent's representative will reply. These are known as opening submissions.
- The Applicant and any witnesses will give evidence and be cross-examined, and then the Respondent and any witnesses will give evidence and be cross-examined.

- There is also a possibility of re-examination if any further points have arisen.
- Then there will be closing submissions and the judge will give a judgment.
- Sometimes, particularly if the matter has overrun in time, or the judge needs more time, there will be a reserved judgment and you will not know the final order on the day. Usually, you will have the final order.
- Once that has been determined, representatives may make cost submissions. This is where open offers are useful.

Strategy and Cost Implications

Open Offers and Without Prejudice Offers.

Open offers of settlement are put before the judge when the judge considers the papers for final hearing. You do not need to make any open offers early on but it is generally advisable to do so. The case summary filed before each hearing includes confirmation of any open offer made by a party, the date of all open offers made, and the date of response. The offer filed closer to final hearing must be what you are prepared for the judge to order. Very often the judge will end up making an order between your and your spouse's open offers. If you want the best hope of seeking costs against your spouse, make a good open offer early on and the court may then make an order for costs in your favour from the date you make the offer, if the matter ends up at final hearing. Do not assume, even if you have the most intransigent spouse, that the court will make an order for costs. The usual order is no order for costs, i.e. each party meets their own legal costs. However, each party will be expected to engage in trying to resolve matters amicably. The court have now stated that they will take a broad view of conduct and will generally conclude that to refuse to openly negotiate reasonably and responsibly will amount to conduct in respect of which the court will consider making an order for costs. This includes what is called a "needs" case where a party litigates unreasonably, resulting in the costs incurred by the parties to become disproportionate to the award made by the court.

Without Prejudice offers can only be disclosed on the issue of costs after the final order has been made by the judge. The Without Prejudice offer will therefore invariably be a higher offer to your spouse, i.e. a carrot that you will make somewhere along proceedings, again ideally early on, to try to get an agreement with your spouse without incurring further costs.

Both Without Prejudice and open offers can be made at any time throughout the proceedings but if you wish to rely on them on seeking costs, you must have already made your financial disclosure.

Prior to each hearing your legal representative, normally Counsel, will prepare a position statement setting out your position. These statements include a requirement at each hearing to provide short details of what efforts the parties have made to negotiate openly, reasonably and responsibly.

Disclosure

There is an ongoing duty of full and frank disclosure in financial proceedings. Any material changes need to be disclosed to the other party and the court at the earliest opportunity. For instance, you must disclose if you decide to cohabit, or you get a promotion, or you become due an inheritance – anything that is clearly relevant to your circumstances.

Privileged documents are excluded from disclosure in evidence. These are, for instance, Without Prejudice letters written in a genuine attempt to settle your matter. A letter marked Without Prejudice, giving financial information in the hope it can be kept away from the court's evidence, may not be privileged. In this situation, the court may be addressed as to whether privilege should be waived.

Confidentiality

Regarding documents belonging to your spouse, do not try to get your spouse's financial documents yourself as you could risk conduct being raised against you and an adverse costs order. The courts don't like this type of self-help which will inevitably undermine trust between you and increase hostility. Also, a civil or even criminal action could ensue if you have tried to surreptitiously remove or download information. However, it can be a difficult one to tackle if your spouse is failing to disclose.

There has been a case for allowing such information, if no force was used to obtain the documents and after taking copies, the originals were immediately returned to your spouse. The fact of these coming into possession should be immediately disclosed. But the general premise is if you pass documents to your solicitor that belong to your spouse, they should send them to your spouse's solicitor without considering them. Your spouse's solicitor must read the same and disclose anything relevant in accordance with the duty to the court of full and frank disclosure. If your spouse does not have a solicitor, then your solicitor will retain the documents unread and seek a direction from the court.

The Court of Appeal's decision in the case of **Tchenguiz v Imerman; Imerman v Imerman** in 2010 provided that if one spouse takes confidential documents belonging to the other, then they may be committing criminal offences and may also be breaching their spouse's confidentiality, which could give rise to civil proceedings. What constitutes a confidential document is not entirely clear from the judgment and is highly fact-specific. For example, a document left lying around in the kitchen, living room or bedroom may not be viewed as confidential, whereas the same would not be said if the document were left in, for example, the spouse's study or on their computer. Not only would you risk facing criminal prosecution or civil proceedings for breach of confidentiality, the same may apply to your solicitor who deals with such a document.

Top Tips

DO

1. File your form at court even if your spouse is failing to file their form E. I would invariably recommend serving your form E on them so you can show you have completed your disclosure, and this may assist later with any possible cost applications.
2. Try to exchange your form E and questionnaires (with replies if you can) earlier than the date given by the court, if possible, to potentially be able to utilise the first hearing as an FDR hearing.
3. Be prepared for each court hearing by going through the court bundle in advance of the hearing so you are familiar with it.
4. If a remote hearing is listed ensure basics are dealt with, ie you are in a quiet room with no-one else present, and ensure you remain undisturbed through the hearing, your computer is fully charged, you are ready to join on time and can mute and unmute when you need to speak. Have a glass of water present, but no food or drinks, and make sure you have a paper and pen in case you need to make notes.

DO NOT

1. Think you can hide assets. Solicitors are used to checking transaction trails. There can be cost implications, and in serious cases you may be held in contempt of court.
2. Be tempted to rummage through your spouse's paperwork. This is not permitted.
3. Do not enter into combative correspondence or instruct your solicitors to do so. This will be expensive and is frowned on by the courts. If you end up going to a final hearing, correspondence is unlikely to be put before the court, or worse, it may go against you as conduct or in respect of costs.

Forgiveness

It may not come straight away, it may take time to process a lot of what has happened, but forgiveness really is the key to moving on. I have seen many clients, and indeed friends, embroiled in their story of the other person. Also, it is easy to become identified with your role. I particularly think the labels of victims, or the other as perpetrators or narcissists, keep one stuck. I always found it helpful to look at it from the perspective of how other people view your ex-wife or husband and take some comfort from that. If they think the sun shines through them, it probably does and it just did not for you. But this is your problem and your perception. No one is bad to everyone (especially to their mother or father)!

I find it really helpful to look at our own children or animals to understand forgiveness – we have an unconditional love for them. They may be naughty, but we always forgive them. My cat, for instance, has bitten me in the past but I have not banished him and still continue to love and care for him. A child can do naughty things or be spiteful, but it is all simply overlooked with love.

And then we must forgive ourselves – for the choices we have made to get to this point. We may have regrets but there is no point in beating ourselves up. Why not forgive and care for ourselves if we are prepared to forgive others? There are many situations where it is easy to be eaten up with guilt but we did our best with what we knew at the time, and if we now think we did not – well, we still did – we just did not have as much wisdom and clarity at the time when we made our choices. We will always have learnt something.

My Dad reminded me of an annual custom in the Jainism faith called " michhami dukkadam" which is wording from the ancient Prakrit language, where a person will ask of all other people that if any harm has been done by them, knowingly or unknowingly, to the other, may it be forgiven. How lovely to ask for forgiveness.

Take a Breath and Reduce Stress

Going through financial proceedings is a stressful time. Proper breathing can help alleviate some of the stress. The reality is as soon as our breath goes – that is it, life is over. It is a good time to reflect on this – our spouse may have left, we may be disappointed things did not work out, or that we are now facing an uncertain financial future. We may have been married for 5 years, 10 years, 20 years or 30 years and the marriage is over, but our life really isn't over, however we may feel. We take it for granted that we are breathing. We are still breathing – we are still alive – our movie is still running. So, let us embrace this miracle of life – this is not a time to take it for granted – as we may have done in the past for both our relationship and ourself. This is much more important – there is no time other than this one to be grateful and really feel our life, in our breath. Why do we always feel invigorated after the gym, a swim or cycle ride? We are using our breath by breathing deeply. We are feeling life through us, and through being alive. Our cells rely on oxygen for energy, so the more oxygen we can breathe in, the better for both our energy and bodily health.

We are likely to feel a variety of emotions during the proceedings. I had never really taken the time through the majority of my life to see how breathing changes depending on how I am feeling. It is said that every emotion and every thought have a corresponding reaction in the breath. I could immediately relate to this when I thought of the times I had experienced anger as the breathing quickens then. But I had not reflected on each emotion. For instance, with fear, I have noticed that my breathing becomes anxious and almost irregular; with sadness, that the exhale is longer, almost a sigh. I had not considered this any deeper but in the same way our emotions are linked to our thoughts, and our thoughts are also linked to our breathing. When I am feeling happy, joyful thoughts, my breathing is composed and almost effortless.

Pranayam (breathing)

From the physical yoga exercises, it is beneficial to introduce specific breathing exercises to your practice known as Pranayam exercises. Prana means life force. Ayama means to lengthen or work on it. These are viewed as yogic exercises or asanas in themselves in India, but in the West they are often taught as a precursor to the physical yoga asanas. I have used them for a few minutes with Hatha yoga in the past, but only recently started to understand how important methods of breathing can be.

If prana or the life force is unable to move properly through the body resulting in blockages or imbalances, sickness may result, so the exercises maintain good health and vitality. The way we breath may also have an effect on how we perceive things, so it is both mental and physical optimum health that is the real potential.

Most of us breath in a shallow way, from only the upper part of the lungs. As a result, we do not get the benefits of lungs that could be full of oxygen and the pranic life force.

Anulom Vilom (alternate nostril breathing)

Anulom vilom is my favourite of these to start with, calming down the mind. Anulom vilom is also known as alternate nostril breathing. Anulom means with the grain and vilom means against the grain. It reduces stress and calms the nervous system. It is gentle. In Ayurveda, this exercise is believed to balance the three doshas which are mind-body types or constitutions known as Pitta, Vata and Kapha, which, if imbalanced, lead to physical and mental ailments.

It is good to sit cross-legged but you can also sit on a chair with your back straight. You do not need to have had an empty stomach for a few hours for this one so it is flexible. It can be done a few times during the day whenever you need it or before you start any physical exercises, or indeed before meditation. You begin by closing the right nostril with the thumb of your right hand. Your hand is kept upright, with fingers between your eyebrows over the third eye (known as the seat of intuition) towards the middle of your forehead. You start by exhaling through the left nostril. You then inhale through the same left nostril, release the thumb, and exhale through the right nostril whilst closing the left nostril with your ring or little finger, or both together, whichever feels more comfortable. You then inhale again through the right nostril and once inhaled, close the right nostril and exhale through the left nostril again. You alternate in this way and carry on for a few minutes. There are advanced postures whereby you then have pauses between inhale and exhale, and the exhale becomes longer.

I love the Shilpa Shetty's yoga practices and often still come back to her DVD which is great to follow and an inspiration to look at! The anulom vilom has slightly different finger postures but is easy to follow. Here is a link to the exercise.

https://www.youtube.com/watch?v=ndSgDt1mwE8

Kapalabhati

This is seen as a pure detoxifying exercise. Kapal means head, and bhati means to shine. So, the idea is that you develop a glow of good health with this detoxifying exercise and you literally glow with radiance on your face. It must be done on an empty stomach, ideally first thing in the morning or at least three hours after eating. It should be done with a teacher initially as it is a very powerful exercise. It is understood to remove toxins from the body and air we have inhaled. It aids digestion and removes acidity. There are also beliefs that it removes blockages in the heart and lungs and improves the brain function. It also removes that stubborn and harmful fat around the middle, if done with regular practice. There are those yogis that say all our ailments originate from our digestion so there is a strong belief in this exercise or asana. It is also spiritually designed to activate the chakras to lead towards a greater awakening.

Again, it is good to sit cross-legged but you can also sit on a chair with your back straight, or stand. The technique uses active exhalation and passive inhalation. After an inhale, there is a complete expulsion of air from the lungs on an exhale by contracting the stomach in and expelling the air out through the nostrils. It can be done quite vigorously and you can get lightheaded if it is overdone. If you have any medical issues at all, including high blood pressure, avoid this exercise.

The real master for Kapalabhati is known as Ram Dev. Here is a link with English subtitles.

https://www.youtube.com/watch?v=Az_RG03FFbk

Joyful Breathing

I have also tried joyful breathing, which was really powerful. A session for some can clear some deep down emotional blocks. It is nice to be supported as you let your emotions come out. I would recommend a class, or one-to-one initially, to get the right technique, as the effects can be profound. I joined a class and literally felt blissed out but others had varying effects and a few were moved to tears as deep-seated emotions were released.

This technique is breathing in and out through the mouth which feels strange initially. The breath out is as if you are demisting a pair of glasses, and the in and out breath follow each other without pause. Again, there is quite an emphasis on a full exhalation of the breath. It is clear that you are oxygenating the lungs with these breaths which is invigorating.

Judith Kravitz is the founder of transformational breathing and through her website you can gain more information about facilitating sessions.

http://www.transformationalbreath.com

Case Scenario 1

The situation. Harry was in his late 50s when he met his husband Tyler abroad. Tyler was several years younger than him in his 40s, and he fell in love. Harry wanted to show him he was committed and so he entered into a civil partnership, then they decided to marry. They had been married for three years. There was no pre-nuptial agreement, and Harry had his own home, mortgage free, and a good pension. Tyler wanted Harry to pay him lots of attention and support him financially even though prior to the marriage, he had worked. Soon it became apparent they had little in common and Harry felt he had made a mistake only a few years after they married. Tyler took it very personally and refused to seek work or move out of the house. Harry almost felt paralysed, treading on eggshells whenever he saw Tyler and he became emotional throughout communications. Harry felt uncomfortable in his own home so he decided to leave and rent elsewhere. Whatever Harry offered by way of financial settlement, Tyler rejected.

How we helped him. We advised Harry that as his house became the marital home, potentially there were a range of orders that could be made. The house could be sold and divided equally. Alternatively, the court may only divide equally the equity that had built up in the home over the period of their relationship and giving him credit for what he brought into the marriage. We discussed possibly the best case scenario would be that he could give a lesser lump sum to Tyler to meet his housing needs.

Harry made an application to court and the matter settled at the FDR hearing. He paid Tyler a lump sum for him to leave his house and find rented accommodation, and a deposit to place on subsequent shared ownership accommodation, and to cover a period for him to find work.

We helped Harry look practically at the options available to him. We discussed ways he may be able to raise a lump sum without having to sell his house and liaised with his financial advisors.

We helped him gain perspective that after a few years his financial situation would recover sufficiently so he had no major financial worries and we achieved a clean break order so his husband could make no future claims.

By agreeing settlement, he was able to get the final divorce order and have further cordial relations with his ex-husband.

How he coped. Patience. He wanted financial matters to be resolved and division agreed as soon as he decided he wanted a divorce. His husband was having none of it and, after gruelling sessions in mediation, lots of attempted negotiations between solicitors in correspondence, he had no choice but to let the court process evolve and eventually settled matters at court.

Where he is now. As a result of this experience, he managed to develop a more positive outlook generally in life. He eventually found peace in being true to himself. He initially felt bitter at having to pay a considerable sum after only a few years of marriage and vowed never to remarry! However, he also felt wholly relieved to have concluded the relationship, to be single and he counted his blessings.

Case Scenario 2

Situation. We acted for Nadeem. He had been married for 31 years and both trust and communication had broken down with his wife Khushi. He had shares in a family business which he transferred to his brother just before he separated from his wife and he had many rental properties in his name. His wife had not worked through the marriage. They had four children, the two elder children at university, the younger two completing their A level equivalent education. He sought to argue that a large proportion of his properties were non-marital properties and that they were his business assets. He also stated that he was simply transferring back to his brother, shares in his brother's business. His wife did not believe him and as soon as she brought divorce proceedings, she almost immediately issued financial proceedings and also sought an injunction order preventing him from transferring other assets. They started with proceedings from the outset and Nadeem was aggrieved by his wife's actions. The children sided with their mother, Khushi.

It was not an appropriate case for mediation. At the first appointment in financial proceedings, the court gave directions for valuations of all the properties held, and also for Nadeem's brother to be joined to proceedings. At the next financial dispute resolution hearing, Khushi's representatives argued that they had not received sufficient disclosure and raised a further questionnaire; the FDR hearing was ineffective in trying to settle matters. Nadeem's case was subsequently listed for a final hearing. Whilst often at a final hearing matters settle at the court door, no settlement was achieved, and both parties went before the judge. After their respective barristers gave submissions, they both gave evidence. The judge took into consideration all the assets, and also the value of the holding transferred by the husband to his brother.

How we helped him. We advised him of the implications of letting the judge decide at final hearing. Whilst the court made an order in favour of the wife, we managed to stave off an application by her barrister that Nadeem should be ordered to pay all her legal costs, which at this point were over £30,000.

How he coped. As we advised Nadeem throughout, it is futile to try to put assets out of reach of the other spouse –the court will want to take those assets into account. Furthermore, assets built up during the marriage, whether or not they are in the sole name of one party or seen by them as business assets, are generally taken into account. The final order made was still fair, and Nadeem realised that the order could have been a lot worse.

Where he is now. Nadeem remarried and ensured he protected himself with a pre-nuptial agreement. He also went into the marriage with the wish to make the marriage work as a partnership and make his spouse happy. He approached his second marriage with affording her freedom to express herself fully and he had less expectations of her and her role as homemaker. He eventually patched things up with his children and saw them more frequently.

Evening Meditation

Put aside 15 minutes in your quiet place, an hour or two before you go to bed. A smile can lift another but it can also lift and heal yourself. This is a tao meditation which is soft and beautiful.

Sit in a chair comfortably with your feet on the floor and back erect but not rigid. Hold your hands comfortably in your lap and close your eyes. Feel your feet connected to the ground, to the earth, and lightly press the tip of your tongue to the roof of your mouth.

Now, see an image of yourself three feet in front of you, looking towards you and smiling lovingly at you. If you need to, bring to mind an event that happened in the past, or your favourite place, to find your smile.

Become aware of the midpoint between your eyebrows, the third eye centre, and relax that area. Imagine that loving smiling energy now being drawn through that centre, into your body. Let the smiling energy flow around your face, and your head, and then flow down your neck, and towards every organ of your body. You smile to your heart. Draw the smiling energy through your lungs, your liver, pancreas and spleen, kidneys, and your reproductive organs. Then take the energy through your legs to your feet. Once again, draw in more smiling energy from your smile, and imagine it bathing every blood vessel, your lymph nodes, your muscles and tissues. Smile to every single part of your body and then imagine the energy collecting at your navel. You may want to move your hands to gently cover your navel, then feel the smiling energy circulating. Rest here for a while. Take your time as you rise from meditation and take your smile with you as you have a lovely warm drink, relax into the rest of your evening, slowing down and preparing for a good night's rest.

Concluding Thought of the Day
I smile to myself and others.

Chapter 9

SIDE LEGAL ISSUES, INJUNCTIONS, CONTENTS AND NON-ATTACHMENT

Introduction

In this chapter we go over some of the side legal issues that may need to be addressed. If you are suffering as a result of domestic violence, I provide an outline of injunctions which will often need to be addressed at the outset. There are a few matters such as making a new will, lasting powers of attorney, and checking the deeds to your home and other properties, that should be done as soon as you decide to divorce. The issue of your belongings and contents in the home will need to be discussed between you. You may also want to revert back to your unmarried name. We look at the practical side of decluttering, and the emotional and spiritual side of letting go and non-attachment. We meet Jessica whose issues over house contents and her parrot ended up in court! We then start our day with our morning meditation on letting go, and our positive statement for the day that we let go of anything that no longer serves us.

Injunctions – Safety

An injunction is a court order. There are two types of order that are sought from the court to keep you safe.

- A "non-molestation order" protects you or your child from being harmed or threatened.
- An "occupation order" covers who can live in the family home or enter the surrounding area.

Try to avoid these, if you can practically move out of your current situation. Invariably proceedings that start with injunctions, in my experience, continue to be inflammatory throughout future proceedings and communications. However, if you fear you are in danger, then you absolutely must protect yourself with an injunction order and report to the police. The court can also put in place special measures at hearings to keep you separate.

Domestic violence is a pattern of coercive and controlling behaviour or abuse, and can manifest itself psychologically, physically, emotionally, sexually and financially. Following the introduction of the Domestic Abuse Act 2021 a broad ranging definition of domestic abuse is now recognised. Often this behaviour has crept up in degrees over the relationship period – this makes it more difficult to leave an abusive relationship. The heat has literally been turned up so that a pattern becomes established, and the person on the receiving end often loses their self-confidence. Domestic violence occurs, regardless of background, education and status. I think it has been helpful that many celebrities have stepped forwards to say they have experienced such behaviour. It happens behind closed doors and needs to be brought into the open to be dealt with as swiftly as possible.

If you are suffering from any type of control, I would suggest you leave the home and take refuge elsewhere before seeking an injunction, so you know you will be safe. You should call the police; they are very helpful and have special teams that now deal with domestic violence issues. You must also seek the immediate advice of a solicitor. You may be eligible for public funding to take you through court proceedings.

If you do not know which way to turn, I would first advise that you contact the National Centre for Domestic Violence – www.ncdv.org.uk - Tel number 0800 970 2070 or text NCDV to 60777 and they will call you back. Also, http://www.refuge.org.uk/get-help-now/phone-the-helpline/ operate a 24 hour national domestic abuse helpline freephone Tel number 0808 2000 247. If a phone has been taken away from you, which can sometimes happen, get out as soon as you are able to and go to a neighbour and ask them to call the police for you. Alert friends or family regarding any control issues so they can call the police if you are not in touch daily. The charities Shelter and Women's Aid may also help with temporary and urgent accommodation and assistance.

Procedure

Non-molestation Order

A non-molestation order can be applied for which prohibits your spouse from using or threatening to use violence, or intimidating, pestering or harassing you or the children.

- A form FL401 has to be completed and filed, accompanied by a witness statement stating in detail what has happened, and a draft order you are seeking. There is no court fee.
- Then a court hearing date will be fixed.
- If there is a risk of significant harm or you would likely be deterred from making or pursuing the application, your solicitor will advise that you go to court ex parte, which means without giving your spouse notice, to get an urgent order to cover you from non-molestation by your spouse.
- If granted, the court will then invariably fix an on notice hearing, giving your spouse (the Respondent) the opportunity to file their statement and attend court.

- Your solicitors must immediately arrange for personal service, normally by a process server on the Respondent, of the application and other documents, and hearing date.
- A statement of service, i.e. proof, will have to be filed at court so it must be done formally.
- You may both be called to give evidence and be cross-examined before any final order is made by the court. If there is a particular vulnerability, the court can direct an intermediary be engaged to assist with questioning.

The court need to be satisfied there is evidence of molestation, you or the children need protection and the court need to intervene to control the Respondent's behaviour.

Molestation can cover a wide range of behaviour, including control, using abusive language, to threats of, or actual, violence. The court have regard to all the circumstances including the need to secure the health, safety and wellbeing of the applicant and any relevant children. The order normally lasts for a specified time but in severe situations it can be indefinite, i.e. until further order. You can apply for an extension of the order if the order is, in effect, for a set duration, provided you apply before it is due to cease. You should apply in good time and have justification for the extension.

If a Respondent breaches a non-molestation order without reasonable excuse, it is a criminal offence and they can be arrested. The order must be personally served by process servers on the Respondent. Also, a copy must be provided to the police station.

A Respondent may offer a compromise to give an undertaking to the court which is a promise not to do certain things. The court will not accept an undertaking in serious situations. If an undertaking is given and breached, the person cannot be arrested as the breach is not a criminal offence. However, it is contempt of court, which can be punished by committal to prison.

Occupation Order

Often an occupation order is also applied for at the same time. This can set out who lives in the family home and regulates its occupation. It can also restrict your spouse from entering the area surrounding the home.

- The same form FL401 must be completed with a full witness statement as before. Again, there is no court fee.
- The need for personal service of the proceedings and any subsequent order made are also the same. Additionally, the mortgagee or landlord also needs to be served by first-class post. It is less likely for this order to be made without giving notice to the Respondent as it interferes with their property rights. This will only be granted in limited circumstances in the interim if there is significant risk that if it is not made immediately, the Applicant may be prevented from bringing the application, or when the Respondent is deliberately evading service, and the delay will severely prejudice the Applicant or children.
- Again, a hearing date is set and the Respondent will file their own witness statement in response.
- The court apply a "balance of harm" test, in which it balances the likelihood of significant harm to one person, which can include children, against the likelihood of significant harm to the other party, if a court order is, or is not made. If significant harm is likely to be suffered by the Applicant or any children, they must make the order. The court also have the power to make an order if the balance of harm test is not satisfied by taking into account other factors. They are as follows:
- the housing needs and resources of the parties and any relevant children,
- financial resources of the parties,
- likely effect of making or not making an order would have on the health, safety, and wellbeing of the parties and any relevant children,

- and the conduct of the parties in relation to each other or otherwise.

The order is known as a Draconian remedy as it can effectively exclude a spouse from their home. This order is normally for six months, 12 months or until determination of financial matters on divorce. It can also impose obligations to pay rent or mortgage and maintenance and repairs on the home.

Breach of an occupation order is not a criminal offence but if it has a power of arrest attached to it then the police can arrest the party if they breach it. A power of arrest will be attached if the Respondent has used or threatened violence against the Applicant or child, and they would not be adequately protected without it. In addition to the order being served personally on the Respondent, a copy should also then be lodged at the police station.

Joint Tenants and the Marital Home

Joint Property

Your properties will ultimately be dealt with in a financial order. However, some advanced measures are useful to protect your position whilst finances are going through. If your property is joint, it can be held as "joint tenants" or "tenants in common".

When you purchased property jointly with your spouse, you may not recall whether you purchased it as joint tenants in law and equity, or tenants in common. Tenants in common specifies what share of the property in equity you each hold and passes as part of the estate under your will. If in doubt, contact the solicitors that dealt with the conveyancing of your purchase. Your current solicitors can also undertake a search of the Land Registry register to commence initial enquiries.

Joint tenants (sometimes called "beneficial joint tenants"):
• you have equal rights to the whole property
• the property automatically goes to the other owner/s if you die
• you cannot pass on your ownership of the property in your will
Tenants in common:
• you can own different shares of the property
• the property does not automatically go to the other owner/s if you die
• you can pass on your share of the property in your will

As you are divorcing, you may no longer want your property to transfer to your spouse if you die whilst financial matters have not concluded. Most people purchase property in joint names as "joint tenants". If you die, the house automatically passes to your spouse. It is usual at the outset of your divorce to sever the joint tenancy. Your spouse is served with a *notice of severance* so your share of the property passes to your estate under your will. Your solicitors will prepare this for you. Your solicitor will then arrange for your spouse to be served with it, normally by recorded delivery as proof of postage and delivery can be retained for future reference, or they can sometimes arrange personal service, even though this is not strictly necessary, to ensure it has been received.

The notice of severance of tenancy needs to be served on your spouse, a record kept, and notice registered on the land registry title. Your solicitors will deal with this. At the same time, it is important to make a new will to cover this. If your spouse is not in good health, you may not want to sever the tenancy if there is a likelihood your spouse may in fact pass away before you, as their share would automatically pass to you.

Property only in your Spouse's Name

If the marital home is in your spouse's sole name, you must register a Matrimonial Homes Rights notice at the Land Registry to cover your rights of occupation and forewarn any potential purchaser.

As you can only have one Matrimonial Homes Rights notice, if there are several properties in your spouse's sole name, for the remaining properties you will need conveyancing solicitors to apply for a restriction or notice on the register, alerting third parties who may wish to buy the house from your spouse of your interest.

These are all interim measures as you will ultimately ask the court to decide property matters in a final financial remedy order, and then any notices and restrictions will be lifted and the timing of this will be referred to within the final property orders made.

Wills

When you are divorced, this does not invalidate any will made before. It just means that any provision for your former spouse lapses. You should update your will as soon as you know you are separating so you state who you are going to leave your estate to, particularly if you do not want your spouse to benefit whilst you are in the midst of divorce proceedings. If you have joint property, you make a will, and at the same time your solicitors should be instructed to serve a notice of severance of joint tenancy, so your share of the house becomes part of your estate that falls under your will.

If you marry or remarry, this does automatically revoke any previous will made so it is very important to make a new will either in contemplation of marriage if you do have imminent plans, or when you re marry.

Lasting Powers of Attorney

A lasting power of attorney (LPA) is a legal document enabling you (the donor) to appoint one or more persons to make decisions on your behalf. It continues to take effect in the event of your incapacity. There are two types of powers of attorney:

- one for health and welfare (form LP1H)
- one to cover financial matters (form LP1F)

It is also a good time to complete these as you are considering your position if you were to die, but also if you are unable to act in your lifetime which can include if you were mentally incapacitated. You need to know your health and finances are in good hands as your spouse will no longer be an appropriate person to act on your behalf. It is likely to be a member of your family that you appoint as your attorney to act for you, but you can have several people. There are quite clear but long forms. You can complete these yourself online or get guidance from solicitors if you do not know what wording to include. They must be validly executed and registered with the Office of the Public Guardian before they are effective.

They can be completed online at https://www.gov.uk/power-of-attorney

If you choose more than one person to be your attorney, you can decide whether they will act jointly or severally. If you are appointing a few attorneys, consider if they can act independently, and practically how it will work. It is a good idea to have more than one person named in case someone cannot act, or perhaps moves away. You can also provide for replacement attorneys.

Certificate Provider

A certificate needs to be completed, normally by a professional, i.e. your solicitor, or possibly your doctor, to confirm that you understand the purpose of the lasting power of attorney and the scope of authority you are giving, and there is no pressure or fraud or anything else that should prevent the lasting power of attorney from being made. It can also be completed by someone who has known you for more than two years but they must know you well enough so they are satisfied you understand. There are several people disqualified from being the certificate provider so it is always best to have a professional sign the certificate. The certificate provider cannot be a member of your family nor an unmarried partner of yours or your attorney, nor employee or business partner of you or your attorney.

Strict execution formalities apply. You, the certificate provider, and attorneys must sign in a set order: you sign first, then the certificate provider and then the attorneys. The signatures for you and the attorneys must be independently witnessed by persons over 18 when you each sign.

Change of Name Deeds

If you changed your name when you married, you may wish to revert back to your unmarried name. A change of name deed is a simple document that can be prepared by your solicitor and needs to be signed in your previous name and new name, and witnessed. Most institutions will want a certified copy of the change of name deed and certified copy of the final divorce order to update their records. Ask your solicitor to prepare and certify at least six copies of each, as often institutions don't return them.

The Small Stuff – Home Contents

When it comes to house contents and personal possessions, it is incredible how couples can fight over items that cost a fraction of the cost of the fight through solicitors. Do not sweat the small stuff. Treat it as a practical exercise. Make a list of things and items in the home and suggest in one column what you would like and in another column what you expect your spouse would wish to retain. Ideally, if you can sit down and do this list together, this is the best approach. Do not put all the major items in your column and everything you don't want in his or hers. Be fair, generous and think how you would want him or her to behave towards you.

Otherwise, if this does not work and you are literally still fighting over your possessions, try a selection method. You have your list of items in front of both of you and then one of you chooses first (toss a coin if you can't decide who is to go first) and pick one item, then your spouse chooses an item, and you carry on alternating until you have gone through the list.

Whatever you do, keep the issue of contents out of court. There is nothing more that judge's dislike than having to deal with a contents application. They and you have better things to do. I have heard of cases where the judge has literally said they will buy the item or auction items, as it is so frustrating for them. I have only ever been involved in one case that finally went to a hearing, and my view is it was a complete waste of effort, time and money; the parties could have fully furnished a house with new contents for the money spent.

There is a specific law that relates to contents – Married Women's Property Act 1772. It differs from the general principles that apply to other capital and assets. Therefore, if you have purchased an item with your funds, you retain ownership, particularly if you brought the item into the marriage, or it was inherited from your family. With gifts, the ownership passes to you if your spouse has given it to you as a gift. The court may differentiate if the item is a significant heirloom from your spouse's family, so it should ultimately return to its progression through the generations. If you have purchased items jointly, or from a joint account, you own them jointly unless there was a specific agreement that one person would retain ownership.

They do say that possession is nine-tenths of the law. This practically ends up being very true. If you have an aggressive spouse, I advise that you remove any special items and personal belongings into your possession as soon as you leave the home. There have been many occasions where suddenly the spouse says he or she does not know where something is, and if disposed of it's too late. If you decide to move out, take anything that is important with you. Also, always take your paperwork so that doesn't miraculously go missing. Of course, if there are children who are remaining in the house and you are leaving, keep items in the house that are needed for them.

At the end of the day, remember they are just things and things can always be replaced. How many of those things do you actually need?

Sometimes it can be freeing to start afresh and begin to lose your attachment and importance to things.

Top Tips

DO

1. Get help straight away if you are suffering from domestic violence.
2. Check how your home, and other properties, are held at the outset and check with your solicitor whether any immediate steps need to be taken to protect your position.
3. If you are moving out, move out with your possessions.

DO NOT

1. Spend a great deal of time, energy or money fighting over possessions and house contents – it is a waste.
2. Leave making your will until the end of your divorce – treat this as priority.

Decluttering and Non-attachment

Non-attachment

Your home. It will all come down to non-attachment. If you have a property, one of you will have to move out or you will both have to move if the house needs to be sold. It is not always just the physical surroundings that you have become attached to, but the memories of situations that have taken place in the house. Also, very often, it is the status that you have become identified with.

Declutter

Your home contents. It's a really good time to declutter which can be therapeutic too. If you are not sure whether to get rid of items which you are still emotionally attached to and may regret parting with, think about putting them with your close relatives. Maybe put them in their garage or loft, then when you get them in a few months, or a few years, you can easily let go if you are finding it difficult at the time to decide.

Let Go of Spending

If money seems tight, as it often is when you change from a double-earning household to a single-earner household, just try to be as careful as you can with money. Do so as quickly as possible so you do not get into debt. Do more things that are free or cost less money– go for a walk or run in the park; cycle; read a book; watch inspirational stories on YouTube; invite friends round for a drink or a cup of tea rather than going out for dinner or to the pub; cook from scratch more rather than buying ready-made meals. Think about what is really important – a roof over your head, food and your health. It is also good for children to appreciate the little things and the value of money. Your lifestyle may change temporarily or you may make changes for good.

Concentrate on people rather than possessions.

Case Scenario

The situation. Jessica and Tim had a very acrimonious breakup. They had been married for seven years. They did not have children. Jessica had left Tim for a life with his best friend Phil. Money was very tight. Whilst Jessica had put in a lot more money when they bought the marital home together Tim still sought an equal share. Most of the contents of the house had been purchased jointly, but Jessica also had some family heirlooms, and Tim had also received art items which he stated were gifted by Jessica to him.

How we helped her. We acted for Jessica and prepared a list of the very extensive contents of the home indicating the items that Jessica wanted to retain. Tim would not agree to the division and he prepared his own list of the items he wanted to retain. It became clear that they wanted to each have the same large items.

We indicated at court that the issue of contents could not be resolved, and the court ordered that the parties prepare a Scott Schedule. A Scott Schedule has several columns. The left-hand column is the description of the item. In the next column the Applicant, namely Jessica in this case, puts detail as to why they should retain the item and their argument as to ownership. The Respondent then completes the next column with a reason why he, in this case Tim, should retain the item with arguments as to ownership, and how he responds to what Jessica has said. The far right-hand column is then left blank for the judge to make a decision on the item.

We had suggested that Jessica and Tim simply alternately choose an item from the house, but they could not agree on this.

In the end, the judge made a decision regarding each item, and where there was still dispute over a jointly owned item which the parties could not resolve, he gave a direction that the item should be auctioned for sale and proceeds divided equally if they could not come to an agreement within 14 days of the hearing. Although some items were of a reasonably high value, most items were hardly worth putting on the list. For instance, a soft toy dog!

The parties also owned a parrot and could not decide who would keep it. Again, the judge directed that unless they came to an agreement within 14 days, he would decide who the parrot should live with and make an order that the other person receive an amount from the proceeds of the contents to purchase another parrot! We were not exactly sure that the court were able to make such orders but the exasperated judge was clearly coming to the only practical solution.

How she coped. Jessica realised soon after the hearing that her dear parrot meant more than the contents and Tim agreed she should retain the parrot. She realised the value of life.

Where she is now. Jessica made a new life and moved to the countryside with her partner, Phil, where they set up a kennels. She lived her dream looking after animals for others, and although she kept various heirlooms, did not spend her time acquiring more possessions.

Morning Meditation

When you wake, take yourself to your quiet place where you won't be disturbed. Take a seat either on a chair or cross-legged on a cushion for 15 minutes. Close your eyes and take a few deep breaths. Keep your back erect but not held, and hands loosely in your lap. Breathe in for the count of two, and out for the count of two. Continue this for a few rounds of breath. Then breathe in for the count of two, and out for the count of four. Continue breathing in this way, with a longer exhale. Let go of any tension you may be holding on the exhale. Then bring to mind all the items you may be disposing of or leaving behind. Look at them in your mind and tell yourself you are ready to let them go. Then carry on with your breathing, with a longer exhale. Let those items go, let any memories go, let it all just fade away. Carry on breathing for a few minutes before you rise from meditation.

Opening Thought of the Day

I let go of what no longer serves me.

Chapter 10

PRE- AND POST-NUPTIAL AGREEMENTS AND FINDING LOVE AGAIN

Introduction

A pre-nuptial agreement is entered into prior to a marriage whereas a post-nuptial agreement can be entered into after you have married. Both seek to regulate financial affairs in the event the marriage ends. They are contractual bespoke documents drawn up by solicitors which you will enter into with the intention to be legally binding. They will be executed as a deed. However, you cannot oust the court's jurisdiction to deal with financial matters on divorce. In this chapter we also discuss what is true love, as you find love again. We meet Rhianna before she is due to marry and due to her hectic schedule before she married, her decision to enter into a post-nuptial agreement. We conclude with an evening meditation and thoughts towards yourself, your future spouse and everyone out there to be well, happy, peaceful and loved. Let your love radiate!

Pre- and Post-nuptial Agreements

Pre-nuptial agreements arc often entered into in second and subsequent marriages, particularly where one or both of you want to protect assets brought into the marriage, often including inheritance and trusts. Also, increasingly in first marriages particularly where one party has family wealth, the family often want to protect their position. You can differentiate between matrimonial and non-matrimonial property, i.e. assets owned prior to the marriage. It is also helpful to enter into this agreement if there are other countries you reside in or have properties in. It is important to get legal advice in all jurisdictions, as in some countries, pre-nuptial agreements will be binding. They tend to be seen as a mechanism for a more financially dominant party to try to limit the settlement the other party may receive on divorce but are also entered into to give more certainty.

They most often cover:

- what will happen to the home if you split up.
- any other properties
- pension, maintenance, assets held jointly or solely by each of you, and debts.
- how anticipated assets and inheritances will be dealt with.
- how any provision may change if you have children.
- setting out what your contributions have been and will be during the marriage.
- a financial summary of each of your current assets (based on the financial disclosure). This is helpful as, by the time of any divorce, it is often forgotten what your exact positions were when you married.

A pre-nuptial agreement is not currently binding under the law of England and Wales. However, the courts are increasingly taking these into account and being persuaded by pre-nuptial agreements upon divorce, particularly where the marriage is short. Sometimes they will also be upheld.

It is essential when the court considers whether the agreement should be upheld, or what weight to give to it, that there has been full financial disclosure, you have both taken independent legal advice and understand the implications of the agreement, there has been no undue pressure on one person to enter into the agreement, and it must be a reasonable agreement in all the circumstances.

Even if the agreement is held to be valid on future divorce, the court retains a broad discretion and may make an award in excess of needs if the circumstances of the case require that for "fairness". However, it is still better, in my view, to have this document so at least it was clear what your intentions were when you married. You then have the prospect of it being upheld or at least considered on divorce. Only sign it if you are happy to be bound by it, as simply changing your mind when you get to divorce is too late – the court may find it reasonable and uphold it. You will have to give good reasons to explain why an order should not be made in those terms.

Normally, agreements are entered into more than 21 days before a marriage, following a series of discussions between solicitors to ensure there is ample time for consideration. This helps to illustrate there is no undue pressure. If time is short, you can still enter into a post-nuptial agreement once you have married.

You can also include provision in the agreement for review periods, for instance, in five years' time, or a trigger event such as the birth of a child. To an extent, there is a bit of crystal ball gazing to try to cover all eventualities and changes in circumstances. Therefore, it is a good idea to review the document, maybe annually, at the same time as reviewing whether you want to change provisions in your will. A current agreement based on current circumstances is more likely to be upheld by the court on divorce.

Top Tips

DO

1.   Execute a new will to reflect the terms of any pre-nuptial agreement (which can be done in contemplation of marriage) as marriage automatically invalidates previous wills. Your will can then reflect any terms of the agreement.

DO NOT

1.   Try to draw up an agreement purporting to be a pre-nuptial agreement between you. You must have legal advisors to draw this up properly.

True Love

Despite my profession, I am a great believer in love! But I do believe there are karmic relationships. On some level have we allowed the suffering to take place? Other relationships that did not work perhaps we were meant to experience to open ourselves up to something we did not know about ourselves, for instance, our inner strength. Or perhaps to make it clear what we do not want and therefore give us clarity in what we do want and to give us a greater awareness generally. Then there are those relationships that really are true love which of course are about us ultimately being the source of that love. If we have restored peace in ourselves, we bring to our relationships joy, love and compassion. They, in turn, are loving and full of joy.

On a human level it is about putting aside all expectations of what the other should and should not do or be or not be. Acceptance of who they are and also who you are. I do think it is imperative that you feel whole and happy to be single before you meet someone else. They are not going to complete you; you are already complete. Can they enhance your life experience? Then let them in. If you do not feel good in their company, do not try any harder to make things work. Life is far too short and far too important to waste time. Learn whatever lesson you are meant to learn with them and move on quickly from the relationship and with compassion to the other.

Warren Buffett, American magnate and philanthropist, once said that the two most important decisions you will make in life are:

- what career to choose,
- and who to marry.

For careers we often receive some advice but may take time to find our true calling. For our life partner, we are often totally unprepared with any form of guidance. There are no classes. How many of us researched books and relationship patterns as we fell in love spontaneously and unconsciously? As we stumble into these decisions, it is no wonder that we often end up in major events such as divorce. We are either lucky in making the right choice in the most compatible life partner, or often have to just learn through our past mistakes.

As one of my closest friends once said of a good relationship – it is just easy. Another of my friends said there are no rough edges. If it is a struggle, it is not the relationship for you or you are not in the right place for this relationship. Always work on yourself first and you will have happiness.

When defining true love, I often reflect on Thich Nhat Hanh's book *True Love*. It is an essential read. It outlines that, according to Buddhism, there are four elements of true love.

- The first is maître; loving kindness which is not only wanting to make someone happy but also the ability to do so.
- The second is karuna; compassion, which is both the wish and again the ability to ease the pain and suffering of the other.
- The third is mudita; joy, if there is no joy in love it is not true love. If you are crying all the time or make the other cry, this is the opposite of true love.
- The fourth and last element is upeksha, freedom. In true love the person you love feels free on both the inside and outside.

I often reflect on these uplifting aspects.

The most important overall message is to be there truly for the other, which includes the practice of deep listening – really listening to the other and coming to understand what they want. Being present in their presence. Thich Nhat Hanh uses a lovely phrase: "Dear One, I am here for you." What could be a greater gift than this? To me, this encompasses everything a person could ever wish for, for someone to always be truly there for them. Not preoccupied in their presence, not taken for granted. It is such an unconditional giving. It makes sense that this type of relationship will flourish and bring joy to both. It is a relationship full of awareness. I also like the reference Thich Nhat Hanh makes to let the other know when you are suffering, and there is no room for pride. There is the potential to develop complete unity from a place of understanding and openness.

If we reflect on true love and love for a young child or a pet, it is unconditional, and it comes back to bringing this into our personal relationships. Also, to children as they develop. That way, they will always feel loved and secure.

I have read that relationships are partnerships and not amalgamations. Each partner assists in creating conditions that are wholesome and supportive of the other. It is important to always treat the other with respect, courtesy, support, be faithful, share decisions, and offer yourself to be there for the other.

Case Scenario

Situation. We acted for Rhianna in respect of a pre-nuptial agreement. She was due to marry her fiancé Max in three months' time. She owned a property jointly with her parents in which she had a one-third interest, and she also held a 25% interest in her aunt's property under a family trust. In addition, she had significant inheritance prospects from her aunts and uncles. Her fiancé Max had no property but he did have a good job, and they already had a young child together who was aged three. As her aunt's trust was complex, it took time establishing whether, and when, she could realise her interest under the trust. Rhianna travelled abroad a lot, and time elapsed from taking instructions to having a finalised draft pre-nuptial agreement, which she reviewed only four weeks prior to the marriage.

How we helped her. We advised it was important, and generally good practice, not to enter into a pre-nuptial agreement within 21 days of the marriage, and to allow sufficient time for discussions/revisions. We therefore discussed, also due to busy schedules for her and her fiancé, that we amend the agreement into a post-nuptial agreement, to be entered into after their marriage. This would allow full financial disclosure to be exchanged, and schedules exhibited to that agreement. We also advised that new wills needed to be prepared as marriage automatically revoked previous wills.

Max took some advice from solicitors but decided to respond to us himself. It was agreed that as the property held with her parents would continue to be the marital home for herself, Max and their daughter, that her husband would be entitled to an equal interest. The equal interest would relate to the current one-third share, and in the future likely to the whole of the property as her parents would probably transfer their interest to Rhianna. It was then agreed that Max would have no claim under Rhianna's interest in her family trust, aunt's property, and any other future inheritance would remain solely for her benefit. They were both happy with the agreement as Max would be paying the bills on the marital home so it would be fair in the future that the property would be shared. We also allowed for a review of the post-nuptial agreement when they had another child, and further reviews in five and ten years, as it was likely by then that Max's resources would have built up, whereas Rhianna would be the main carer of the children.

Rhianna had the peace of mind knowing that she had a good chance of the court upholding the provisions in the post-nuptial agreement in the future, and if this did not happen it would still be a factor that she could ask the court to consider and give weight to. Rhianna and Max were both happy that they had clarity at the outset on finances, and that they both knew where they stood in the event of any future separation or divorce.

How she coped. The certainty of future security and knowing she had good communication with Max to broach these issues.

Where they are now. In a happy marriage knowing where they both stand... and now with another baby!

Evening Meditation

Find a quiet place where you will not be disturbed. Sit comfortably with your back erect, either on a chair with your feet on the floor or on a cushion sitting cross-legged. Place your hands loosely in your lap. Close your eyes. Take a couple of deep breaths. Then start to settle into your breath. As you take your next breath say to yourself, may I be well, may I be happy, may I be peaceful, may I be loved. Take a few breaths and focus on those words. Then turn your attention to your fiancé/e or spouse. Say to yourself, may you be well, may you be happy, may you be peaceful, may you be loved. Focus on those words for the next few breaths and send them loving thoughts. Then take your attention to your family and friends and say the same words. Then turn to your wider community, saying these words to your neighbours and community. Finally, to all living beings, wish for everyone to be well, happy, peaceful, and loved. Send loving thoughts to all living beings. Take your time as you rise from meditation and prepare for a good night's sleep ... hopefully beside your loved one.

Concluding Thought of the Day
May we all be well, happy, peaceful and loved.

Chapter 11

COHABITEES (COHABITANTS) AND PARTNERSHIPS

Introduction

Post-divorce I have had many clients vowing never to remarry – although time does heal and history is forgotten. It may be that you find a new relationship and decide to live together. The law is particularly complex for cohabitees (defined in law as *cohabitants*). In many ways, financial obligations and claims are limited in these circumstances so please do seek advice at the beginning of your relationship with a view to entering into a cohabitation agreement. If you enter into a civil partnership, the financial position and claims are the same as for married couples. However, if you live together without entering into a formal civil partnership, if you separate, your claims are currently limited to property rights and claims relating to children. Unlike divorce, or dissolution of civil partnerships, there is no such thing as a common-law marriage, and there is no automatic right that applies if you separate, even on the death of the other. This is a particularly bitter bill to swallow if it is the end of a long-term relationship, which is just as painful as the end of a long marriage. I also recommend entering into a separation deed if you separate.

Regarding the law that applies to cohabitees, there is about to be a brighter side; look out for a change in law as this is expected over the next few years. This will increase financial claims between cohabitees. The Cohabitation Rights Bill 2019–2021, had its first reading in the House of Lords on 5th February

2020. Second reading date to be announced, and there are several further stages to go through. It is still some way to being enacted.

I also cover in this chapter other options if you find yourself no longer in a partnership. Enjoying solitude and having the company of a pet. We help Beatrice to reach an agreement with her long-term partner and understand that even after many years together with several children, how starkly contrasted her situation is with her position if she had married. We conclude this chapter with a simple meditation to bring us into the present. Each present moment is a gift.

Civil Partnerships

(same-sex and opposite-sex couples)

- If, as an opposite-sex couple, you have a registered civil partnership from December 2019, under the Civil Partnerships, Marriages and Deaths (Registration, etc.) Act 2019, you can finally seek financial redress if your relationship breaks down in the same way as married couples and same-sex civil partnerships.
- Same-sex civil partnerships were recognised in this way 15 years prior, pursuant to the Civil Partnership Act 2004.
- The same financial remedies as for married couples on divorce can be sought from the court on the dissolution of a civil partnership. The same procedures apply, and the same factors for determining financial division (section 25 Matrimonial Causes Act 1973) apply.

Couples Living Together without Registering as Civil Partners

If you have not formalised your relationship into a civil partnership, as the majority of cohabitees have not, then the range of financial claims open to a spouse on a relationship breakdown are currently simply not open to you. There is still a high public mistaken belief that couples have rights from a "common-law marriage". You have significantly less rights than married couples. These rights are limited to interests in property or claims for children, which can result in very little financial compensation even after a long period together. This particularly comes as a shock for the many cohabiting couples who have been together for a long period of time where one person has cared for the children and the other has been the main breadwinner. With no interest in the family home, the main carer may have to rely on claims on behalf of the children. For a long partnership without children, unless a property interest in their partner's home can be successfully claimed, the financially weaker party is also often left high and dry when they break up.

Cohabitees (cohabitants) rights

The option to enter into a civil partnership is not an appropriate course for the vast majority of cohabiting couples who have decided they have no wish to marry or otherwise formalise their relationship. Often, the relationship has developed organically into cohabitation and an economically intertwined relationship. There will also be situations where one person may refuse to make the relationship formal.

Couples living together are defined as cohabitants in statute law. Their rights are generally limited to property and children. Even regarding property, the claims a spouse can make are far wider reaching than for a cohabitant who is limited to principles from the law of trusts, which determines their beneficial interest. The cohabitant cannot claim maintenance for themselves on relationship breakdown but have some further possible claims where there are children. They also do not automatically benefit if their partner passes away. It is really important, therefore, to protect your financial position with a cohabitation agreement, a declaration of trust in relation to property, and wills that provide for each other.

Cohabitation Agreement

It is essential, in my view, to enter into a cohabitation or living together agreement either before you start living together or early on in the relationship.

Formalities

- It will be prepared as a deed.
- You must have both received independent legal advice.
- You must have both entered into the agreement freely and voluntarily.
- There should be full disclosure of your assets before it is entered into, to counter any allegations of undue influence and ensure it is upheld in the future.
- It is important that it is formally recorded in writing in this way to avoid future dispute over how assets are held and how contributions will determine any further shares, as these are matters that would be considered by the court in any future dispute over property.

Property Rights for Cohabitees

Property rights are governed by the law of trusts. An application is made under the Trusts of Land and Appointment of Trustees Act 1996 in the event of future dispute. These proceedings are expensive so it is better to have a written cohabitation agreement on which you can rely if all the correct steps have been taken. A clear definition of your property interests in the agreement will usually determine your beneficial interests if you separate.

With property, it is important to distinguish between "legal ownership", which is the name on the Land Registry title to the property, and "beneficial or equitable ownership", whereby you may still have an interest if your name is, or is not, on the deeds.

Property in Joint Names

The general premise is if you bought a house in joint names it is joint in both "legal ownership" and "beneficial or equitable ownership". If it is held as joint tenants, it is presumed you hold a 50% share, and on death your share automatically passes to the other by way of survivorship. On any future dispute, this presumption would have to be displaced by you if you want to contend you should have a greater share. Merely contributing unequally to the deposit will not be enough to be certain you will end up with a greater share in the future. It will turn on your shared intention, which can be expressed, or implied from conduct. As a relationship continues over many years, the initial intention may be blurred or may change. Don't leave it to the other person's goodwill later down the line.

If, when you purchase, it is stated on the transfer deed you are "tenants in common" you can have unequal shares in the property defined and your share does not automatically pass to the other if you die. You can outline from the beginning exactly what shares you both want, but again it is important to consider whether either of you are going to make future payments and how these would affect the percentages. What if one of you stops paying the mortgage – should this affect the share? So, these matters should be considered in detail when you purchase a house together.

Property in your or your Partner's Sole Name

If you live in your partner's home and make contributions, ask the question, will this give you an interest? Don't rely on the other person's good nature and promises. It is much better to cover everything in a legal agreement. Also, if you own the property, ensure you cover yourself against future property claims, if you do not intend that your partner should have an interest. Be certain and put these matters down in a cohabitation agreement to avoid later challenges.

What the Agreement can Cover

The agreement can cover:

- who owns what and in what proportions.
- what financial arrangements are being made when you are together, including, for instance, who is going to pay the mortgage, the bills.
- whether these are going to be seen as future contributions.
- how property and assets should be divided if you split up.
- whether this would change if you have children.
- maintenance if there are children.

Couples with Children

There is no right to spousal maintenance but if there are children then there can be additional claims under the Children Act 1989, whereby a former partner may seek an allowance if it is needed by them to care for the child. The emphasis is on the child's welfare.

There can be other claims on behalf of the child for a lump sum to cover capital expenses and settlement of property. The court can order that accommodation is provided for the primary carer and the child. However, if this is ordered, the property would go back to the paying party when the child reaches 18 or completes full-time tertiary education. The court can also provide a capital allowance for setting up the home.

Child maintenance is always open through the government child maintenance service, and top-up orders from the court are available for higher income situations, disability expenses and school (and possibly university education) fees.

When the courts are considering what financial orders to make on divorce or dissolution of a civil partnership under Section 25 of the Matrimonial Clauses Act 1973, the court is required to give first priority to the interests of any dependent minor children. That is not the case when the court is considering proceedings under the Trusts of Land and Appointment of Trustees Act 1996. The economically weaker party may bring an application under the Children Act 1989 Schedule 1, but the claims are not as far reaching as for divorce.

Cohabitation Rights Bill 2019 – 2021

The Resolution Cohabitation Committee has continued to push the agenda for law reform and to raise awareness amongst the public of the lack of legal rights and remedies for cohabitants on a separation and the steps they can take to strengthen their position, such as entering into a cohabitation agreement. Even with the growing majority of cohabiting couples, I still see few people coming in to arrange a cohabitation agreement, even though without this they often have nothing tangible to rely on for financial certainty.

The Cohabitation Rights Bill 2019–2020 will significantly change the position and redress the situation for the majority of couples if it is enacted. It is not yet law but keep an eye out for any updates. The purpose of the Cohabitation Rights Bill is to provide protection to financially disadvantaged cohabitants and to make provision for them on the death of their partner. The bill provides protection for cohabitants who have lived together for a minimum of three years or who have a child together. Either cohabitant may apply to court for a financial settlement order upon the breakdown of the relationship to redress a financial benefit or an economic disadvantage resulting from the period of cohabitation. It also gives cohabitants the right to succeed to their partner's estate under the intestacy rules and the right to have an insurable interest in the life of their partner.

A financial settlement order may require the payment of a lump sum, the transfer of property, a property settlement, the sale of property, or pension sharing.

The other crucial point is that the Cohabitation Rights Bill allows the parties to agree, in writing, to opt out of its provisions. The bill allows couples to choose to opt out of the financial settlement provisions, therefore preserving freedom of choice. Cohabitation agreements or deeds of trust would be honoured by the opt-out agreement. However, this does not prevent an application for an order being made – the court may vary or revoke the opt-out agreement if it determines that the agreement is "manifestly unfair" to the applicant.

The application for an order must be made before the end of the period of 24 months starting with the date on which the former cohabitants ceased living together as a couple unless the applicant satisfies the court that exceptional circumstances would justify a late application being made.

The financial settlement provisions, as set out in the bill, are still more limited than for married couples or for those who have entered into a civil partnership. The starting point is for the applicant to show that:

- he or she has made qualifying contributions, whether financial or in work care or kind, to the parties' share of family lives,
- as a result of such contribution, the party has derived and retained a financial benefit, actual or potential, whether in capital, income or earning capacity, or the applicant has suffered or would in the future suffer an economic disadvantage,
- the court could intervene to award a financial settlement if it considered it just and equitable to do so having regard to a number of discretionary factors.
- There is the introduction of three new terms: "retained benefit", "economic disadvantage", and "qualifying contributions".
- A "retained benefit" is defined as "a financial benefit which has been acquired, retained or enhanced by or for the respondent during the parties' cohabitation or in contemplation of the parties' cohabitation, whether in the form of capital assets of any kind, income, whether actual or potential or earning capacity".
- An "economic disadvantage" is defined as "a past, present or future financial loss, burden or cost sustained by the

applicant during the parties' cohabitation or in contemplation of the parties' cohabitation or likely to be sustained by the applicant following its breakdown".

- A "qualifying contribution" is defined as "any financial or other contribution made by the applicant to the parties' shared lives or to the welfare of members of their families during the parties' cohabitation or in contemplation of the parties' cohabitation or likely to be made by the applicant following its breakdown".

So, for instance, where one partner has been put at a financial disadvantage by contributing to the purchase or upkeep of their partner's home without receiving any repayment or interest from the other, or has given up their job to look after children, the disadvantaged partner could seek a court order to rectify the imbalance.

The discretionary factors a court may consider will be as follows:

(a) The welfare, while a minor, of any child of both parties who has not attained the age of 18.

(b) The income, earning capacity, property and other financial resources which each of the parties has, or is likely to have in the foreseeable future (including any pension, allowance or benefit paid or to be paid to either party or the eligibility of either party for a pension, allowance or benefit).

(c) The financial needs and obligations which each of the parties has, or is likely to have in the foreseeable future.

(d) The welfare of any children who live with or might reasonably be expected to live with either party.

(e) The conduct of each party if, but only if, it is of such a nature that it would be inequitable to disregard it.

(f) The circumstances in which the applicant made any qualifying contribution, in particular, if the respondent shows that the applicant made such contribution despite the respondent's express disagreement that it should be made.

There are similarities with the section 25 Matrimonial Causes Act factors. Albeit with section 25 factors, first consideration is given to the welfare of any minor children, and the provision in paragraph (f) is unique to cohabitants.

Will

You should also execute a will otherwise a claim would have to be made against the cohabitant's estate as there is no automatic provision on death. Cohabitant's claims are limited depending on how long you have lived together (two years continuous period is the minimum with some exceptions if you can show you were being maintained by the deceased). If you want to provide for them, include specific provision under the terms of your will. Equally, if you do not want to provide for them, an appropriate clause in the cohabitation agreement is best to confirm that it is not intended that claims will be brought against your estate, together with a statement with your will stating the reasons. Also, do consider pension and life insurance nominations as these assets fall outside of your will. Review and update your lasting powers of attorney.

There will be changes under the Cohabitation Rights Bill. At present, if one partner dies without having made a will, his or her partner will not fall under any class of persons eligible to automatically receive a share of the estate of the deceased partner. This means that the surviving partner would need to bring a claim under the Inheritance (Provision for Family and Dependants) Act 1975 to benefit at all. This relies on the surviving partner having the means to bring such a claim and being able to evidence their eligibility to make such a claim. The bill provides for the qualifying cohabitant to benefit even if no will provision has been made, and also amends the Life Assurance Act 1774 to formally allow cohabitants to take out life insurance on the lives of each other.

Declarations of Trust

A Declaration of Trust (also known as a Deed of Trust) is a legally binding document in which the legal owners of a property declare that they hold the property on trust for the beneficial owners and sets out the shares in which the beneficial interests are held. In relation to property, you may have already instructed the conveyancing department to ensure the property is held as tenants in common and a declaration of trust is entered into, but do not treat this as sufficient. A cohabitation agreement will make it clear on any future court application that you have considered the whole position and if there is a dispute, the cohabitation agreement can often shed light on the intentions and give greater clarity to the background history and contributions intended to make a difference to beneficial interests.

I would suggest that you set up both a cohabitation agreement and declaration of trust.

Separation Deed

If you separate, do ensure that a formal separation deed is entered into, similar to that if you were married and decided to separate. This is more important for cohabitants as there is no equivalent subsequent divorce procedure. The deed will ensure that no future claims against you or your property come back to bite you. You can also cover children issues. Your solicitors will prepare a deed, ensure there is reciprocal financial disclosure, and your partner obtains independent legal advice to protect your position.

Children

If you are an unmarried father, provided your child was born after 1st December 2003 and you are registered on the birth certificate, you automatically have parental responsibility. Otherwise, the mother can agree to enter into a parental responsibility agreement to confer this on you, but if she does not agree, you will need to make an application to court. The mother automatically has parental responsibility. If you both have parental responsibility, you both have the right to be involved in major decisions such as where the child should live, schooling, medical treatment and religion to be practised. You cannot change the surname of the child without the other's consent. In the event of separation, you can make an application for a child arrangements order in relation to time spent with the children, who they are to live with, as explained in previous chapters, the same as for married couples.

History of Cohabitation

We are definitely living in a time of historic change for family law. The year 2019 in particular set the scene for major changes. Legislation is gradually acknowledging how we now choose to live in our relationships. Opposite-sex couples living together as cohabitees have eventually been afforded the same financial protection as married couples, if they choose to enter into a civil partnership. However, cohabitees who do not register a civil partnership have nowhere near the same rights as married couples, regardless of the length of their relationship. This is also set to change with the progression of the Cohabitation Rights Bill 2019–2021. Although, noticeably, the rights are still not paralleled to those of married couples. There are valid arguments for this, couples choosing to live together precisely because they do not want the full intertwining of marriage.

There has been significant progress in recent years recognising modern-day relationships, initially in 2004 with the introduction of Civil Partnerships for same-sex couples living together. However, there has been much lobbying for the change to occur, same-sex marriages only having been legalised in England and Wales in March 2014.

The state of the law in relation to cohabitees is still at odds with public expectations. In January 2019, NatCen Social Research published findings from the British Social Attitudes Survey showing that 46% of the public still mistakenly believe there exists a "common-law marriage" which protects cohabitees. Of those in cohabiting relationships, 48% believe this to be the case and 55% of those lived in households with children, who would be the most vulnerable in the event of such a relationship breaking down.

The Cohabitation Rights Bill was introduced previously in 2017 by the House of Lords and was in the process of being considered for some time but made no progress. It is believed by some that successive governments did not want to encourage people to live together rather than marry. Critics of marriage question why governments continue to support and promote it when it has such a high failure rate.

Top Tips

DO

1.   Enter into a cohabitation agreement when you decide to live together, and if you separate, enter into a separation agreement. Treat financial aspects of your relationship formally and always obtain legal advice.
2.   Execute wills.
3.   Review your documents if the law changes.

DO NOT

1. Take your partner's word for it that they will make sure you are looked after or that they will divide finances fairly if you break up. The situation can be very different from their original promise if you separate. Many things change with time.

Going Solo or Partnerships

As you move forwards to your next chapter of your life, perhaps reflect on one matter. Have your happiest times been in or out of a relationship? I do not doubt that a relationship can enrich our lives but it can also hold us back. And we have many relationships, our children, our family, our friends, our pets. Do we really need a significant other?

My belief is that we are whole in ourselves, that we do not need another to complete us or our life. Separation is an inevitable part of this human existence. Can we not just love everyone around us without discrimination, and go wider than a partner, friends and family. We will eventually leave them all on our deathbed. Maybe we should just love humanity. Let's all just support and love one another.

This is ultimately your personal choice. Whilst I think a personal relationship will inevitably come with challenges, a relationship may also bring further growth. It is nice to have company, as long as you are also comfortable in your own space too.

There is a tremendous freedom to life that I personally enjoy without being in a relationship. However, in true love, there is great spiritual support and growth. Whichever is your path, may you find joy.

Look after a Pet

I initially thought of introducing this a bit tongue in cheek but I have since reflected on the benefits. How marvellous if you have the time to look after another living being, a cat or a dog or any other animal. You consider whether this would be a good time to introduce them to your loving arms. The benefits of helping a rescue animal, and at the same time being able to pour out your love to them, are beneficial to you both. Pets reduce stress. They are great companions for adults and children. They also teach children about the responsibility of looking after an animal. Unfortunately, they will not last forever, but to provide a home, and for them to be your companion, will make memories you will never forget. Financially, you need to be able to afford to look after them properly. You also need to give your time. Adopting any animal is a commitment in the same way it is to a human being.

I was discussing divorce with someone I know who said if his wife ever wanted a divorce, he would just get a dog. Whilst we laughed, there is a lot of truth in this for many people. As he said, they are always happy to see you when you get home! It is nice to have another living being to care for.

If you decide it is too much responsibility to care for a pet full time, an option is perhaps to help out at a rescue centre, or with a neighbour. This is also really good for children, to have an unconditional bond at this time.

I can truly say that time spent with my cat has given me the most wonderful moments of my life!

Case scenario

Situation. Beatrice lived together with Herman for 15 years. They had four children and expected to spend the rest of their lives together. They had discussed getting engaged but neither of them particularly felt a need to do so. However, the relationship changed over the years. Beatrice looked after the children, was a teaching assistant and worked part time in the local school. Herman was an IT consultant, had done well financially over the years, and almost denigrated Beatrice's time spent working. He also set up a successful company which he sold and amassed great wealth. He wanted to move to a larger house but when Beatrice viewed it, she did not like it. She subsequently found out that not only had he purchased the house, but also that she was not mentioned in his will. He said he had provided for the children. She was very upset about this as she thought they had been partners for such a long time they would be providing for each other, as well as the children.

When she came to us for advice, she was disappointed to note that she had no claim against the second property purchased by Herman, and that in relation to the "marital" home (which is how she viewed the main property), as she had made no capital contribution, she was basically reliant upon claims on behalf of the children in the event of separation together with the possibility of an allowance for her, pursuant to the Children Act. She had tricky claims under the Trusts of Land and Appointment of Trustees Act 1996 as there had been no express declaration of trust and it would be difficult to imply this if there was no common intention. She was wholly reliant upon the goodwill of Herman for her financial future, despite the length of their relationship.

How we helped her. We subsequently prepared a deed of separation providing her with an interest in their home. She would continue to receive maintenance for the children but she had no alternative but to seek full-time employment at the school to cover her future needs.

How she coped. She learnt a great deal of independence through this process. She also budgeted her income and got a great deal of satisfaction from the money she earned.

Where she is now. Her children are grown up. She decided to undertake further qualifications to become a teacher and now enjoys her career. She also enjoys dancing in her spare time. After many years of being single again, she met the love of her life and they decided to marry!

Morning Meditation

When you wake, take yourself to your quiet place where you won't be disturbed. Take a seat for 15 minutes. Close your eyes and take a few deep breaths. Keep your back erect but not held, and hands loosely placed in your lap. Bring yourself into the present moment. Be conscious of your breath; maybe you can feel your heartbeat. Bring awareness to this moment. Whoever is in your life at the moment, you may feel their presence around you. Just be aware of any sounds around you. Continue to be present, no past, no future. Just enjoy this moment, nowhere to go. It doesn't matter how you got here, you are just here. Carry on breathing for a few minutes before you rise from meditation. Take that sense of presence into your day and into any interactions you have with others today. Try to be fully present in everything you say and do.

Opening Thought of the Day
I am present and aware.

Chapter 12

HISTORY OF DIVORCE V. YOUR FUTURE (MOVING ON AND EMBRACING CHANGE)

Introduction

We have come a long way, and it has taken nearly 50 years for the law to change from fault, to no-fault divorce. You have come a long way to get through your own divorce. You may be interested in how the law evolved. Patience seems to go hand in hand for all of us that have supported the change in law, and patience remains the requisite attribute needed for your divorce. In the same way the law has changed for the better, I hope your journey has evolved in the right direction. I go a little deeper spiritually to talk about your growth, and your opportunity to move from fear to joy, and have a bright new future. We do not consider any other case scenario, as this is now your case, and how you want it to evolve. We finish with a meditation on deep gratitude for all we have. I am deeply grateful to you for taking the time to read my book which I hope has helped you in some way.

Origins of Divorce in England and Wales

The divorce legal process started in the ecclesiastical courts (run by the Church) until divorce was transferred to a new civil court, the Court for Divorce and Matrimonial Causes, following the Matrimonial Causes Act 1857. In those times, as it took place in London, it was only the wealthier couples that could afford to divorce. But by the 1920s, with the help of legal aid, it started to open up to ordinary people and by the 1960s, divorce was dealt with by local county courts.

This continued to be the case until 2015 when divorce centres were opened throughout England. Divorce applications, previously known as "divorce petitions", and financial applications could be submitted to dedicated centres to free up court time for other cases, and with the intention the procedures would be streamlined through these centres. Unfortunately, divorce cases took inordinate amounts of time through the divorce centres, and by 2019 even undefended petitions were often taking a year to process. With the move towards online divorce, several centres were closed within five years and others amalgamated. It is likely that the only centre that will remain long term will be the Bury St Edmunds divorce centre.

No-Fault Divorce

There was a previous move towards no-fault divorce but it failed to be enacted. The Family Law Act 1996 allowed for no-fault divorce provided couples took part in compulsory mediation meetings but the divorce sections of the Act did not become law.

The Divorce, Dissolution and Separation Bill Act 2020, was introduced as a Bill on 13th June 2019 by the House of Commons, and passed through the House of Lords and finally to Royal Assent in June 2020. By the autumn of 2021 it took effect.

Fault

A few definitions of fault are: an unattractive or unsatisfactory feature, especially in a person's character; a weakness in a person's character; being responsible for an undesirable situation; in the wrong; a mistake, especially something for which you are to blame.

No wonder, with the strong personal associations and accusations, fault-based divorces have been difficult pills to swallow on the receiving end.

History of Fault

Before 1857, divorce was largely open only to men and had to be granted by an Act of Parliament which was hugely expensive. Whilst the Matrimonial Causes Act 1857 allowed ordinary people to divorce, as mentioned still in reality it was open to the wealthy in London until the 1920s. The sole ground for divorce was adultery. But even under the new law in 1857, women divorcing on the grounds of adultery not only had to prove their husbands had been unfaithful but also had to prove additional faults, which included cruelty, rape and incest, whereas a man could rely upon adultery alone. A Private Members' Bill in 1923 made it easier for women to petition for divorce for adultery but it still had to be proved. In 1937, the law was changed and divorce was allowed on other grounds including drunkenness, insanity and desertion.

It took a long time before change really came and the Divorce Reform Act 1969 established the ground for divorce as irretrievable breakdown of marriage which is still used to this day. It also introduced two no-fault facts upon which this could be based, allowing couples to divorce after they had been separated for two years (or five years if only one of them wanted a divorce). It was only at this point, separation became an option to the fault-based grounds.

Then, in 1973, the Matrimonial Causes Act was passed which consolidated previous laws and confirmed the ground for divorce as irretrievable breakdown of marriage. It outlined the following five factors and that one of them would have to be proved for the court to be satisfied that the marriage had broken down irretrievably.

The five facts upon which petitions have been based from 1973 to 2022 up until no-fault divorce came in, were that your spouse had:

- committed adultery.
- behaved in such a way that you could not reasonably be expected to live with him or her (unreasonable behaviour).
- deserted you for over two years.
- lived apart from you for two years or more and your spouse consents to the divorce.
- lived apart from you for five years or more (no consent was required).

One or more of these facts had to be relied upon.

As a result of these facts, a husband or wife who wanted to immediately divorce, had to resort as Petitioner to filing a petition based on the other spouse's unreasonable behaviour or adultery, because the alternative was waiting two years for a consent divorce, or five years if no consent was forthcoming. The finger of blame was pointed at the Respondent spouse at the beginning of proceedings and the legislation fuelled conflict. This often then set the scene of animosity, which sometimes resulted in defended divorce proceedings, or otherwise influenced the discussions regarding children and finances.

Particulars of unreasonable behaviour became particularly tricky, most clients saying that over years they had drifted apart for a variety of reasons. I know myself and colleagues who tried to ensure the particulars were not too inflammatory but sufficient for the court to accept the marriage had broken down irretrievably. Some clients would write reams, for some there would be hardly anything. But get it wrong and their spouse was going to take umbrage and potentially defend, or if not defend, still be sour through further negotiations. In recent years, until the case of Tina Owens in July 2018, most solicitors would limit particulars to five or six general paragraphs of reasons or incidents the Petitioner wished to rely on. The particulars in the Owens' case outlined standard reasons that often came up with clients; the husband in this case was said to have prioritised his work life over home life, there was no love and affection, and they had grown apart. Mrs Owens took the matter to the Supreme Court where her petition was rejected on the basis the marriage had not irretrievably broken down and she would practically have to wait for five years separation before being able to petition for divorce. It was a shocking and unwelcome decision for a lady in her late 60s who wanted to come out of a 40-year marriage that had come to an end, and for solicitors and their clients who wanted to file tamely phrased petitions to achieve a more amicable divorce. The publicity surrounding the case had an effect on highlighting the existing campaign for a change of law to no-fault divorce.

Adultery became slightly less inflammatory in more recent years as it was soon directed by the courts that a third party should not be named unless it was likely the petition would be defended. However, the finger of blame and reason for marriage breakdown was still clearly pointed at the Respondent, and the third party added as Co-respondent in some cases.

Only with the introduction of no-fault divorce did the terminology change from Petitioner to Applicant, and divorce application rather than a divorce petition. The subtle change in language also makes a difference.

Resolution (an organisation representing over 6500 family law solicitors) took the lead in campaigning for a change to a system of no-fault divorce appropriate to modern-day society so couples could be supported by the legal system to resolve differences as amicably as possible.

England and Wales Statistics

Whilst many couples are choosing not to marry, it is still estimated approximately 42% of marriages in England and Wales will end in divorce. The Office for National Statistics releases annual figures for divorce. The latest published in England and Wales are for 2020. There are annual releases available and the next release may be around October 2022. In 2020 there were 102,438 divorces of opposite-sex couples and 1154 divorces of same-sex couples. Same-sex couples have been able to marry in England and Wales from March 2014 and a rise in the divorce rate has been seen over the last few years.

It was estimated that there were 8.9 divorces of opposite-sex couples per 1000 married population in 2019. Divorce rates were highest among both men and women aged 45 to 49 years. The average duration of a marriage for opposite-sex couples is 12 years as at the time of the divorce.

Wives issued 62% of petitions. Wives have consistently petitioned the majority of opposite-sex divorces. The most common ground used by wives (49%) and husbands (35%) was the fact of unreasonable behaviour. This was also the most common ground for same-sex couples used by 63% of women and 70% of men.

Statistics in Other Jurisdictions

US. The statistics in the US for 2018 were that 50% of all marriages would end in divorce, and that of those 41% would be first marriages. Apparently, the professions most likely to divorce are gaming managers, bartenders and flight attendants. Those least likely are those in medical, technology and finance professions. It may be likely that hours of work and security do understandably have an impact on a relationship.

Australia. In 2018, 49,404 divorces were granted in Australia, approximately two divorces per 1000 people. The median age for males was 45.9 years and for females 43.2 years. The average marriage duration was 12.3 years.

China. As of 2017, the divorce rate in China is 3.15 per 1000 population. The divorce rate has been increasing since 2000.

No-Fault Divorce in Other Jurisdictions

Russia. Russia has led the way when it comes to no-fault divorce.

No-fault divorce was introduced in 1917 by the Bolsheviks following the Russian Revolution. Divorce was obtained by filing a mutual consent document with the Russian Registry Office, or by a unilateral request of one party to the court. Before that, similar to the UK, it was ecclesiastical law of various denominations that controlled divorce.

US. On 1st January 1970, the Family Law Act was signed by then Governor Ronald Reagan, and California passed the first no-fault divorce in the country. By 1983, every other state apart from New York and North Dakota had passed their own forms of no-fault divorce law.

After many years of opposition, on 15th August 2010, the New York State was the last state in the US to adopt the law permitting no-fault divorce.

No- fault divorce laws in the US now allow either party the freedom to sue for divorce with the claim of "irreconcilable differences".

Australia. In 1975, the Family Law Act adopted no-fault divorce in Australia. The only ground for divorce is irretrievable breakdown of marriage, evidenced by a twelve-month separation.

Canada. In Canada, no fault was introduced in 1986. Before 1968, the only grounds for divorce were adultery or cruelty and in 1968 the Divorce Act was amended to permit divorce for other reasons, including separation for at least three years. The Divorce Act was amended in 1986 to reduce the separation period to one year and at the same time with no requirement to prove fault by either spouse. The fault grounds for divorce are also available.

China. China introduced no-fault divorce under the New Marriage Law in 1950. The current marriage law provides that divorce shall always be granted if sought by both husband and wife. Divorce is also granted if one party can present evidence of incompatibility, such as separation for at least two years.

Germany. In 1976, divorce law was changed to make no-fault divorces the standard. Until 1976, divorce was only possible if a spouse had acted wrongly, referred to as the principle of guilt *Schuldprinzip*.

Ireland. In Ireland you need to have been separated for four out of five years before you issue divorce proceedings with no prospect of reconciliation. Separation may also be possible in the same house where there have been separate living arrangements. There is no element of fault.

Scotland. In Scotland you must prove that there is an irretrievable breakdown of your marriage by either both agreeing to the divorce and having lived separately for at least one year, or have lived separately for at least two years whereupon no consent is required. Adultery and unreasonable behaviour facts are also still available for irretrievable breakdown of marriage.

Jersey. It will be interesting to see if Jersey moves towards no-fault divorce in the near future. The Law Commission has recommended that no-fault divorce, without the need for the parties to live apart, should be adopted. However, this has not yet been taken up by the Government of Jersey although a consultation process was underway during 2019. In Jersey, divorce is only available after three years of marriage except in exceptional circumstances. The grounds for divorce include some similar to the facts previously used in England and Wales for irretrievable breakdown of marriage. This covers that the Respondent has committed adultery, desertion for two years or has behaved in such a way that the Petitioner cannot reasonably be expected to live with the Respondent. Additional grounds are incurable mental illness or serving a prison sentence of more than 15 years or life. A divorce may also be granted if the parties have lived apart for a year and the Respondent consents to the divorce, or if the parties have lived apart for two years immediately before the divorce proceedings are started with no consent required.

How is it Likely that the Introduction of No-fault Divorce will affect Divorce going forwards in England and Wales and Globally

There is speculation that the introduction of no-fault divorce may result in a rise in divorce rates. This may be likely initially but may even out over time.

Statistics in the US seem to point to an increase in divorce since the beginning of no-fault laws. However, it is clear that the laws have been popular with the people. A few states – Louisiana, Arkansas and Arizona – can choose before they marry if they want a covenant marriage giving options to limit the grounds and options should they divorce, or the no-fault option. Approximately 97% of couples choose to go the no-fault route in Louisiana.

There also appears to be positive justification for supporting no-fault divorce. States in the US that adopted no-fault divorce laws saw a decline in the rates of domestic violence. Additionally, it is understood that abused spouses may feel more empowered to leave their marriage if they do not have to publicly testify or detail information on abuse that may have occurred during the relationship. It is accepted that those who may have suffered domestic violence may find it difficult to open up about their experiences. With no-fault divorce, they do not have to and they have the power to get out of the marriage. By giving individuals who have suffered abuse the ability to unilaterally dissolve their marriage, it cannot be underestimated how powerful the effect of no-fault divorce is in giving them a way out of a bad situation. How many before would have been scared to detail their spouse's behaviour in the divorce petition, knowing they would encounter both recrimination and denial?

There are also good indications that the process lessens emotional harm to children and shortens the time it takes to get the divorce, thereby shortening the time in a stressful situation.

There may be some that believe that marriage vows lose their value. Many opponents of no-fault divorce have cited the rise in divorce rates as evidence of the policy's social impact upon the institution of marriage. However, I cannot think of anybody who thinks that outlining their spouse's fault in an already very emotional breakup situation could be beneficial in any way.

It is also interesting to look at the system in the US prior to no-fault divorce. The family court judges found that feuding couples would be more likely to distort facts or even perjure themselves rather than acting reasonably to prove the other at fault. It was quite clear that good faith and integrity often went out of the window as a result of the old fault system.

No-fault divorce will also eliminate the need for parties who want to be divorced but who did not really have sufficient fault-based grounds, to fabricate grounds simply in order to be divorced. This was seen in some of the states in the US before the no-fault introduction. As states gradually introduced no-fault divorce, there would also be forum shopping, with the couple moving from where they would have to allege fault to reside in a different state that had already implemented no-fault divorce for the period of residence required to obtain it.

No-fault divorce laws are seen as a way for couples to avoid lengthy and costly legal proceedings, draining them financially and emotionally as they seek to assign blame to one another in a court of law. Another benefit of removing fault as the basis for a divorce, was the court's approach to related matters such as property distribution and child custody, would now be decided on the basis of what was equitable as opposed to who was at fault.

The trend has been clear worldwide, and no-fault divorce is the way forwards in society. They are gaining popularity. It appears almost impossible that a country, once they have made that decision in law, will subsequently pass a reversal or change in law to divorce based on fault, or to include fault. It would present as a backwards step and it would be hard to see who would advocate the readmission of fault.

It is interesting how many countries still allow fault divorce grounds in addition to no fault. For instance, several states in America and the countries of Canada, China. In Australia, a residual "fault" element remains in relation to child custody and property settlement issues.

It will be interesting to see if Scotland also change facts in their petition which currently cite similar facts to those previously used in England and Wales.

Conclusion

Divorce remains a tough personal journey. However the introduction of no-fault divorce moves the law concurrently to match the times we live in. The legal process supports the changes in our personal situation with awareness and without the outdated concepts of fault and recrimination.

Happy Endings

Please do not make your divorce define who you are. It is an experience you were meant to grow and learn from, and maybe you or your spouse or both of you had outgrown the reason to remain together. It is a major change. However, you can decide now how you want to spend the rest of your life. Please do not spend it looking back. Look at today and be grateful for what you have. If you have food and shelter you have so much more than so many of our fellow human beings. If you are fortunate to have good health and even more fortunate to have family and friends, you have so much abundance so count your blessings and look forward to a great future.

Patience

The experience of divorce will have taught us a great deal of patience. That is a really helpful attribute to take further into life. I have stood back in many situations and find that they ultimately naturally come to a conclusion. We try to control each other, our circumstances, the time that things should happen as we expect it to. But, despite our efforts, positive or otherwise, there are times when we have to be patient for a situation to play itself out. By having patience for ourselves and the situation, we may still find it tough at times, but somehow one day we wake up, it is in the past and we can hardly remember what happened.

You really can reinvent yourself at any time. Be the best that you can be. Do the things that make you happy. Watch funny movies and laugh as much as you can. And laugh again! Treat life lightly when you can – it was never meant to be serious all the time. If you still find those darkest times in your life, watch a comedy. Have a distraction for a while to lift your mood and then use effort to take you towards your next more positive thought. Before you know it, you will move from fearful thoughts, to loving thoughts.

You can stand on your own two feet. You don't have someone taking a contrary view. What were the small things that you wanted to do that you did not have a chance to do when you were together? We often lose our self-identity in a relationship and compromise for the sake of the relationship. Take this stage as your freedom and explore life to its fullest. It may mean doing more hobbies, but the things that really give meaning and ultimate happiness as you take yourself out of your own situation, are using your unique talents to help others. So, do what you can in small ways. Help your family, help the community, and ultimately help the world.

Concluding your Journey Within

Imagine you are journeying inwards:

- The first outer circle is unconscious behaviour and one of fear. In this mode we often act as if we are in a state of survival. We may complain and show negative emotions such as anger and feel anxious or fearful. We feel out of control. We may feel powerless and often undisciplined to be able to look after our own wellbeing, and that of others. It is from here that we can spread gossip and keep circling bad news. We often act unconsciously, with learnt and recurring patterns of behaviour.
- The second is the education and awareness circle where we build up knowledge and become aware of our emotions, the situation and how to act. We start to give up control. We cultivate a much more positive outlook where we see the best in others and evaluate information in a much more balanced way. We act in a much more evolved way.
- Then we move inwards towards the third growth area. We feel positive emotions and have become more disciplined with our own wellbeing and more interested in the wellbeing of others. We have empathy with, and are interested in helping others, and use our unique talents in the best way possible.
- Then we conclude in the fourth inner circle of joy. We have an abundance of love and positivity. We have equanimity and compassion towards all living beings. We show gratitude for everything and everyone. We live more simply. We live in the oneness of our existence with all our fellow living beings, our mother earth and the universe. With this comes peace. This is our inner circle, as this is truly who we are.

We all experience suffering, sickness, and ageing towards our ultimate death. As I finish this book, we are hopefully through the coronavirus pandemic, which has taken many beloved ones' lives across the world. It has also taught us to look out for each other and help others where we can. It has taught us empathy and compassion. It has taught us to become a little wiser, a little less concerned with our material needs, and focus on our families' and communities' wellbeing. Many of us have personally used this time to move from a state of fear, through learning and growth, to ultimate joy. Many of us have learnt to live more simply, to do less – and to count our blessings. So, let's not forget, and carry on doing this. A divorce in the scheme of our lives, is not the most catastrophic event of our lifetime.

Top Tips

DO
Embrace every single moment of your new life.
DO NOT
Look back.

Case Scenario

This is now finally your story, your experience. How will you go through your divorce? How will you cope? What will you have learnt at its conclusion? How do you see your life now moving forwards? Hopefully, like many of the people we met through their journeys, you will choose to move forwards positively. They show us it is possible.

Moving On and Embracing Change

Change is an experience only easy for the enlightened; those that understand the impermanence of every situation, every cell, every life. Wisdom and acceptance are the keys to any situation. The more you resist, the more you will suffer. Let the divorce be a catalyst for change. Consider your intentions in everything you say and do. Will it benefit yourself and others? Transform your life. Make the best possible of the situation and broaden your outlook. Move forwards with the good of you and others in mind. Move from fear to joy.

As you move on, consider what will bring meaning to your life. If we do not build up our inner strength through spiritual practice, what will happen at the end of our life? We enter this life alone and empty handed. We leave this life alone and empty handed. Our loved ones may only grieve for us. We have no other person or possessions that can help us. This life is not to teach us fleeting happiness, it is to teach us true happiness, joy and eventual peace. My wish is that, through change, we all move from a state of fear to ultimate joy. I hope my writing has helped and supported you in some way through your divorce journey. I am giving you a virtual personal hug at this moment; be strong and I promise you will get through this. You may feel you have lost a significant love, but you will always be loved.

Always be kind. Be gentle on yourself and others.

Be happy, be well, be peaceful, be loved.

Final Evening Meditation

This is our final meditation. Have a nice relaxing bath or shower and do this meditation before bedtime. Find a quiet place where you will not be disturbed. Light a scented candle and place it on a table in front of you. Sit comfortably with your back erect, either on a chair with your feet on the floor, or on a cushion sitting cross-legged. Place your hands loosely in your lap. Close your eyes. Take a couple of deep breaths. Then start to settle into your breath. Bring to mind a few things you are grateful for. It may be the fact that you can see; it may be good health; it may be your children; it may be the fact you have got through the other side of your divorce. It can be anything. Continue to breathe. Then think again. What are you grateful for? Who or what do you appreciate? It may be your family, your new home, it may be food. It may be the scent of your candle wafting through the room. Bring to mind naturally what you are grateful for. As you continue to breathe, and you continue to look out with gratitude, you will realise there are so many things to be grateful for. Gratitude and appreciation are two of the most beneficial mindsets to keep going into your future. Make a promise with yourself that you will always keep the attitude of gratitude. Decide you will appreciate every day. Take your time and open your eyes. Look at your candle flame and contemplate with awareness that this light is in all of us, also a light that goes out at some point. It reminds us to appreciate everything and each other. Be so grateful for what you have experienced so far, and what you will experience. As you blow out the candle, reflect on where you are now. Affirm to yourself every time you light it, it is a new day, a new life, for which you are blessed. As you rise from meditation, prepare for a very good night's sleep, and a very good future.

| **Concluding Thought of the Day** |
| I am grateful for my life and everyone and everything in it. |

Acknowledgements

With thanks to my parents in giving me the foundation for my career and encouraging my creative paths, and my friend Simi for valued friendship help and continued support in bringing this book into fruition. Thanks to Sharon and all my friends for being my champions.

Thanks Karin for your invaluable critique, Julie for detailed editing, Yasir for perfect illustration and Rohit for your valued technical support.

With gratitude to Austin Kemp, K J Smith, and all present and past employers and colleagues in developing my expertise, and my clients in broadening my mind.

Bibliography

Byron and Mitchell, K. a. (2002). *Loving What Is: Four Questions That Can Change Your Life.* London: Rider.

Chopra, D. (Director). (2014). *Guided Meditation on Gratitude* [Motion Picture].

Chopra, D. (Director). (2015). *Meditation for the End of the Day* [Motion Picture].

Dhamma.org. (2020). From https://www.dhamma.org/en/about/vipassana.

Dispenza, J. (2014). *You are the Placebo.* London: Hay House.

Divorce, Dissolution and Separation Act (2020). c11 UK Public General Acts .

Eden, D. (Director). (2015). *Daily Energy Routine* [Motion Picture].

Eden, D. (2020). From https://edenmethod.com.

Federation, U. R. (2021). From http://www.reikifed.co.uk.

Foundation, T. B. (2020). From http://www.transformationalbreath.com.

Grace-Bishop, K. (Director). (2011). *Loving Kindness Meditation* [Motion Picture].

Hanh, T. (2006). *True Love.* Boston: Shambhala Publications Inc. .

Hicks, E. a. (2004). *Ask and It is Given .* London : Hay House .

Kübler-Ross, E. (1969). *On Death and Dying.* Routledge.

Kataria, D. (Director). (2013). *100 Laughter Yoga Exercises* [Motion Picture].

Kataria, D. M. (Director). (2013). *TEDMED Live Talk by Dr. Madan Kataria at the other song* [Motion Picture].

Ltd, D. Y. (2021). From https://druyoga.com/.

Nirula, N. a. (2000). *The Joy of Reiki.* Delhi: Macmillan Publishers India Limited.

O'Morain, P. (2014). *Mindfulness on the Go.* London: Yellow Kite.

Owens v Owens (Supreme Court UKSC 41 2018).

Publications, T. (2020). From https://tharpa.com/uk/.

Ramdev, P. B. (Director). (2016). *Quick 10min. English* [Motion Picture].

Sadhguru (Director). (2017). *Isha Kriya- Guided Meditation With Sadhguru* [Motion Picture].

Statistics, O. f. (2019). *https://www.ons.gov.uk/peoplepopulationandcommunity/birthsdeaths andmarriages/divorce/bulletins/divorcesinenglandandwales/2019.* From https://www.ons.gov.uk.

Tchenguiz v Imerman; Imerman v Imerman (Court of Appeal EWCA Civ 908 2010).

Tolle, E. (1997). *The Power of Now.* Vancouver: Namaste publishing.

White v White (House of Lords UKHL 54 2000).

Yoga, C. (2020). *https://www.carlingfordyoga.ie/category/yoga/.* From https://www.carlingfordyoga.ie.

Printed in Great Britain
by Amazon

43932572R00159